THE LANGUAGE
OF ARGUMENT
Seventh Edition

DANIEL McDONALD
University of South Alabama

📖 HarperCollins*CollegePublishers*

For Irene

Acquisitions Editor: Patricia Rossi
Project Coordination and Text Design: Ruttle, Shaw and Wetherill, Inc.
Cover Design: Kay Petronio
Production/Manufacturing: Michael Weinstein/Paula Keller
Compositor: Ruttle, Shaw & Wetherill, Inc.
Printer and Binder: R. R. Donnelley & Sons Company
Cover Printer: The Lehigh Press, Inc.

THE LANGUAGE OF ARGUMENT, Seventh Edition

Copyright © 1993 by HarperCollins College Publishers

Library of Congress Cataloging-in-Publication Data

McDonald, Daniel Lamont.
    The language of argument / Daniel McDonald. — 7th ed.
      p.   cm.
    Includes bibliographical references.
    ISBN 0-06-500583-X (student edition) — ISBN 0-06-500584-8
(instructor's edition)
    1. College readers.   2. English language—Rhetoric.   3. Persuasion
(Rhetoric)   I. Title.
PE1417.M43   1992
808'.0427—dc20

92-23334
CIP

92 93 94 95 9 8 7 6 5 4 3 2 1

CONTENTS

PART THREE EIGHT RULES FOR GOOD WRITING

RULE 1: FIND A SUBJECT YOU CAN WORK WITH

Exercises 270

RULE 2: GET YOUR FACTS

Visit the Library 271 • Use Your Telephone 273 • Write for
Facts You Need 274 • Exercises 274 • Alternate Exercises
275

RULE 3: LIMIT YOUR TOPIC TO MANAGEABLE SIZE

Exercises 278

RULE 4: ORGANIZE YOUR MATERIAL

The Introduction 279 • The Body 280 • The
Conclusion 281 • Exercises 282

PREFACE

The purpose of this edition remains the same: to teach students to read argument and to provide materials around which they can write their own argumentative essays. The selections cover a range of provocative issues. Some are notably persuasive; some are not. Most of today's hot topics are represented.

This book is no larger than the previous one, but it has changed. I've kept 20 selections from the sixth edition and added 80 new ones. The 100 titles should be gratifying to numerologists and, indeed, to any teacher who wants students to have a lot of argument to look at. The subjects are intended to create excitement and controversy in the classroom.

I have had to avoid areas that are too topical. This book won't appear until a year from the time I send in the manuscript. And it must be relevant three years after that. Therefore, I have few titles on political subjects. These become old news quickly. Students today don't know about Watergate or Iran/Contra. Those two years from now will have little interest in Desert Storm.

The "Argument for Analysis" section has 51 short (or relatively short) works: essays, editorials, letters, photographs, cartoons, and advertisements. Students can be asked to write on any of these, giving either an analysis of the argument or a response to it. Teachers could conceivably assign a different title to each member of the class.

In the same way, the 87 brief arguments in the "Exercises for Review" section should be useful. A teacher could divide a class into teams of four or five and give each a dozen examples to work on.

These short selections should produce a good result. I am not concerned that students know all the facts about some area of controversy (abortion or secular humanism or nuclear power). I'll be happy if they can read an argument and say, "That's an unrepresentative sample," or "Where did those statistics come from?," or "Post hoc rides again!"

The book will be a useful writing text. The back pages give "Eight Rules for Good Writing." And the preceding essays should teach a lot, too. With eight or ten exceptions, the arguments illustrate good writing; they are models students can learn from. The badly written pieces stand out. The writers lack a purpose or get lost in metaphor or academic language or long sentences. When students complain an essay is dull or obscure, ask them what features make it that way. They can learn from that.

The opening section of the book has changed. Originally, I called it "Logic and Composition"; now I've titled it "Persuasive Writing." It takes up issues of readability. The seven selections are more and less compelling. They illustrate the line "An argument can't be persuasive if it isn't read."

I am indebted to a number of people. Jim Dorrill, the English Department chair at the University of South Alabama, has been continually supportive. Mary A. Coan, Charles Harwell, Gene Knepprath, Sylvia Mitchell, Patricia Rossi, Lynda Thompson, and G. R. Wilson offered materials that found their way into the book. Mike Hanna, Kathy Damico, and Irene McDonald are a continuing intellectual resource. I thank them all.

I also wish to thank the following reviewers for their suggestions for the seventh edition: Christina Murphy, Texas Christian University; Steven Strang, Massachusetts Institute of Technology; Julia Dietrich, University of Louisville; Joseph Sanders, Lakeland Community College; Rachel Schaffer, Eastern Montana College; and George R. Mahoney, University of Wisconsin.

Daniel McDonald

PART ONE

FORMS OF
ARGUMENT

Japonica
Glistens like coral in all of the neighbouring gardens,
And today we have naming of parts.
—Henry Reed

PERSUASIVE WRITING

"Too often 'justification' is nurtured by inane rationalization viewing experimentation in a laboratory setting as salutory."

—From an animal-rights tract

Good = effective.

Most writing is persuasive writing.

When you write, you want something. You want people to be more informed and to accept your point of view. You want them to do something. You want them to see you in a positive way. Good writing is writing that gets the effect you want. *(which doesn't make what you want right)*

A study of the techniques of persuasion will make you more concerned about your audience and about forms of writing that have a good or bad effect on them. It will keep you from speculating vaguely on some topic that cannot be proven with evidence. It will help you know when you're making sense. *↳ being understandable.*

WIN YOUR AUDIENCE

To make a persuasive case, you have to know your audience. This will help you choose your words and shape your style. *— stereotype?*

One body of readers—say, a group of fraternity men—may respond to a direct appeal in strong language; another group—say, members of a Methodist congregation—may reject your whole argument if you use a word like "crap." One group will respond to wit, another to biblical quotations, and still another to a spread of statistics. Some readers will be offended if you write "Ms.," "ain't," "black," "symbiotic," "Dear Sir," or "and/or." Most audiences will be bored if you write vaguely about "Civic Responsibility" or "Tomorrow's Promise," but some audiences and occasions may call for rhetorical generalities. A detailed analysis of a social problem would be out of place at a political rally. The writing that would produce a great letter or advertisement might be unsuccessful in a sociology term paper. Some people will be impressed by "symbiotic relationships" and "a thousand points of light," some won't. You have to know your audience. *↳ recognize it? George Bush / Ray Jones*

A central feature in argument is creating a personal voice to express

3

your views. Too often individuals with a strong case fail to be persuasive because of a writing style that makes them sound like a computer, a demanding top sergeant, a condescending aristocrat, or a stubborn child.

Most readers respond favorably to a concerned and courteous tone. So let your writing sound like a human voice. When addressing a committee, refer to the members in your presentation. ("I'm sure you ladies and gentlemen recognize how complex this question is.") When writing a business letter, try to use a direct, personal style. ("I'm sorry about your problem, Mr. Baker, and I hope we can do more for you next time.") Routinely, work to avoid a hostile tone. Don't write, "You must do this," when you can say, "We would like to have you do this promptly" or "I need this by Wednesday." Never write, "I will not do this," when you can say, "For these reasons, I cannot do this now." Don't protest, "You're too ignorant to understand my point"; say, "I am sorry I did not make myself understood."

This tone can be difficult to maintain. At times you will want to rage out with righteous indignation or ego-gratifying scorn. Don't do it. Remember that anger never persuaded anyone. In argument, nice guys finish first.

The point deserves repetition. An Alabama attorney looking back on a lifetime of courtroom experience said, "When I was young, I thought that lawyers won cases. Later I believed that facts won cases. Now I think that clients win cases. When the facts aren't overwhelmingly against him, the jury will find for the person they like best." (The celebrated trials of Jean Harris, Larry Flynt, John DeLorean, and Bernhard Goetz seemed to work on that principle.)

The persuasive force of sweet good-nature can hardly be overstated. Americans twice elected Ronald Reagan as president because, among other reasons, they perceived him to be a nice person. Occasionally, lawyers have to press a personal injury suit against Disneyland or Walt Disney World. The attempts fail because Disney is too fixed in the public mind as sweet, clean, and moral. One frustrated lawyer said, "You might as well try to sue Mother Teresa."

DEFINE THE ISSUE

A study of logic shows the importance of defining your issue. Some topics you may want to discuss are flatly unarguable. They would produce vague speeches and incoherent essays.

Some issues rely more on a definition of terms than on evidence. When two people argue about whether Vice-President Dan Quayle is handsome, for example, they are not disagreeing about his hair, teeth, or clothes, but about a definition of *handsomeness*. If they can agree on a definition, they will probably agree about Dan Quayle as well. Similarly, the question of whether capital punishment is wrong hinges not so much on the character of the act (the pain, the possibility of error, the protection afforded society) as on the definition of *wrongness*.

Aesthetic and moral questions are often unarguable because individuals cannot agree on the terms involved. The meaning of any word is what a body of people say it is. (A telephone is called a *telephone* because English speakers regularly use that word to denote it.) But in these special areas, people do not agree. What is handsomeness? What is beauty? Theoreticians have sought objective standards, but the quest seems fruitless. Is a Greek temple more beautiful than a Gothic cathedral? Is Bach's music better than Madonna's? Who can say? The decision rests on a subjective judgment that does not lend itself to evidence.

When friends tell you they prefer Frank Zappa's music and the taste of Miller Lite, you can't argue with them. It's a good time to change the subject.

Like beauty, the idea of goodness is not easy to define. Seeking an objective basis for calling actions right and wrong, authorities have cited scriptural precedents; they have based systems on the inalienable rights of each human being; they have insisted that nature provides a moral example. But these definitions have not been universally accepted. If two individuals could agree that morality resides, say, in a natural law, they might then *begin* to talk about capital punishment. In general usage, however, moral terms remain so ill-defined that such issues cannot be argued meaningfully at all. (If you have to write on beauty or morality, focus your essay on some concrete example—say, arson or pop art or Vanna White—and work in as many "for example" and "for instance" references as you can.)

Moral and aesthetic questions are further removed from argument because they often produce emotional responses. Two individuals who agree in defining *handsomeness* might, for example, still disagree about Vice-President Quayle because one objects to his conservative politics or his personal style. It is, of course, unreasonable to let emotions color such a judgment, but it happens all the time. You might be completely persuaded that capital punishment is cruel and barbaric yet, at a given moment, argue that hanging is too good for a child murderer or a political terrorist.

Vague definitions make argument impossible in many areas. Saab has been proclaimed "the most *intelligent* car ever built," and Royal Copenhagen "the only *elegant* musk oil cologne." The advertisement insists "Only Tareyton has the *best* filter!" Are these claims true? Until the key words are defined, the statements are no more subject to being proved with evidence than is "Razzle dagons, popple stix." Nonsense is neither true nor false.

Many areas of modern controversy hinge on definitions of terms. Do animals "talk"? Can children "sin"? Is running a "religious" experience? Is prostitution a "victimless" crime? Do computers "think"? It depends on how you define the words.

Only when terms are defined and mutually accepted can you begin gathering evidence to prove something. You can, for example, argue whether O. J. Simpson or Walter Payton was the better football player because their records, the merits of their supporting and opposing teams, and the qualities of a good running back are generally agreed upon. Is it true that smoking causes lung cancer, that President Bush knew about the illegal events of the Iran/contra scandal, that Gordon's is the largest-selling gin in the world? The questions can at least be argued.

MAKE YOUR CASE

Finally, the study of argument will let you know when you are making sense. It will tell you if your sample is sufficient to support an inductive conclusion, if the expert you want to quote is a reliable authority, if your words express the meanings you want, and if your statistics are relevant.

A survey of logic will make you a more perceptive reader. You will be better able to recognize strengths and weaknesses in particular arguments. It will be harder for people to lie to you.

The essays in this book will show you writing patterns to imitate and to avoid. You can't become a good writer simply by knowing how words are spelled and where commas go. You need a clearly defined topic, a body of information, and a concern for the interests of your reader. *What you have to say is of the essence in good writing.* The study of logic should make what you have to say more meaningful.

And knowing how to write will make your ideas more persuasive. Of the seven arguments that follow, some are convincing and some are not. None is helped or hurt much by the facts defining the issue. Invariably, the successful arguments have a focus and a voice; they use language and layout that make them easy to read. The unsuccessful ones use techniques that turn off the reader.

Observe these techniques and learn to avoid them. An argument can't be persuasive if it isn't read.

EXERCISES

Can you argue the truth of these statements?

1. All men are created equal.
2. Mexico City's Copper Dome is higher than the Empire State Building.
3. Smokers make better lovers. *than whom?*
4. It is wrong to say "between you and I."
5. Bacardi Black—"The taste of the night."
6. Time is a trapezoid.
7. Babe Ruth was a better baseball player than Dizzy Dean.
8. "Blessed are the pure in heart, for they shall see God."

by authority *w wan*

9. All prisoners eligible for parole should be tested for the AIDS virus.
10. "Only Armorall works like Armorall."   *How does it work?*
11. A diamond is forever.   *Is it unique?*
12. No woman is happy with the way she looks.
13. Immorality is corrupting every area of our nation. Only a moral renaissance can save America now.   *How many areas?*
14. One way to relieve the gasoline shortage is to legalize marijuana.   *How connected?*
15. Stolichnaya—"The only vodka imported from Russia."
16. L'Oreal—"Why be gray when you can be yourself?"   *yourself, meaning gray?*
17. SURGEON GENERAL'S WARNING: Smoking Causes Cancer, Heart Disease, Emphysema, and May Complicate Pregnancy.
18. Vacation in Florida—"The Rules Are Different Here."   *From what?*
19. "Quite Simply, Mink Will Change Your Life"—ad for Mink International.

Revert to pp. 3-6

Does this mean we ignore whatever we can't argue?

COLOR ME
PRO-CHOICE

Mitchell Farnum

I don't spend a lot of time with homosexuals, chain-smokers, feminists, porn-buyers, atheists, vegetarians, or problem drinkers—but when the issues get legal, I am with them. I am pro-choice.

I think adults should have options.

I want options. I want my Marriott room to have a Gideon Bible and porn movies. Let me decide if I want to buckle my seat-belt, or drive to 11:00 Mass, or swing out to the dog-track. Let me send my kids to public school or to Holiness Tabernacle Academy. I may invite Jews and blacks to join my private club, but don't tell me I have to accept orientals or women or somebody's cousin. It's *my* club.

I don't like people with oppressive theories. They come around telling everybody what to do. Local 7-11's shouldn't sell *Playboy*. Poor women can't have abortions. Nancy Cruzan should stay hooked to that machine for another seven years. Consenting adults must go into their bedrooms and behave sensibly. Who needs this crap?

I want to make choices, even dumb ones. If I buy my Big Mac with the large order of fries (and extra salt), that's OK. If I don't buckle my seat-belt, so what? If I smoke a pack or two a day, leave me alone! I've got my rights. And among them is the right to take the consequences of what I do. Man, it's *my* life!

Also, let me believe what I want to. You're hearing from a man who subscribes to the *National Enquirer* and the *Sun*. So the evidence is shaky about UFOs and the Shroud of Turin and vitamin E and the Kennedy assassination? So what? If I want to believe dramatic theories, that's fine. (Tomorrow I may send off $15.95 for a talisman containing Lourdes water.) And you're free to believe your theories. If you want to think Elvis is dead, that's your business.

All this freedom is for adults who can take care of themselves. With people who can't, OK, let's pass laws. I don't mind rules that protect kids and AIDS victims and neurotics and wheelchair people and the homeless. I want laws in areas where we're all helpless—those protecting the environment and the purity of foods. I can live with traffic regulations and *some* antigun laws. I want ex-cons and psychopaths to have trouble buying a gun, but don't tell me *I* can't buy one.

Summing it up, I don't like meddling people. Spare me from censors and pro-lifers and gay-baiters and temperance advocates and antismoking Nazis and anybody who would enforce prayer or "political correctness" in the schools.

But don't get me wrong—I'm not some antagonistic nut. I love a lot of things—babies, Heineken beer, golden retrievers, Willie Nelson, my wife, the Atlanta Braves (with all their faults), and the Roman Catholic Church (with all its faults). And if you want to be Baptist or agnostic or

SOURCE: Reprinted by permission of the author.

gay or vegetarian, great! If you turn on to *All My Children* or Guns and Roses, hey, that's fine with me. It's a big world, friend. Enjoy yourself. Just stay off my back.

DISCUSSION QUESTIONS

1. Whether you agree with it or not, is this argument easy to read? What problems attend an argument that is not easy to read?
2. Specify the features that make this easy to read.
3. What is the author like? Do you find him appealing or unappealing?
4. How intelligent is the author? Is he just mindlessly angry, or is he well informed on the issues involved?
5. Do his extreme positions hurt his case? Do you think he really smokes two packs a day, refuses to wear his seat belt, and believes that Elvis is alive?
6. Were you offended when he said he might not want women or orientals at his poker game? Or when he said, "Who needs this crap?"
7. What is implicit in his complaints that "poor" women can't get abortions? That Nancy Cruzan should stay on her life-support machine "another" seven years?
8. Does the author just want to be left alone? Has he no compassion for the sufferings of people around him?
9. What is the purpose of the last paragraph, in which he affirms babies, golden retrievers, and Willie Nelson?
10. Does this argument sound like writing or talking? How does the author's "voice" help the case he's making?

The fountainhead of leadership

In 1776—a milestone year in the struggles for political and economic freedom alike—a Scottish social philosopher named Adam Smith published *The Wealth of Nations*. In it, he theorized that competition and the forces of the marketplace constituted an "invisible hand" which, if left unfettered, could create a wondrous machine for the creation of riches and a rising standard of living.

For much of this century, Smith's theories and those of Karl Marx seemed engaged in a worldwide struggle for supremacy. For many of the years since World War II, in places as diverse as Eastern Europe, Asia, Africa, and Latin America, the Marxist siren song of government-guaranteed necessities—some sort of roof over every head and at least a little food on every plate—held a great deal of attraction for people who never had even that much. But as the years unfolded, the West prospered and living standards rose. Expectations of a better life, fueled by modern means of communication, roared into those places where the leaders long derided capitalism. Finally, notably in Eastern Europe and the Soviet Union itself, decaying economies, unable to deliver better living standards, helped prompt the sweeping changes now being chronicled in our newspapers and television broadcasts.

The Eastern Bloc, it should be noted, is led by a military superpower, surely a "strong" nation to those who define strength in terms of army divisions or the throw weight of missile-carrying rockets. Even so, the economic weakness of the Soviet Union and its satellites—the inability of their system to deliver the basic goods and services so freely available to Western consumers—is a dynamic force prompting the current unrest.

In describing the sources of a nation's wealth, Adam Smith, in effect, was also describing the <u>health</u> of nations. History—and recent history in particular—demonstrates that a country's economic health equates directly to its strength. America assumed the leadership of the free world because its military and economic power were instrumental in winning World War II. And in the postwar world, this nation's economic strength allowed it to continue as a leading power. Indeed, that same economic base made possible the military muscle that may only now begin to unflex.

But economic power, like power generally, has to be used wisely. In the postwar years, this nation has acted to foster the free-market system, and share its own wealth with its allies and trading partners. The Marshall Plan allowed a war-ravaged Europe to rebuild its factories and infrastructure. The Bretton Woods Conference erected the framework for the postwar monetary system and established the International Bank for Reconstruction and Development and the International Monetary Fund. The General Agreement on Tariffs and Trade set out the ground rules for dealings between trading partners back in 1947, and a new round of negotiations, with the U.S. as a key player, continues today.

Now comes more startling news: The Eastern European trading bloc seeks to link the value of its currencies to those of the West and let its goods be sold at market prices. Some in Eastern Europe want to enter GATT and individual ex-Communist states seek Western joint-venture partners and trade agreements.

The world is truly a different place, and an exciting one. And it's certainly a different one for the U.S., which now confronts a dilemma. America earned its role as a world leader through its economic strength. But today the nation faces serious economic challenges at home and abroad. The budget and trade deficits remain sky-high. We rely increasingly on foreign money to finance our debts. We don't save enough to make needed capital investments. Foreign competitors bedevil our industrial producers.

Are we, in short, becoming too weak economically to retain our leadership position? Or can we successfully adapt to unfolding events? The answers to those questions will be largely of our own making.

Next: Whose lunch are we consuming?

Mobil

Reprinted by permission of Mobil Corporation. Reprinted from *Time*, February 26, 1990.

DISCUSSION QUESTIONS

1. Can you say in one sentence what the main point of this essay is? If so, was it easy to find? *Are we losing our position?*

2. This is one of a series of messages. What seems to be Mobil's purpose in publishing them? *Mobil is the fountainhead of leadership. USA #1*

3. Does the prose sound like writing or talking? Can you hear an author speaking? *Writing*

4. How appealing to the reader is each of these:
   a. The title? *very*
   b. The first sentence? *1776 is a buzz word*
   c. The first paragraph?
   d. The long block paragraphs? *bad* *small type*

5. How were you affected by these features:
   a. The length of the sentences? *bad*
   b. The long introductory phrases and clauses? *bad*
   c. The number of words separating a subject and verb? *bad*

6. Would you have read this essay if you were not assigned to do so? *No* Did you read it even after it was assigned? *Yes*

You read the title and the company name.
Everything else is small print.

THE LITTLE RED
SCHOOL HOUSE

Edward Patterson

The little red school house perched like a miniature ruby on a sea of emerald green that was the remote and verdant farming valley in some distant region of America.

The decree of man's law against the word of God in schools had travelled with devilish speed unmolested through the heavens, hop-scotching from one ice cold and indifferent antenna to another till it reached this tiny village tucked away in some forgotten cranny of the nation. The school principal got his Government's under God decree, however contradictory sounding, to forthwith cease and desist from any kind of worship in his little red school house. He would obey the letter of the law of man.

All his pupils were under his incessant surveillance so seriously did he take his obligation to man over God. He monitored them in study and at play lest they lapse into prayer for any reason. God would be expelled from school from the time the bell ushered in a new day until it exited a finished one.

In his home, the principal had a son of his own, the age of his youngest pupils. He was a hopeless cripple, that terrible sentence in fate's court of justice that has no mercy, that constant reminder of the miracle of birth and its attendant peril. Thoughts of his poor boy at home in prison tortured him remorselessly. God was his adversary, a truant, too, perforce.

In all kinds of weather during recreation periods, the principal meandered down to the creek behind the school. This way he would oversee his pupils lest they seemed to pray. It was an opportunity as well for him to meditate and let loose still another deluge of bitter emotions that ceaselessly assaulted him.

This eventful day, the earliest winter snow had blanketed the good earth. It was especially painful to hear the laughter of children at play like joyful notes from a flute happily pirouetting skyward then dancing as if in a chorus line below a curtain of clouds. He thought of his injured son and sank weeping to his knees. He looked up to heaven as if in prayer but there was only a curse on his lips.

It was then he noticed another little boy kneeling right beside him. The principal, rubbing his eyes with his sleeves in disbelief, jumped up, indignant. But the look on the lad's face stopped him short.

He told him he was sorry to break the rules but that he was praying for the principal himself and his own crippled little boy. Then he took his hand and gently said, "Let school out early. Go home now and greet your son."

The principal went back to the little red school house, rang the bell

SOURCE: Reprinted from the *New York Times*, October 9, 1987. Reprinted by permission of the author.

and dismissed his pupils. Down by the creek, the reverent little boy had vanished.

The principal dashed home. As he reached the gate to the path leading to the front door, a bundle of winter clothes tumbled towards him and leaping, cuddled in his arms.

His crippled son cried out, "Look, Daddy, I'm whole," and then he ran and jumped and somersaulted in a kind of halo around his father, the principal.

From that time on, the schoolday started with a prayer of hope and ended with a prayer of thanks. The loudest voice of all was the principal's. The biggest smile of all was his son's.

But the greatest lesson of all was that the mention of God was as much a blessing and no more a threat in the little red school house than ever it had been in church or temple.

DISCUSSION QUESTIONS

1. This essay originally appeared as an ad in the *New York Times*. The author paid to have it printed. What seems to have been his purpose?

2. How far would you have read if you were not assigned to read the essay? What would have stopped you?

3. How effective are the figures of speech? What is your response to these lines?
   a. "Like a miniature ruby on a sea of emerald green"
   b. "Hopscotching from one ice cold and indifferent antenna to another"
   c. "Like joyful notes from a flute happily pirouetting skyward then dancing as if in a chorus line below a curtain of clouds"

4. Does the story seem to involve real people living in a real place? Does it involve a real problem?

5. Does it seem reasonable that young people, if not carefully watched, would run behind trees to pray?

6. Is this effective writing? Does it fulfill the purpose the author had in mind?

Sometimes, the worst thing you can do to a drug user is the only way to help.

Drug use is a question of extremes. People who use drugs are either addicted or in danger of addiction.

The results of drug addiction are poor performance, absenteeism, theft, robbery, industrial accidents, and death.

And addicts often take others down with them. Loved ones, co-workers, even employers.

Addicts seldom get well or even get into treatment by themselves. Someone has to help. You could be that person. If you're willing to get involved.

When you say, in no uncertain terms, "Get well or get out," you may be awakening the addict to the one reality that can save her.

Threatening to fire an addict is the worst thing you can do to her. Or the best. If it gets her into treatment.

To find out how to set up a treatment program in your company, please call 1-800-843-4971. That's the National Institute on Drug Abuse hot line for managers and CEOs. It's manned by trained Employee Assistance Program planners and designers, from Monday through Friday, 9:00 a.m. to 8:00 p.m. Eastern Time. They won't tell you what to do, but they can outline the options.

Courtesy of Partnership for a Drug-Free America.

DISCUSSION QUESTIONS

1. This document was written and laid out by a professional advertising agency. Consider the features they used to get their message across:
    a. The title
    b. The picture
    c. Sentence length
    d. Incomplete sentences (sometimes called "context sentences")
    e. Paragraph length
    f. The use of "you"
    g. The colloquial diction ("Get well or get out.")
2. Whom is this ad addressed to? Do you think it would be effective with that audience?
3. Is there a message for other audiences?
4. Compare this with the Mobil essay "The Fountainhead of Leadership." What does the comparison tell you about readability and effective persuasion?

THE BALDNESS
EXPERIMENT

George Deleon

The winos who hung around my Brooklyn neighborhood in 1950 were not funny. With their handout hands, reeking breaths, and weird, ugly injuries, they were so self-rejecting that you could bark them away even while you shoved them a nickel. My friends and I didn't think they were funny, but we observed one thing that always busted us up. Almost without exception, they had all their hair.

Seriously: we never saw a bald bum. Have you? When was the last time you remember a street alky stumbler with nothing on top?

Black, white, old, young, short, tall, all of them had a full mop. And hair that wouldn't quit. It leaped up as if it were electrified, or shagged down in complete asocial indifference, or zoomed back absurdly neat, gray-black and glued. Inexplicably, it seemed that boozing burned out the guts but grew hair.

Fifteen years later, I offered this observation to my undergraduate classes in the psychology of personality. Then, one semester, I decided to get past the laugh, integrate my present self with my past self, and actually test the hypothesis that booze grows hair.

I conceived a simple investigation, with the class participating as co-researchers. In the project, we'd get some real data on the density, or rather the incidence, of baldness in a random sample of rummies. The tactic was to beachhead ourselves on the Bowery in New York City, fan out in teams of two, and gradually move up from somewhere around Prince Street to 14th Street, the end of the bum region.

On two successive Saturday mornings, the whole research outfit—me, four men, and two women—met on the corner of Bowery and Houston to carry out the plan. Every other derelict who was not unconscious was approached, talked to, and looked at. Since no one usually walks up to a rummy except cops and other rummies, something seemed to happen when two pretty young students of mine would say, "Sir, I'd like to ask you a few questions." The winos would rock a bit and—no kidding—you could almost see a little ego emerging.

In planning the research, I decided that we should gather as much information as we could that might be relevant to the experiment. We decided to mark down answers to questions about age, race, ethnicity, marital status, family baldness, drinking life, etc. We even asked our subjects where they usually slept (in or out of doors), figuring that, too, might influence their hair growth.

While one team member interrogated, the other circled around the subject, studying the head, raised and lowered, to observe the pate. Subjects were evaluated on a four-point baldness scale as hairy, receding, bald pate, or totally bald.

Interesting problems developed from the beginning; what appeared

SOURCE: Reprinted from *Psychology Today*, October 1977.

to be simple was really complex. When do you call a guy bald? What does "receding" mean? (We dispensed with the use of rulers or vernier calipers, assuming that, bombed or not, the derelict would shuffle off as soon as we pulled out any kind of hardware. We felt grateful that he tolerated the paper, pencils, and questions.) So there was no quantification, no precision. We simply had to make quick judgments.

Our teams interviewed over 60 Bowery subjects, paying them a quarter a pop, all of which came out of my pocket. Back at the school, the data were tallied and, sure enough, the results confirmed my intuition. Only about 25 percent could be called receding or totally bald, with the remainder being pated or hirsute. I had been right all along, and we reported the results to the class.

But it turns out that the skepticism of annoyed youth may actually be the quintessence of good scientific research. After I enjoyed the laughs and took a few bows, a number of students, not on the teams, were quick to raise some sharp objections.

First, and most obvious, was that we needed to study baldness in a group of nonderelicts in order to make proper conclusions. Second, wasn't it possible that the teams had been influenced by my colorful classroom predictions about hairy bums and had tended to judge the subjects as nonbalding?

The criticism was first rate. I knew that because it threw me into an immediate depression. I hated the students who offered it. I also knew that we'd have to do the whole study again with new teams and new derelicts. This time, nonderelicts would have to be included, too, and I would offer no advance hypothesis that might bias, in my favor, the way kids looked at heads.

I waited a whole academic year, got a new personality class, and this time took no chances. During the lectures, it was necessary to arouse the interest of the class in the broad issue of bums and baldness. So I suggested that derelicts were a special group of people who seemed to lose their hair sooner and more completely than other men. In short, I lied. Morality aside, it was a tough one to tell because I feared that it would shape the kids' perception the other way. They might actually see receding hairlines and shiny heads where there really was only hair. But I had to take the risk of betting against myself to make the win more sure.

Out on the turf again a new and larger research squad of six men and six women worked over five straight Saturdays. They did the Bowery in pairs, interviewing about 80 derelicts.

We also went after a comparison group. Any man walking in or out of Bloomingdale's or cruising along 5th Avenue in the 50s was operationally defined as a nonderelict. These fine fellows we decided to call "sterlings." "Sterling" male shoppers in tweeds were stopped on a random basis in front of Bloomingdale's revolving doors. They were put through the whole routine of questions about drinking, age, etc., and their heads were carefully checked out. One difference was that we were too embarrassed to hand them quarters, so we didn't. Then, about a month later, to extend our control group, I sent five squads into a faculty meeting at Wagner College and got the same information on 49 college professors in one sweep.

Happily, the new set of derelict data turned out the same as the old, and the results of the three comparison groups were more striking than expected. When the information was presented simply as nonbald versus balding (which combined receding plus pated plus total), we found that 71 percent of the college professors were balding, 53 percent of the sterlings, and, of the derelicts (both years), only 36 percent (see Figure 1).

There were no ethnic or racial differences, nor were the other factors in the questionnaire very important. Still, age must matter, and it does.

Under age 25, we found 17 (21 percent) sterlings, but only one derelict and no professors. In fact, the average age of the sterlings was 37.5, while it was 47.5 for the other two groups. This makes sense, since it takes a lot of years to become either a derelict or a college professor.

Figure 2 shows the percentage of balding across several age levels. Naturally, the older men in all groups contain a greater proportion of hair losers. But after age 40, the differences among the groups are fascinating. The sterlings and professors reveal similar rising percentages, with the profs leading. The derelicts, however, in the years 41 to 55, actually show a slight decrease, and of the 50 guys on the Bowery past age 55, only 44 percent showed signs of balding as compared with about 80 percent of the oldies in the other groups. So the stereotype of the balding egghead professor is not contradicted by these data. For the Bowery bum, there's no doubt that he simply keeps his hair.

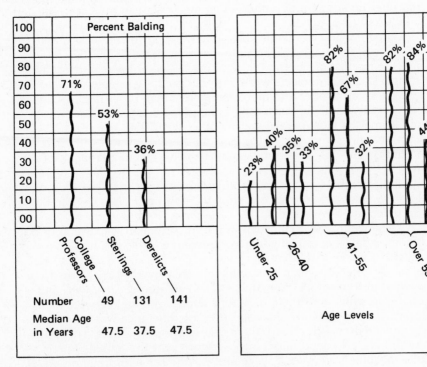

Figure 1   Figure 2

Now comes the hard part: what does it all mean? Though it did not show up in our data, I'm sure that genetics is relevant. Even so, what is the likelihood that only the bums have fewer bald daddies? Not much.

These results also rule out ethnic and racial factors. Hair and air didn't go together, since the derelicts who said they usually slept out were no less bald than those who snoozed in the dorms of the flop-house hotels.

Are the bums breezier and more carefree? Calm or numbed so that they don't feel the stress that most of us do? Is it the food they eat, or don't eat?

No. We concluded that it must be the alcohol and some resulting biochemical activity. It happens, since completing the study, that I've learned that medical literature does point to some interaction between liver damage, alcohol metabolism, the female hormone estrogen, hair growth and retention. Seems reasonable to me.

If so, I'm elated that our finds are valid. But, in a way, it doesn't matter. The whole trip started for me back in Brooklyn, as a joke. Later, my students and I really observed, recorded what we saw, and attempted to draw conclusions. Seeking the truth is always an adventure; the scientist is in all of us.

DISCUSSION QUESTIONS

1. This is the report of a scientific study published in a national journal. Would you have read it if you had not been assigned to do so?
2. Does the article seem written or spoken? Can you hear the voice of the author?
3. How do these features contribute to make the essay readable:
   a. Plain and colloquial language
   b. Sentence length
   c. Paragraph length
   d. Use of specific details
   e. The graphs
4. "Now comes the hard part: what does it all mean?" What does that tell you about statistics? About the author?
5. Do you think the essay gets the effect the author intended?

Why Are We Offering Our Nationally Advertised

GFX-100 INDOOR TV "DISH" ANTENNAS

for only $10

GUARANTEED TO FIRST 10,000 WHO RESPOND WITHIN THE NEXT 30 DAYS

Throw away your old TV rod antenna! The GFX-100 looks like an outdoor satellite "dish," but works *indoors* like ordinary "rabbit ears." *No wiring or installation!* Legal in all 50 states. *You pay NO cable fees because you're NOT getting cable!!! You pay NO satelite fees because you're NOT using satellite technology or service!!!* Works entirely via proven **"RF"** technology. Instantly locks into every local VHF and UHF channel from 2 to 83 to bring you their **movies, sports** and **special events** *just like an ordinary pair of "rabbit ears."* No cable box or special attachments needed! Helps enhance color, clarity, and weak signals. Compatible with all TVs from 3-inch portables to giant 7-footers. Sits on any TV top in less than 4 linear inches of space! Guaranteed not to utilize, replicate, transmit or interfere with any satellite signal. Complies with all applicable federal regulations. Not technical razzle-dazzle but the sheer beauty of its elegant parabolic dish design make the GFX-100 a *marketing breakthrough!* At this price, put one on every TV in your home! One-year money-back guarantee. *(Sorry, limit 3 per address. No dealers or wholesalers, please!) We reserve right to extend above time and quantity guarantees.*

© 1989 E.M.P. Sales. 535 Fifth Avenue, New York, N.Y. 10017

MAIL WITHIN THE NEXT 30 DAYS FOR THIS AMAZING OFFER

□ YES, rush me a TV "Dish" Antenna for the low price of only $10.   (R54220)

SAVE!
□ 2 FOR ONLY $17 (SAVE $3)
□ 3 FOR ONLY $25 (SAVE $5)

Add only $3 shipping for each antenna. NY residents add sales tax. Make check payable to E.M.P. Sales.

TOTAL $ _____ enclosed. Or charge to my
□ VISA □ MASTERCARD/Expire Date: Mo___Yr___
(Enter all 13 or 16 card numbers below)

Card # _____

Mr/Mrs
Ms/Miss _____

Address _____

City _____ State _____ Zip _____

MAIL TO   EMP, TV "DISH" ANTENNA, DEPT. 800-716 BOX 1280, Westbury, NY 11595

- - ALLOW UP TO 6-8 WEEKS FOR SHIPMENT - -

Courtesy of E.M.P. Sales.

DISCUSSION QUESTIONS

1. What does this ad say to the literate person who reads it all the way through?
    a. How many channels will this antenna bring in?
    b. Will it enhance color, clarity, and weak signals?
    c. How is it different from the rabbit-ears one may already have?
    d. What does it mean that the GFX-100 is "a marketing break-through"?
    e. Does the ad ever lie?
2. What does this ad say to the less literate person who just glances at its big messages?
3. Much of the text is offered as a block of relatively small print. Why is it printed that way?
4. What techniques are used to let the buyer respond quickly and easily?

ARE THERE GOOD GUYS
AND BAD GUYS LEFT?

William F. Buckley, Jr.

The progressively popular new line about events in the Soviet Union is that there isn't anything we can do one way or another to accelerate/decelerate what's happening. That is substantially true, but by no means conclusively so. We could, for instance, stir up a dangerous Great Russian nationalist xenophobia by making the wrong moves or even by saying the wrong things. But let that pass for the moment.

What catches the attention is a creeping historical egalitarianism. Some observers have become so enthusiastic about what Mr. Gorbachev is doing that they tend to blame us for its not having happened earlier. That is enough to boil the blood, and my own is eutectic on that subject.

Maureen Dowd of the *New York Times* (she is one of the ablest and funniest reporters in Christendom, if you will pardon the expression) writes about "Watching History from Washington: Awe as Soviet Party Yields Power." And pretty soon she gets to Peggy Noonan, identified as "the speechwriter for Ronald Reagan who wrote many of the former president's most biting Evil Empire denunciations." "We may (says Ms. Noonan) have exhausted our capacity for surprise and delight when we watched children in Tiananmen Square quoting Jefferson and children in East Germany taking pickaxes to the Berlin Wall as East German guards smiled for the camera." Miss Dowd goes on to comment that "Wednesday symbolized for many people in this self-absorbed capital the sense that Washington is more and more a bystander to world events rather than a player."

But now get this. Back to Noonan. "The imperial city of Washington has been taken aback by history because it thinks that it must help the world turn on its axis . . . Perhaps it's salutary to know that the world can change without our permission or encouragement."

A nice metaphor, and metaphors are Miss Noonan's thing. But a nation that 30 years ago worried about hanging on to Quemoy and Matsu; 20 years ago worried about preserving the freedom of a small IndoChinese nation (with good reason: we were unable to do so); goes to the brink of despair trying to bring back 52 State Department employees from the clutches of a Moslem fanatic; has been going crazy for eight years trying to do something about Nicaragua—hardly has got around to thinking that God waits for Washington to wind the clock every day.

Miss Dowd's commentary goes on. "In political circles, where strategists are accustomed to promoting the notion of good vs. evil, the news was discombobulating. The Soviets, the terrifying presence in all those James Bond films and Ronald Reagan speeches, seemed to be trying to kick the traces of their Evil Empire image. 'It's disorienting,' Ms. Noonan said, 'because it's hard to know who to assign the evil role to.'"

Now that is gag time.

SOURCE: Reprinted from the *Mobile Register*, February 16, 1990. Reprinted by permission of the author.

It is one thing to applaud the changes Mr. Gorbachev has licensed, and to pray to the God whose existence he denies that these changes will take organic shape and that some day we Cold Warriors can safely fade away. It is something entirely different to suppose that the dazzling changes in the Soviet Union cast doubt on who is to blame for the nightmare of the past 70 years. Only a few days ago, the Soviet Union acknowledged—for the first time—that it was responsible for a famine beginning in 1932 that claimed more Ukrainian lives than Hitler claimed Jewish lives. There is no way to extirpate the memory of that, an act that was the product of a system to whch Gorbachev continues to swear allegiance.

The millions who died awful, painful, lonely deaths in Gulag, or spent years in Soviet dungeons for the least infraction against Soviet orthodoxy, are not made to have lived painless lives because we think now to wonder out loud "who to assign the evil role to." What was evil about American diplomacy was its inability to mobilize more quickly, to prompt more efficaciously, an end to the awful suffering brought on by the dogmatists, whose influence has not ended (only a few weeks ago, Zimbabwe declared itself a Marxist–Leninist state).

God help Gorbachev. But here is a quote for the day that casts light on the question. It is from the last paragraph of James Burnham's *The Coming Defeat of Communism*, published in 1949, when Gorbachev was a worker at a machine-tractor station:

> The defeat of communism, probable on the facts, is also INEVITABLE, because there are enough determined men in the world—and their number daily grows—who have so resolved. The knowledge and intelligence, which enter into the synthesis of politics, are still needed in order to make that defeat as fruitful as possible a victory, as sparing as possible of blood and treasure. But the issue is no longer in doubt. Doubt is vanquished by the act of will which makes the decision. The future becomes servant, not master.

DISCUSSION QUESTIONS

1. Find the sentence (or two) in which the author summarizes his central message. Where is this passage located?
2. What does it tell you when the author ends his first paragraph with the line "But let that pass for the moment"?
3. The essay uses learned diction, words like "xenophobic," "egalitarianism," and "eutectic." Whom is the author writing to? Does such language encourage you to read on?
4. About half the article is made up of material quoted from Maureen Dowd, Peggy Noonan, and James Burnham. What is the effect of all the quotes? Do they help you follow the argument?
5. Does the length of the sentences encourage you to read on? (One sentence has 88 words.)
6. The author uses a one-sentence paragraph: "Now that is gag time." What does this mean?
7. Why would an author use someone else's long quotation to end an essay? What does Burnham's quote say?

INDUCTION

Induction is the process of drawing a general conclusion from incomplete evidence. Most of the things you know, you know by induction.

You believe, for example, that polar bears are white. But because you haven't seen all polar bears, your judgment is based on limited evidence. The two or three polar bears you have seen were white. Those shown in *National Geographic* or on the Discovery Channel were white. Everyone you know agrees they are white. From this information, you reasonably decide that all polar bears are white.

This process is induction. You consider evidence you have seen or heard to draw a conclusion about things you haven't seen or heard. The intellectual movement from limited facts—called a *sample*—to a general conviction is called an *inductive leap.*

Most conclusions regarding past, present, and future events are based on this kind of leap. You believe, for example, that Balboa discovered the Pacific Ocean, that taking Tylenol eases a headache, and that the Republicans will win the next presidential election. Because you can never secure all the evidence relating to these questions, you reasonably make judgments from the evidence you have.

It is equally reasonable, when you hear induced conclusions, to inquire about the number and kinds of facts that went into making them. For a claim to be credible, its sample must be (1) known, (2) sufficient, and (3) representative. If you are told simply that the FBI is directed by Jewish conspirators, you can withhold belief on the grounds that the sample is not known. No evidence is given to support the accusation. If you hear a famous athlete's low IQ cited to demonstrate that athletes (or members of the athlete's race or nationality) are generally ignorant, you can respond that the sample is not sufficient. One example proves nothing about a large group. And if you hear the cruelties of the Spanish Inquisition used as evidence of the repressive views of Catholics in general, you can insist that the sample is not representative. Spanish practice in the fifteenth century is hardly typical of worldwide Catholicism today.

You should recognize such unsupported claims when you see them. Try to keep them out of your own writing.

IS THE SAMPLE KNOWN?

You frequently hear statements that lack evidence. An advertisement announces that "Ban is preferred by seven out of ten American women." A *Globe* headline reports "Seven Out of Ten Husbands Are Cheating." Rumors whisper that green M&Ms are aphrodisiacs, that McDonald's hamburgers contain worms, and that Procter & Gamble is involved in Satan worship. Such claims can be dismissed if no evidence is offered to support them.

A variation popular with exposé writers is to make an extravagant claim and then point to conclusive evidence—which happens to be unavailable. They argue that superbeings from outer space built Stonehenge and that President Warren Harding was murdered by his wife—then they regret that evidence is lost in the past. They talk confidently about Bigfoot, Atlantis, and the Loch Ness monster—and then lament that proof remains out of reach. (For years, tabloids reported arthritis cures, sacred statues that talk, and other wonders occurring "behind the Iron Curtain.") Popular writers insist that UFOs are extraterrestrial spaceships and that a massive conspiracy led to the attempted assassinations of President Reagan and Pope John Paul II—then they protest that government officials and law enforcement agencies are withholding crucial evidence.

When you become familiar with such stories, you begin to see a pattern. The tabloids and the talk shows tell you about the audio tapes giving intimate conversations between President Kennedy and Marilyn Monroe. They mention a dog who can read and an 87-year-old woman who is pregnant. Where are these amazing wonders? You know where they are. They're elsewhere, in some distant place. You can't get there from here.

All these are inductions with an absent sample.

IS THE SAMPLE SUFFICIENT?

Induction with an insufficient sample is common. You regularly hear charges like these:

> Most labor leaders are crooks. Look at Tony Boyle, Frank Brewster, Jimmy Hoffa, and Roy Williams.

> Running is dangerous. You saw what happened to Jim Fixx.

> Don't talk to me about Puerto Ricans. I lived next to a Puerto Rican family for two years.

Clearly, the indicated samples—*four* labor leaders, *one* runner, and *one* family—are inadequate evidence on which to base any broad conclusion.

Insufficient samples lead to stereotyping. They underlie the simplistic descriptions you hear about blacks, Jews, college professors, Republicans, epileptics, southern Baptists, feminists, Swedish stewardesses, athletes, and cab drivers.

Persuaders commonly try to enhance the effect on an insufficient sample by insisting their examples are "typical" or "average." In argument, the words "typical" and "average" deserve immediate suspicion.

IS THE SAMPLE REPRESENTATIVE?

A sample is called *unrepresentative* when it is not typical of the whole class of things being studied. It is easy to see that you cannot gauge your town's attitude toward a proposed liquor tax by polling only the citizens at a corner tavern or only members of a local fundamentalist church.

Nevertheless, conclusions based on an unrepresentative sample can sound persuasive on first hearing; for example, "Women are better drivers than men; they have fewer accidents." Here the sample is large enough— a substantial body of accident statistics—but it is not broad enough to be meaningful. The conclusion concerns *all drivers*, but the sample group includes only *drivers who have had accidents*. To be representative (that is, typical of the whole area under discussion), the sample must include all four groups involved:

1. Men
2. Women
3. Drivers who had accidents
4. Drivers who had no accidents

This broad sample would show that there are fewer women in automobile accidents because there are fewer women driving. The isolated accident statistics are meaningless if they are not compared to those for all drivers.

Similarly, if you hear that 80 percent of all San Quentin convicts came from homes that served liquor, you can't draw much of a conclusion. The implied judgments describe *everyone*, but the sample includes only *convicts*; there are no general statistics with which to make comparison. Perhaps 80 percent of *all* homes serve liquor. Then, of course, the narrow statistics become meaningless.

Photographic evidence is usually induction with an unrepresentative sample. A candidate's campaign photographs show him and his loving wife walking on the beach with their children. They show him late at night reading important books and thinking deeply about the problems of the day. The pictures you see are chosen from dozens taken by professional photographers and media people who arranged settings, chose clothes, and told the candidate how to stand and what to do. When you see such photos, ask yourself, "What would this candidate look like if I saw him right now?"

You must remember too that photos can be faked. The cover of *TV Guide* (August 25, 1990) carried a glamorous picture of Oprah Winfrey. Later it was revealed that her head had been superimposed on the body of Ann-Margret. Recent literature celebrating multiple UFO sightings at Gulf Breeze, Florida, offered sensational prose and doctored photographs.

Any induced conclusion is open to question, then, if its sample is too small or unduly weighted in some way. Nielsen Media Research claims to know the audience size for American television programs. But because the information comes from 4000 people meters (one for every 24,000 homes), the sufficiency of the sample has been questioned. *The Hite Report* on female sexuality was based on responses to questionnaires mailed to chapters of the National Organization for Women, abortion-rights groups, and university women's centers; on information from women who saw notices in newspapers, the *Village Voice*, *Mademoiselle*, *Bride's*, and *Ms.* magazines, and who wrote in for the questionnaires; and on responses from female readers of *Oui* magazine, which ran the questionnaire in its entirety. Clearly, the sample is not representative of all American women.

Any poll with a selective sample—that is, where some individuals choose to respond to it and others do not—is unrepresentative. Those who choose to respond cannot represent those who don't.

POLLING

People can misuse a poll to make it support a favored opinion. They can announce the results of surveys that were never taken. (Politicians have for years made good use of "private polls" to enhance the prestige of a lagging candidate.) They can phrase a poll question to draw the response they seek (Evangelist Jerry Falwell asked, "Do you approve of the present laws legalizing Abortion-on-Demand that resulted in the murder of more than one million babies last year? Yes _____. No _____."), or they can inflate others' polls. A memorable example occurred in 1972, when Washington television station WTTG asked viewers to write in their opinion of President Richard Nixon's decision to mine North Vietnamese harbors. The final poll result showed 5157 supporting the president and a much smaller number opposing him. Later investigation showed that some 4000 of the votes favorable to Nixon came directly from the Committee for the Reelection of the President.

What is an adequate sample on which to base a reliable judgment? There is no easy answer. It varies with both the character of the question and the degree of probability you want.

You should remember, however, that a small sample—if generally representative—can sustain a broad conclusion. George Gallup assesses the opinions of the American public by polling 1500 individuals. But because his sample is chosen so that every adult American has an equal chance of being interviewed, the Gallup poll, like similar polls, is a reliable source of information. The mathematical probability is that, 95 times out of 100, a selection of 1500 anonymous people will give results no more than 3 percentage points off the figures that would be obtained by interviewing the whole population.

In the past 23 national elections, the Gallup predictions were an average of 2.3 percentage points off the exact results.

In the 1980 presidential election, however, both the Gallup and the Harris polls were 4 percentage points off the final total. Apparently many voters made up their minds at the last minute, after these polls had been completed. Both Carter's and Reagan's personal pollsters, who surveyed opinion right up to election eve, predicted the final results exactly.

In later contests, the polls were impressively accurate. In 1984, Gallup predicted Ronald Reagan would win 59 percent of the vote; he won 59.1 percent. In 1988, it said George Bush would win 56 percent of the vote; he won 54 percent.

OCCAM'S RAZOR

Even in everyday experience, you commonly use very limited information to draw a tentative conclusion. This is not unreasonable. If you see that a friend is not wearing her engagement ring and is behaving despondently, you may speculate that she has broken her engagement. The evidence is not sufficient for you to offer condolences, but it will keep you from making jokes about marriage.

If you hear from a friend that a new restaurant is disappointing, you will probably choose not to eat there—at least until you hear a contrary report. Your conclusion is based on a tiny sample, but it is all the sample you have. As your sample grows, so will your degree of conviction.

With induction, you should remember *Occam's razor*, the maxim that when a body of evidence exists, the simplest conclusion that expresses all of it is probably the best. A classic illustration occurred in 1967, when New Orleans District Attorney James Garrison sought to prove that Clay Shaw, a local businessman, was involved in the assassination of President Kennedy. He submitted that Shaw's address book carried the entry "Lee Odom, P.O. Box 19106, Dallas, Texas," and that the number "PO 19106," when properly decoded, became "WH 15601," the unlisted phone number of Jack Ruby, slayer of Kennedy's assassin Lee Harvey Oswald. (The process involved "unscrambling" the numerals and—since P and O equal 7 and 6 on a telephone dial—subtracting 1300.) Thus Garrison used the entry in Shaw's address book as inductive evidence leading to a sensational conclusion. But Occam's razor suggests a simpler explanation, one that proved to be true: Shaw was acquainted with a businessman named Lee Odom, whose Dallas address was P.O. Box 19106.

You should remember Occam's razor when you read the many books and articles that "reexamine" famous crimes. Routinely, they conclude that people like Lee Harvey Oswald, Alger Hiss, Lizzie Borden, Bruno Hauptmann, Carl Coppolino, James Earl Ray, Sam Sheppard, the Rosenbergs, Alice Crimmins, Jeffrey MacDonald, the Atlanta child murderer, and Sacco and Vanzetti were really innocent. The true criminal was either a shadowy figure whom nobody saw or members of some complex and incredible conspiracy. Occam's razor says that the person with the motive and the opportunity and the gun is probably guilty. It submits that the 16-year-old Greek girl who had an illegitimate baby probably was not captured and impregnated by space aliens.

As you read, carefully examine the facts underlying conclusions. Are they given? Are they sufficient and representative? As you write, support your generalizations as much as you can.

EXERCISES

How reliable are these inductive arguments?

1. In a study of a possible relationship between pornography and antisocial behavior, questionnaires were sent to 7500 psychiatrists and psychoanalysts, whose listings in the directory of the American Psychological Association indicated clinical experience. Over 3400 of these professionals responded. The result: 7.4 percent of the psychiatrists and psychologists had cases in which they were convinced that pornography was a causal factor in antisocial behavior; an additional 9.4 percent were suspicious of such a connection; 3.2 percent did not commit themselves; and 80 percent said they had no cases in which a causal connection was suspected.
2. Do you prefer your hamburger flame-broiled or fried?
3. In an article warning of the dangers of cholesterol, *Time* showed the clogged arteries in the heart of an 85-year-old woman.
4. Listerine Antiseptic advertisement: "Proven most effective against colds."
5. How can you argue that large families frustrate the individual child? Benjamin Franklin was the eighth child of his parents. There were six in the Washington family, and Abraham Lincoln had seven brothers and sisters. The Jeffersons numbered 10; the Madisons, 12; the Longfellows, 8; and the Beethovens, 12.
6. Do you prefer a hamburger that is grilled on a hot stainless steel grill or one cooked by passing the raw meat through an open gas flame?
7. *Psychology Today* asked its readers to answer questions about paranormal activity. The responses showed that 85 percent of the women and 78 percent of the men believe ESP exists. Wow!
8. I don't care what you say about stereotypes. Most of the blondes I know are dumb.
9. Cola drinkers were asked to compare glasses of Coke and Pepsi for taste. The Coke was in a glass marked Q, and the Pepsi in a glass marked M. A majority of those tested said they preferred the taste of Pepsi.

10. Certainly it's obvious from the newspaper reports that rich and famous people have a higher proportion of divorces than the general public.
11. A study of 3400 New York citizens who had had a recent heart attack showed that 70 percent of them were 10 to 50 pounds overweight. Clearly, obesity is the cause of heart disease.
12. Arguing that eighteenth-century English poetry was essentially prosaic, Matthew Arnold offered a passage from "Pope's verse, take it almost where you will":

    To Hounslow Heath I point and Banstead Down:
    Thence comes your mutton and these chicks my own.
13. Don't tell me that homosexuals aren't sick. I'm a psychiatrist with a large number of homosexual patients, and all are deeply disturbed. Every one them.
14. Should every American be tested for AIDS? In a 1987 poll conducted by the *National Enquirer*, 83 percent said yes.

ESSAY ASSIGNMENTS

Write an essay either affirming or opposing one of these statements. The arguments you encounter in your background reading will probably be inductive, and so will your essay.

1. Prisoners should be brainwashed.
2. ESP has been proved to exist.
3. Opera is a waste of time.
4. Rock music is a national danger.
5. Jogging is a perfect exercise.
6. Homosexuals should not be allowed to teach in elementary school.
7. The drinking age should be raised to 24.
8. X is worth saving. (Fill in the X.)

NO ALLUSIONS
IN THE CLASSROOM

Jaime M. O'Neill

Josh Billings, a 19th-century humorist, wrote that is it better "not to know so much than to know so many things that ain't so." Recently, after 15 years of teaching in community colleges, I decided to take a sampling to find out what my students know that ain't so. I did this out of a growing awareness that they don't always understand what I say. I suspected that part of their failure to understand derived from the fact that they did not catch my allusions. An allusion to a writer, a geographical locality or a historical episode inevitably produced telltale expressions of bewilderment.

There is a game played by students and teachers everywhere. The game goes like this: the teacher tries to find out what students don't know so that he can correct those deficiencies; the students, concerned with grades and slippery self-images, try to hide their ignorance in every way they can. So it is that students seldom ask pertinent questions. So it is that teachers assume that students possess basic knowledge which, in fact, they don't possess.

Last semester I broke the rules of this time-honored game when I presented my English-composition students with an 86-question "general knowledge" test on the first day of class. There were 26 people in the class; they ranged in age from 18 to 54. They had all completed at least one quarter of college-level work.

Here is a sampling of what they knew that just ain't so:

Creative: Ralph Nader is a baseball player. Charles Darwin invented gravity. Christ was born in the 16th century. J. Edgar Hoover was a 19th-century president. Neil Simon wrote "One Flew Over the Cuckoo's Nest"; "The Great Gatsby" was a magician in the 1930s. Franz Joseph Haydn was a songwriter during the same decade. Sid Caesar was an early Roman emperor. Mark Twain invented the cotton gin, Heinrich Himmler invented the Heimlich maneuver. Jefferson Davis was a guitar player for The Jefferson Airplane. Benito Mussolini was a Russian leader of the 18th century; Dwight D. Eisenhower came earlier, serving as a president during the 17th century. William Faulkner made his name as a 17th-century scientist. All of these people must have appreciated the work of Pablo Picasso, who painted masterpieces in the 12th century.

My students were equally creative in their understanding of geography. They knew, for instance, that Managua is the capital of Vietnam, that Cape Town is in the United States and that Beirut is in Germany. Bogotá, of course, is in Borneo (unless it is in China). Camp David is in Israel, and Stratford-on-Avon is in Grenada (or Gernada). Gdansk is in Ireland. Cologne is in the Virgin Islands. Mazatlán is in Switzerland.

SOURCE: Reprinted from *Newsweek*, September 23, 1985. Reprinted by permission of the author.

Belfast was variously located in Egypt, Germany, Belgium and Italy. Leningrad was transported to Jamaica; Montreal to Spain.

And on it went. Most students answered incorrectly far more often than they answered correctly. Several of them meticulously wrote "I don't know" 86 times, or 80 times, or 62 times.

They did not like the test. Although I made it clear that the test would not be graded, they did not like having their ignorance exposed. One of them dismissed the test by saying, "Oh, I get it; it's like Trivial Pursuit." Imagining a game of Trivial Pursuit among some of today's college students is a frightening thought; such a game could last for years.

But the comment bothered me. What, in this time in our global history, is trivial? And what is essential? Perhaps it no longer matters very much if large numbers of people in the world's oldest democratic republic know little of their own history and even less about the planet they inhabit.

But I expect that it does matter. I also suspect that my students provide a fairly good cross section of the general population. There are 1,274 two-year colleges in the United States that collectively enroll nearly 5 million students. I have taught at four of those colleges in two states, and I doubt that my questionnaire would have produced different results at any of them. My colleagues at universities tell me that they would not be surprised at similar undergraduate answers.

My small sampling is further corroborated by recent polls which disclosed that a significant number of American adults have no idea which side the United States supported in Vietnam and that a majority of the general populace have no idea which side the United States is currently supporting in Nicaragua or El Salvador.

Less importantly, a local marketing survey asked a sampling of young computer whizzes to identify the character in IBM's advertising campaign that is based on an allusion to Charlie Chaplin in "Modern Times." Few of them had heard of Charlie Chaplin; fewer heard or knew about the movie classic.

Common Heritage: As I write this, the radio is broadcasting the news about the Walker family. Accused of spying for the Soviets, the Walkers, according to a U.S. attorney, will be the Rosenbergs of the '80s. One of my students thought Ethel Rosenberg was a singer from the 1930s. The rest of them didn't know. Communication depends, to some extent, upon the ability to make (and catch) allusions, to share a common understanding and a common heritage. Even preliterate societies can claim the shared assessment of their world. As we enter the postindustrial "information processing" age, what sort of information will be processed? And, as the educational establishment is driven "back to the basics," isn't it time we decided that a common understanding of our history and our planet is most basic of all?

As a teacher, I find myself in the ignorance-and-hope business. Each year hopeful faces confront me, trying to conceal their ignorance. Their hopes ride on the dispelling of that ignorance.

All our hopes do.

We should begin servicing that hope more responsibly and dispelling that ignorance with a more systematic approach to imparting essential knowledge.

Socrates, the American Indian chieftain, would have wanted it that way.

DISCUSSION QUESTIONS

1. Is the author an effective writer? Did you find the essay easy to read? Does she write with a personal voice?
2. She uses an inductive process to reach the conclusion that young college students are generally uninformed. What is her sample? How big is it? How representative is it?
3. What does she do to make the results of her small sample more convincing?
4. What kind of test did she give? Was it just a list of names to identify? Were there multiple-choice questions?
5. How important do you think it is that students be able to recognize allusions? What's so bad about thinking that Stratford-on-Avon is in Gernada?
6. What conclusion does she draw about "the ignorance-and-hope business"?

Courtesy of the American Cancer Society.

DISCUSSION QUESTIONS

1. The author uses irony. What is really meant by the claim that "Smoking is very glamorous"?
2. If the author is making a statement about how smokers look, what is the evidence?
3. Where do you think the Cancer Society people and their photographer found this woman? Give reasons for your answer.
4. Put in terms of inductive argument, is the sample known, sufficient, and representative?
5. What does this argument tell you about photographic evidence in general?

BAN
BOXING

Robert E. McAfee

As a practicing physician, I am convinced that boxing should be banned.

First, boxing is a very visible example that violence is accepted behavior in our society—outside the ring as well as inside. This sends the wrong message to America's youth, and at a time when so many kinds of violence are on the rise, it is a message we should stop.

Second, boxing is the only sport where the sole object is to injure the opponent. Think about what a knockout really is: It is a cerebral concussion that knocks the victim senseless! Boxing, then, is morally offensive because its intent is to inflict brain injuries on another person. And it is medically indefensible because these injuries so often lead to irreversible medical consequences, such as a subdural hematoma, nonfatal acute intracranial hemorrhages, "punch drunk syndrome," progressive neurological disorder and serious eye conditions.

Third, medical science can't take someone who has suffered repeated blows to the head and restore that person to normal function. Many physicians, with new methods of brain scanning, have seen an otherwise young and healthy individual sustain serious and permanently disabling injuries due to boxing, sometimes in just one fight. This causes many physicians to conclude that our society should ban boxing. And sadly—slowly but surely—as many of our nationally known veteran boxers can no longer hide the long-term effects of brain injury, the public is beginning to understand what only doctors and family members previously knew.

What about the argument that injuries occur in other sports? Quite simply, in those sports, injuring the opponent is not the accepted method of scoring or winning. And in those sports, there is an attempt to wear protective equipment that will minimize injury. But scientific evidence shows there is no really effective way to prevent boxing injuries that may have a lifetime effect—even from one fight.

And finally, to those who say boxing "gives poor kids an opportunity to get out of the ghetto," I have a better suggestion. Let's take each young person with that precious, undamaged brain and combine some education with that same commitment to excellence he has for boxing. I guarantee that youngster better success over a lifetime—and perhaps a longer and healthier life, too.

Boxing is morally and medically offensive. So as a physician, I believe boxing should be banned.

SOURCE: Reprinted from *USA Today*, December 27, 1990. Reprinted by permission of the author.

DISCUSSION QUESTIONS

1. How effective are the author's introduction and conclusion? Is it clear what he is talking about?
2. The author makes three arguments against boxing. What are they? Is one of them more compelling and persuasive than the others? Why is that?
3. The author challenges two arguments made by people who defend boxing. What problems arise when a person does this?
4. What might the author have done to make his argument more interesting and readable? Why is it duller than it should be? How can you avoid this problem in your own writing?

Elizabeth Richardson
Model/High Jumper

"So I have a vitamin gap, big deal."

"I used to take vitamins. But then I got too busy. I work long hours and—sure, I skip meals sometimes."

Elizabeth Richardson is part of an alarming statistic. 97% of Americans don't eat a balanced diet. And the problem starts right with breakfast, or more accurately without it. It's the meal we skip most often.

And dieters are even more at risk.

Cutting out meals, even whole categories of food.

But even eating three meals a day is no guarantee your body is getting all the vitamins and minerals it needs.

Problems like physical stress and illness rob you of vitamins and minerals. So do smoking and drinking. And, birth control pills, pregnancy and lactation also increase nutritional needs.

For instance, many of us aren't getting enough calcium for healthy bones. Or enough iron for healthy blood. Or enough of the B vitamins essential to every cell in our bodies.

The fact is, most people reading this ad probably have one or more vitamin or mineral gaps to fill.

And, scientists are now studying the nutritional role of vitamins, minerals and other nutrients in helping to protect against diseases such as cancer, heart disease and osteoporosis.

So why live at risk? Fill the gap. Take vitamin and mineral supplements every day. Is it a big deal? You bet your life it is.

Council For Responsible Nutrition. An association of the nutritional supplement industry.

Courtesy of the Council for Responsible Nutrition.

DISCUSSION QUESTIONS

1. The argument is based on two claims: "97% of Americans don't eat a balanced diet" and "most people reading this ad have one or more vitamin or mineral gaps to fill." What evidence supports these statements?
2. Is this ad addressed to all Americans, i.e., Americans of both genders and all economic groups? Cite your evidence.
3. Who is Elizabeth Richardson? Is she real or fictional? Does it make a difference?
4. What can you infer about Elizabeth Richardson (real or fictional) by looking at the picture and the text? What is going on in that picture?
5. Identify the eight activities that can "rob you of vitamins and minerals." Is it self-evident that all people involved in such activities need to take vitamin supplements?
6. What is the evidence that vitamins and minerals help prevent cancer and heart disease?
7. "The fact is, most people reading this ad probably have one or more vitamin or mineral gaps to fill." "So why live at risk?" Do sentences like these require much evidence?
8. Who is the Council for Responsible Nutrition? Is it a federal agency like the National Research Council? Does it make a difference?
9. Did you find the prose easy to read? Look at the words, the sentences, and the paragraphs. Is this good writing?

CHOICE OF SCHOOLS:
NO QUICK FIX

Richard D. Miller

Simple solutions to complex problems. The insistence on quick fixes. Political horses to ride to get through the next election. These conditions are rampant in American society, and perhaps the best illustration is what has become known as school choice.

"Choice" is as American as apple pie. Perhaps that's why politicians who have traditionally supported the rise of tax credits and vouchers and the dismantling of the public schools have chosen it to describe their efforts.

A well-chosen word can be a mask, a cover, a ploy to distract people from the true intent of an effort, no matter how damaging to the public good.

As conceived, choice would make it possible for students and their parents to choose to attend any school. On the surface, that sounds innocent enough. However, look more closely at the implications for American society.

- Our nation's public schools have been the fountainhead of democracy. It is in our schools that children and youth of many races, creeds, and social and economic backgrounds come together to bring life to our motto, E Pluribus Unum, "Of the Many. . .One." Choice, as currently described, would divide our nation.
- When given an uncontrolled choice of schools, only the most motivated will move, leaving behind a ghetto of the unmotivated.
- If a student decides to attend a school many miles away, then how will parents become involved in their child's school? Economically, many parents are working two jobs and often can't afford a car or extra public transportation. Most proponents of choice have little or no experience with the social and economic conditions that sap energy and drain the family budget by having to cover the cost of childcare, transportation and other expenses.
- Imagine, with choice, the recruitment that would take place. Each public school would need a sizable marketing budget to attract students. Of course, those communities that are not quite so wealthy would be out-promoted.
- In short, as conceived, choice would drive this nation even further in the direction of a two-tiered society, rich and poor.

The American Association of School Administrators believes that all children should receive the best education possible. Because we have been child and education advocates since 1865, we cannot tolerate the elitist view that some schools should be excellent and others should be allowed to deteriorate and disappear.

SOURCE: Reprinted from the *Mobile Register,* September 5, 1990. Reprinted by permission of the author.

Here are the types of choice AASA supports:

- Alternatives or "choices" offered within a school building, since children have different learning needs and styles.
- Magnet or specialty schools that provide true educational choices and excellent programs, in some cases, outside regular attendance areas. Choice should be based on the content of the program or the instructional approach, not on whether schools are deemed to be good or bad, since as we stated earlier, all schools must be excellent.
- In some cases, for reasons of convenience or hardship, students and their parents need the option of attending classes in another public school, even if that school is in another district.

Of course, any program of open enrollment must consider whether space is available in a receiving school and whether racial balance is sustained or upset.

Any decisions on open enrollment or choice should be made locally, not imposed by state or federal officials. Local school leaders can predict the impact of any proposal of this type. There, parents can make their wishes known.

DISCUSSION QUESTIONS

1. The author is executive director of the American Association of School Administrators. Is he speaking for himself or for his organization? Does it make a difference?
2. The author gives four reasons why "choice of schools" is a bad thing. Specify the reasons. Are they all equally persuasive? Are they, in fact, different reasons?
3. The author rejects "choice" as an "elitist view." Why is that a bad thing?
4. On occasion, the author resorts to emotional language: "political horses," "a mask," "a ploy," a "quick fix." Does he do it often? Would it help him to do it more?
5. In two sections of the essay, the author uses "bullets" to indicate a list. He uses four bullets to mark his arguments against "choice." He use two bullets to show the procedures AASA supports. Is this a good way to write? Would it be effective if you used bullets (or numbered lists) in your writing?

Every day is Earth Day with nuclear energy.

Nuclear energy is America's second-leading source of electricity. Every day, nuclear energy generates one-fifth of America's electricity— enough to light over half the homes in the U.S.

Nuclear energy doesn't emit greenhouse gases. Because nuclear plants generate electricity cleanly, every day nuclear energy helps reduce greenhouse gas emissions from utilities by 20%.

Nuclear energy helps reduce air pollution. Every day, by using nuclear-generated electricity Americans help reduce airborne pollutants by over 19,000 tons.

Nuclear energy helps reduce our dependence on foreign oil. Every day, nuclear energy helps cut our foreign oil use by over 850,000 barrels and reduce our foreign oil payments by $16 million.

Nuclear Electricity
and
Energy Independence

For more complete information on nuclear energy, send for this free booklet.
Write to: U.S. Council for Energy Awareness
P.O. Box 66080, Dept. ED01, Washington, D.C. 20035

©1990 USCEA

As seen in April 1990 issues of Newsweek, The Wall Street Journal, The New York Times, The Washington Post, Forbes, The Economist, and Congressional Quarterly, and in May 1990 issues of Business Week, TIME, Sports Illustrated, U.S. News & World Report, Business Week, and The Atlantic.

Courtesy of U.S. Committee for Energy Awareness.

DISCUSSION QUESTIONS

1. The ad is laid out with four pictures illustrating the four arguments for nuclear power. Is this form compelling and easy to follow? Why didn't the author just write a short essay?
2. The "Earth Day" title emphasizes the environmental advantages of nuclear power. Do all four arguments relate to the environment?
3. How effective are the statistics supporting the environmental argument? Do the illustrations help or hurt the argument?
4. What is paradoxical about this argument? What is the main complaint of critics of nuclear power?
5. Why all the emphasis on the amount of nuclear power *now* being generated? Does this support the case for the safety of nuclear power?
6. What is the greenhouse effect? If the information in this ad is true, does it make a strong argument for nuclear energy?
7. Why does the author throw in the final argument about the political/economic advantages of nuclear power?

"DR. JACK KEVORKIAN
IS NOT ABOVE THE LAW"

OAKLAND COUNTY PROSECUTOR'S OFFICE

FOR IMMEDIATE RELEASE
December 3, 1990

Oakland County Prosecutor Richard Thompson announced today that Dr. Jack Kevorkian has been charged with first degree murder in the June 4th death of Janet Adkins.

Michigan statute 750.316 clearly provides, "Murder which is perpetrated by means of poison, . . . is murder of the first degree . . .". The 1920 Michigan Supreme Court decision, *People* v *Roberts,* interpreting that provision of the statute, held that a husband who mixed and placed poison near his wife at her request so that she could drink it, was guilty of first degree murder when she died as a result of drinking the poison. To date, the *Roberts* case has not been reversed by the Michigan Supreme Court, nor has it been revised by legislative action.

Thompson said,

"I have a constitutional duty to faithfully enforce the laws of this state as enacted by the legislature and interpreted by the court, regardless of the tragic and emotional aspects of this case. Under our constitution, the legislature is empowered to declare what is a crime. And as a prosecutor, I have no legitimate authority to ignore or stipulate away duly-enacted laws.

"Dr. Kevorkian was the primary and legal cause of Janet Adkins' death. He cannot avoid his criminal culpability by the clever use of a switch.

1. He constructed the 'suicide machine' for the sole purpose of causing death.
2. He saw Janet Adkins for the sole purpose of causing her death.
3. He used his physician's license to obtain drugs for the sole purpose of causing her death.
4. He attached the suicide machine to Janet Adkins for the sole purpose of causing her death.
5. He attached the electro-cardiogram to Janet Adkins for the sole purpose of insuring she was dead before he called the authorities.
6. He shook the bottle with the lethal drugs to insure that there was a good flow.
7. He instructed Janet Adkins on how to hit the switch.
8. He removed the safety cap from the switch.
9. He was present throughout the entire process.
   Janet Adkins was not terminally ill or suffering pain. For me not to charge Dr. Kevorkian under these circumstances would be a corruption of the law and turn Oakland County into the suicide mecca of our nation.

SOURCE: Press release from the Prosecuting Attorney's Office, Oakland County, Michigan. Reprinted with permission.

"Dr. Jack Kevorkian is not above the law; and if he wants to change the law, he should address the legislative branch of government. If physicians are to have a license to kill in addition to their license to heal, that license must come from the legislature, not the prosecutor."

DISCUSSION QUESTIONS

1. This argument involves Dr. Jack Kevorkian's suicide machine. The machine allows a person to throw a switch and inject a lethal dose of poison into his or her bloodstream. Janet Adkins, a victim of Alzheimer's disease, used the machine on June 4, 1990. Does this impress you as murder or suicide? Can it be both?

2. Specify the number of places where the author says he *has no choice* but to bring charges against Dr. Kevorkian. Why does he emphasize this? What accusation is he trying to avoid?

3. How effective an argument is the list of nine reasons for charging Dr. Kevorkian?

4. Are all nine reasons equally persuasive? Which seem more compelling? Do any seem weak?

5. The author says Dr. Kevorkian "cannot avoid his criminal culpability by the clever use of a switch." What does he mean by "a switch"? Do you think this is a good choice of words?

6. Does the author's system of indenting and enumerating seem an effective way to present information? Wouldn't a carefully written paragraph do just as well?

DEDUCTION

Deduction is the opposite of induction. Where induction moves from specific facts to a general conclusion, deduction moves from a general truth to a specific application. Because there are many kinds of deduction—some quite complicated—this discussion aims to be little more than a useful oversimplification.

The vehicle of deduction is the syllogism. This is an argument that takes two existing truths and puts them together to create a new truth. Here is the classic example:

MAJOR PREMISE: All men are mortal.
MINOR PREMISE: Socrates is a man.
CONCLUSION: Socrates is mortal.

In everyday life, you'll meet many examples of deductive thinking. The syllogism is often abbreviated, with one of the parts implied rather than stated.

You haven't registered, so you can't vote. (IMPLICIT MAJOR PREMISE: Anyone who does not register cannot vote.)

No man lives forever. Even old Dan Thompson will die someday. (IMPLICIT MINOR PREMISE: Dan Thompson is a man.)

Anyone can make a mistake. After all, Roger is only human. (IMPLICIT CONCLUSION: Roger can make a mistake.)

Many informal arguments can be resolved into syllogistic form. You do this so you can analyze them more systematically.

A deductive argument is considered reliable if it fulfills three conditions: (1) the premise must be true, (2) the terms must be unambiguous, and (3) the syllogistic form must be valid. These requirements will be considered in turn.

ARE THE PREMISES TRUE?

First, the premises must be true. Because the major premise of a syllogism is usually derived by induction (that is, it is a general statement drawn from specific facts), you can judge its reliability by asking whether the facts that produced it are known to be sufficient and representative. Here is a vulnerable example:

> Gentlemen prefer blondes.
> George Bush is a gentleman.
> George Bush prefers blondes.

This syllogism reaches an unreliable conclusion because the major premise is unproven. The generalization about blondes exists only as a cliché (and as a title by Anita Loos); it was not induced from any known sample. You have heard the common argument for lowering the drinking age:

> Anyone old enough to fight is old enough to drink.
> Eighteen-year-olds are old enough to fight.
> They should be old enough to drink.

This syllogism will be persuasive to anyone who accepts the major premise. Many people find the premise unacceptable.   *Does my = most?*

Political partisans regularly use dubious major premises (a war hero would make a good president, a woman would make a poor one, etc.) to produce the conclusions they want.

IS THE LANGUAGE UNAMBIGUOUS?

The terms of deductive argument must be clear and consistent. If definitions change within a syllogism, arguments can be amusingly fallacious:

> All cats chase mice.
> My wife is a cat.
> Therefore . . .

> All men are created equal.
> Women are not men.
> Therefore . . .

This kind of argument can be genuinely misleading. The advertisement "See *Dangerous Liaisons*, the Academy Award Winner" was based on this syllogism:

> The Academy Award-winning movie is worth seeing.
> *Dangerous Liaisons* is this year's Academy Award-winning movie.
> *Dangerous Liaisons* is worth seeing.

Here the phrase "Academy Award-winning movie" is ambiguous. In the major premise, it refers to the movie voted Best Picture of the year; in the minor premise, to a movie winning one of the dozens of lesser awards given annually. *Dangerous Liaisons* won an award for costume design.

Ambiguous examples are not always frivolous. Consider these syllogisms:

> Killing an innocent human being is murder.
> Abortion kills an innocent human being.
> Abortion is murder.

> A private club should have the legal right to accept or exclude anyone
> it wants.
> The Junior Chamber of Commerce is a private club.
> The JCs should have the legal right to accept or exclude anyone they
> want (translation: they shouldn't have to admit women).

These syllogisms went all the way to the U.S. Supreme Court, where the
terms "human being" and "private club" were analyzed carefully.

A provocative advertisement is based on this syllogism:

> You should be anxious to buy a genuine diamond ring for only $5.
> We are offering a genuine diamond ring for $5.
> You should be anxious to buy this ring.

The advertisers offer a ring containing a 0.25-carat diamond chip. This
isn't a diamond in the sense you usually think of one.

IS THE SYLLOGISM VALID?

A reliable syllogism must have a valid form. This requirement introduces
a complex area of discussion, because there are many types of syllogisms,
each with its own test of validity. Commonly, "valid form" means that the
general subject or condition of the major premise must appear in the
minor premise as well. It is easy to see that this argument is false:

> All murderers have ears.
> All Methodists have ears.
> All murderers are Methodists.

What makes the argument unreliable syllogistically is the fact that the term
"murderers" does not recur in the minor premise. A major premise about
"all murderers" can only lead to a conclusion about murderers. Similarly,
the premises "If Taylor loses his job, his wife will leave him" and "Taylor
does not lose his job" produce no necessary conclusion. The condition
"lose his job" does not occur in the minor premise.

When an invalid syllogism appears as argument, it usually maintains
that things with one quality in common share a kind of identity. Such
argument takes extreme forms:

> The father of Miss Smith's baby has blood type O.
> Mike Hanna has blood type O.
> Therefore . . .

> The American Communist Party opposes resumption of the draft.
> Larry Burton opposes resumption of the draft.
> Therefore . . .

Because the crucial term does not appear in both premises of these syllogisms, their conclusions are no more valid than the claim that all murderers
are Methodists.

DEDUCTION **49**

These three tests, then, permit you to judge the reliability of a deductive argument.

Some deductive arguments involve several syllogisms. Consider this example:

> When a man becomes emotionally disturbed, there is a recognizable change in his voice patterns.
> When a man tells a lie, he becomes emotionally disturbed.
> When a man tells a lie, there is a recognizable change in his voice patterns.

> When a man tells a lie, there is a recognizable change in his voice patterns.
> Senator Ted Kennedy is a man.
> When Senator Ted Kennedy tells a lie, there is a recognizable change in his voice patterns.

> When Senator Ted Kennedy tells a lie, there is a recognizable change in his voice patterns.
> There was a recognizable change in the Senator's voice patterns (as recorded on a PSE device) during his interview on the *Today* show.
> Senator Kennedy lied during his interview on the *Today* show.

This kind of reasoning produced the *National Enquirer* headline: "Senator Kennedy Lied about Rape Case." Notice that all three syllogisms have doubtful premises, and the last has an invalid form.

You can construct sequence syllogisms to analyze the advertising claims "For all you do, this Bud's for you" and "Why be gray when you can be yourself?"

INDUCTION OR DEDUCTION?

Because most syllogisms begin with an induced major premise, certain arguments can be analyzed as either induction or deduction. Consider this example: "Tony Chapman doesn't drink; he'll make some girl a fine husband." You can read this as a syllogism and attack the implicit major premise "Anyone who doesn't drink will make a fine husband." Or you can treat it as induction and argue that the sample (the fact that Tony Chapman doesn't drink) is insufficient to sustain a conclusion about his prospects as a husband. With such arguments, it is best not to quibble over terms; either approach is satisfactory.

When you evaluate a syllogism, don't judge it as true or false, but as reliable or unreliable. An unreliable conclusion may nevertheless be true. From the doubtful major premise ("Anyone who doesn't drink . . .") you cannot reasonably deduce that Tony Chapman will make a fine husband. But he might, in fact, make a very fine husband. In rejecting the syllogism as unreliable, you simply say that the claim is not proved by this argument.

You can recognize the distinction between truth and a reasonable conclusion by recalling a passage from Eugene Ionesco's *Rhinoceros*. In the play, the logician argues, "All cats die. Socrates is dead. Therefore Socrates is a cat." And his student responds, "That's true. I've got a cat named Socrates."

Recognizing the syllogistic form of an argument will help you to analyze its reliability. It will also help you to structure an argumentative essay. In deductive writing, the first paragrah offers the major premise, and the last paragraph, the conclusion. The body of the theme tries to demonstrate the minor premise. (This is, for example, the structure of the Declaration of Independence.)

EXERCISES

How reliable are these deductive arguments?

1. Of course Susan is a poor driver. She's a woman, isn't she?
2. A medical procedure that preserves life and health should be legal. Abortion preserves life and health that would be endangered in a clandestine operation. Abortion should be legal.
3. Professor Costello's new book on marriage should be pretty informed. After all, he's been married four times.
4. Both Catholics and Protestants are Christians. No one can be both Catholic and Protestant. Therefore, no one can be a Christian.
5. We should not pass laws that can never be enforced. Laws prohibiting smoking in public places can never be enforced. Laws prohibiting smoking in public places should not be passed.
6. The Easter Island statues could not have been carved, moved, and erected by mere humans. The work must have been done by superhuman agents.
7. The Easter Island statues were carved, moved, and erected by superhuman agents. Space travelers who could visit the earth must be superhuman agents. So the Easter Island statues must be the work of space travelers.
8. Genuinely oppressed people (like blacks) have lower academic scores and shorter life spans. Women do not have these. Women are not oppressed.
9. The Book of Revelation says the Antichrist who will introduce the last days is identified by the number 666. Count the letters in the name R-o-n-a-l-d W-i-l-s-o-n R-e-a-g-a-n. What do you get?
10. I know I'm not supposed to lust after my neighbor's wife. But Mary Davis lives way over in Biloxi, and she and Billy Miller aren't married.

11. My condition is beyond the help of medical science. Fortunately, Dr. Harris is a quack.
12. The Roman Catholic Church should follow the example of Jesus. Jesus chose only men to preach his gospel. The Church should never permit women to be priests.
13. "Any public school curriculum on sex education should meet a four-point test: It should be true, healthy, legal, and constitutional. The only classroom teaching that satisfies all four is to teach children sexual abstinence until marriage."—Phyllis Schlafly
14. "If you don't like fast driving, why don't you go to Russia?" —Charles Bowden
15. The Bill of Rights says I have a God-given right to "life, liberty, and the pursuit of happiness." This means I have a God-given right to protect my life. I have a right to own a gun.

ESSAY ASSIGNMENTS

Write an essay either affirming or opposing one of these statements. The arguments you encounter in your background reading will probably be deductive, and so will your essay.

1. There's nothing wrong with buying a term paper.
2. Evolution is a foolish theory.
3. Cable TV should not be permitted to show uncut, R-rated movies.
4. Teachers have no right to strike.
5. America needs stronger libel laws.
6. There should be no required courses in college.
7. The miracles of Jesus prove he was God.
8. X is a disease; it should not be punished but cured. (Fill in the X.)

DEATH PENALTY
DETERS VIOLENT CRIME

Senator Strom Thurmond

Does the death penalty have a legitimate role in our efforts to punish vicious criminals? I believe that it does.

I am convinced that the death penalty is an effective deterrent. The threat of capital punishment does deter violent crime. Not only does it deter individual behavior, it has value in terms of general deterrence as well.

By associating the penalty with the crimes for which it is inflicted, society is made more aware of the horror of those crimes, and there is instilled in the citizens a need to avoid such conduct and appropriately punish those who do not.

In addition, capital punishment serves the society's legitimate interest in retribution. Justice requires that criminals get what they deserve. Justice demands that such inhuman action not be tolerated. The death penalty recognizes society's belief that there are some crimes which are so vicious, heinous and brutal that no penalty lesser than death will suffice.

The American people agree with me. A recent Gallup Poll shows that public support for the death penalty is at the highest point recorded in more than half a century, with 79 percent favoring the death penalty for murder. The public opinion on the issue of capital punishment must not be ignored.

Briefly, I want to discuss a few specific cases where the death penalty is clearly warranted. I believe a discussion of these cases will help my colleagues to understand why we need a federal death penalty.

In Ogden, Utah, Pierre Selby and William Andrews robbed a hi-fi shop and in the course of their armed robbery, forced five bound victims—three of whom were teen-agers—to drink cups of poisonous liquid drain cleaner.

Selby also tried to force Orren Walker, the father of one of the teen-agers, to pour the drain cleaner down his own son's throat. When Walker refused, Selby attempted to strangle him to death with an electrical cord and then repeatedly kicked a ballpoint pen deep into his ear. Selby then proceeded to shoot each one of his victims in the head.

Another case which was truly heinous and depraved occurred in January of 1988 in a Landover, Md., apartment. Kirk Bruce and two alleged accomplices, in an orchestrated plan, shot and killed four men and a woman. Bruce's victims were shot execution style with close-range shots to the head. Some were shot as many as eight times. Others were chased into rooms of the apartment and gunned down.

One victim, who survived to testify at Bruce's trial, was hiding beneath a bed but was discovered and also shot in the head. She lay there

SOURCE: Reprinted from the *Mobile Register*, July 18, 1990. Reprinted by permission of the author.

critically wounded when one of the murderers came back into the room, told her he knew she was still alive, and shot her again.

Finally, the case of Robert Alton Harris should be mentioned. We must not forget the heinous crime Harris committed. On July 5, 1978, just six months after he completed a 2½-year prison term for beating a man to death, Harris decided to rob a bank in San Diego.

Looking first for a getaway car, he spotted two teen-age boys parked at a fast-food restaurant. Harris forced the youths at gunpoint to drive to a nearby reservoir, where he shot and killed them as they begged God to save them. Later, he ate their unfinished hamburgers.

These cases truly provide examples of individuals who should face imposition of the death penalty. In all of these cases, the defendants received the death penalty.

However, under current federal law, were these cases to occur on federal land, the death penalty could not even be considered. The law-abiding citizens of this nation demand action on federal death penalty legislation, not life imprisonment legislation. They deserve to have a death penalty which will deter violent action against them and will provide swift, appropriate punishment for individuals who choose to commit heinous crimes.

DISCUSSION QUESTIONS

1. The author expresses a number of syllogisms. One is this:
   Any law that deters crime and protects the public is just.
   The death penalty deters crime and protects the public.
   The death penalty is just.
   What evidence supports the minor premise?
2. Do the three stories of cruel murderers support the claim that the death penalty deters crime?
3. Another syllogism:
   Justice demands that murderers be executed.
   The death penalty executes murderers.
   Justice demands the death penalty.
   What evidence supports the major premise?
4. Syllogism:
   When the public supports a law, it is just.
   The American public supports the death penalty.
   The death penalty is just.
   What evidence supports the major premise?
5. Are the stories of the three horrible murders intended to make a rational argument? To produce a rational response?
6. Is this an example of good writing? Consider the first paragraph, the languages, the sentences, the paragraph divisions. Did you find this easy to read?

The Bill of Rights Guaranteed Freedom of Choice

...but you're <u>not</u> getting it!

Americans are celebrating the 200th year of the Bill of Rights. It was passed by Congress on September 25, 1789 to guarantee freedom. It was designed by our forefathers to protect Americans from the excesses of an oppressive majority, the tendency of power groups to misuse and abuse their position. Because of the Bill of Rights, one of the most important qualities of the American democracy has been preserved – personal privilege and privacy.

Yet, 200 years after this great document came into being, would you believe an important personal privilege is not being preserved? It is the privilege and right to select the physician of your choice to care for your physical health. Your body – what is more personal? Would you believe that the U.S. government has succumbed to self-serving power groups like the American Medical Association? It has done it by just ignoring certain human rights or using bureaucratic interpretation

of existing laws to reduce the benefits due Americans. It happens in Medicare services for the elderly, in veterans' benefits, in some insurance programs, and in other areas of health-care payment programs.

For example, our current Medicare program highly restricts reimbursement to senior citizens for needed chiropractic procedures from their family doctors of chiropractic, in spite of the fact that the method of treatment is safer, more effective and less costly for certain types of health problems.

As we celebrate two centuries of wisdom and protection from the heavy hand of power influence on government, let us look at one of the most personal of personal rights and demand that it be protected.

You be the one who determines who will touch your body and protect your precious health – NOT THE GOVERNMENT OR SOME POWERFUL SELF-INTEREST GROUP.

If you agree, write your congressman

And if you would like to have a copy of the U.S. Court of Appeals' recent decision finding the American Medical Association (AMA) guilty of conspiracy in violation of antitrust laws, write the American Chiropractic Association.

ΛCΛ   **AMERICAN CHIROPRACTIC ASSOCIATION**

1701 CLARENDON BOULEVARD • ARLINGTON, VA 22209 • 1-703-276-8800

Courtesy of the American Chiropractic Association.

DISCUSSION QUESTIONS

1. The ad offers a syllogism. The major premise is "Under the Bill of Rights, a citizen should have free choice in making personal decisions." Give the minor premise and the conclusion.

2. Are the terms consistent in this syllogism? What does "freedom of choice" mean? Doesn't every citizen have the right to choose chiropractic medicine if he or she wants to?

3. The ad claims that chiropractic medicine is often a "safer, more effective, less costly" treatment. What evidence is given to support this? Need such evidence be given?

4. According to the ad, what is the motive of the American Medical Association in working to limit government funding to traditional medicine? What other motives are possible?

5. "You be the one who determines who will touch your body and protect your precious health." Do you have that right at present? Do you have the right to choose an Indian guru, a TV vitamin hustler, a faith healer? Can you insist that the government pay for such treatment?

DEATH PENALTY ARGUMENTS:
AN EMOTIONAL SMOKE-SCREEN

Senator Mark Hatfield

Over the years we have heard arguments for the death penalty from time to time and, of course, most of them are a recitation of gruesome murders and gruesome, horrible, horrendous acts of violence of which none of us approve, none of us can condone, and all of us condemn.

All these arguments have done is to raise the emotional smoke-screen, which prevents us from seeing the real issues and making wise decisions.

Let us take this one by one, at least for a few issues:

Deterrence is usually offered as a justification for the death penalty, despite the fact that this shopworn argument has absolutely no empirical data to support it.

In fact, the American Sociological Review has conducted a study, and here is the empirical data. In a painstaking analysis, between 1940 and 1986, Baily and Peterson, who conducted this particular study, proved that there was absolutely no justification to argue deterrence.

They analyzed and looked at those states which have capital punishment and those which do not have capital punishment. The conclusion was that you are more likely to be murdered in a state with capital punishment than in a state without capital punishment.

The FBI in 1987 conducted a similar study, and the average murder rate per 100,000 citizens in the 37 states with the death penalty was 6.94. The average murder rate in the 13 states without the death penalty was, however, 5.1. In 1988, the murder rate in the states with capital punishment rose to 7.05 percent, whereas in those states without the death penalty, the murder rate dropped to 4.72 per 100,000. I think those statistics would indicate that deterrence is nothing but a shopworn argument.

We also live in an imperfect world, and human beings are fallible in their judgments. But the death penalty is final. There is no room for correction.

In this century alone, according to a study published in 1987, more than 350 people in the United States have been erroneously convicted of crimes potentially punishable by death—116 of them were sentenced to death; 23 were actually executed. No room for correction. Twenty-three innocent lives were taken under the authority of a state.

The vast majority of the free world has rejected such a barbaric form of punishment. By adopting and implementing the death penalty, the United States stands virtually alone, always touting our human rights commitment.

SOURCE: Reprinted from the *Mobile Register,* July 18, 1990. Reprinted by permission of the author.

We stand against all of Western Europe. In contrast, we stand with such countries as Syria, Afghanistan, Iraq, Iran, South Africa, Libya, China, Cuba, Vietnam, North Korea, Lebanon, Albania and Angola. I think we are out of touch with the human rights attitudes throughout the world today as we maintain this gruesome action of the death penalty.

We also must recognize that the public does have some outrage, and reason for outrage, when they see heinous crimes committed and those who are convicted for a life sentence are out in five to 10 years.

We are always talking about that action as it relates to the support for the death penalty, but let me call attention to a University of Louisville study taken in 1989 where they found that in the state of Kentucky, 69.1 percent of the people generally supported the death penalty.

But when they were asked if they would accept a mandatory life sentence in lieu of the death penalty, only 36 percent of them supported the death penalty.

I saw a headline in one of the Southern newspapers recently, "Killer Executed, Crowds Cheer."

Is that not an interesting indictment on our society, a primal urge for revenge, sadistic revenge? That does not ease the pain of the victims or bring back the lives of the victims.

I believe that (a mandatory life sentence, without parole) becomes a little more palatable to those who are concerned about human rights around the world.

It puts the United States, I think, into a very much stronger position in the world for human rights.

DISCUSSION QUESTIONS

1. Half of this essay is given to challenging the claim that the death penalty deters crime and protects citizens. (This was the minor premise of Senator Thurmond's syllogism.) What evidence is offered to challenge this premise?
2. What conclusion can you draw from the fact that states without the death penalty have lower levels of violent crime?
3. The author bases a syllogism on the major premise "A law is unjust if it is capable of making irredeemable errors." How persuasive is this premise?
4. What do you know about the 360 cases where individuals were unjustly convicted, or the 23 individuals who were unjustly executed? Are these numbers very persuasive without additional information?
5. Another syllogism:
   > Countries known for human rights violations (Iran, Iraq, North Korea, Cuba, Angola, etc.) inflict the death penalty.
   > The United States inflicts the death penalty.

   What conclusion can be drawn from this?

6. The author quotes a southern newspaper that headlined "Killer Executed, Crowds Cheer." Is this a paradoxical reference from an author who rejected death penalty arguments as an "emotional smokescreen"?

7. Is the author an effective writer? Consider the introductory paragraph, the "voice" of the speaker, the length of the paragraphs, the unity of the whole work.

JOHN SAAD IS PRO-LIFE

HE IS THE KIND OF MAN
WE NEED IN MONTGOMERY

JOHN SAAD
SENATE DISTRICT 34

Paid Pol. Adv. by Tony Norman, Mobile, Alabama

Advertisement from the *Catholic Week*.

DISCUSSION QUESTIONS

1. Here the syllogism is obvious:

    We need a man who is pro-life in the state senate in Montgomery.

    John Saad is pro-life.

    We need John Saad in Montgomery.

    Is this a reasonable argument?
2. Are the premises true?
3. Are the terms unambiguous?
4. What does the picture prove?
5. Would this ad be equally persuasive in a different periodical?

SHOULD DIRTY LYRICS
BE AGAINST THE LAW?

Bob Martinez and Ira Glasser

PRO: INTERVIEW WITH BOB MARTINEZ, GOVERNOR OF FLORIDA

Why Should 2 Live Crew Be Prosecuted?

Well, in Florida, we have a law prohibiting the sale of obscene material to minors. And that was the focus of our inquiry in this case. The law is clear. And these lyrics are clearly obscene. It is audio pornography. It's brutalizing women. It's bestiality. They're not innuendoes, they're raw words, so raw that none of the print media have even reproduced them. There's nothing redeeming about it.

How Are "Community Standards" Decided?

The people, through elected representatives, have collectively decided to pass a law where a judgment can be made. We must rely on laws, recognizing all laws can be appealed. But the community should have a right to set standards for what's acceptable.

Shouldn't Parents Be Responsible for What Their Children Listen To?

Parents ought to feel that their children can go into any record store and not be able to buy this material. They can't buy liquor and they have to be 18 years old to see nude movies. We do have a responsibility to protect our young.

Do Criminal Prosecutions Run the Risk of Backfiring?

No. I suspect that if these individuals were engaged in the same behavior but were not well-known, they might never have been found out. They shouldn't be treated differently from the average citizen just because they are entertainers.

Is There an Element of Racism Underlying This Prosecution?

The Florida law does not speak to sex or race. It speaks to obscenity. Now, if there are any other records out there available to minors that violate the state law of conduct set by our community, then action has to be taken.

CON: INTERVIEW WITH IRA GLASSER, EXECUTIVE DIRECTOR OF THE AMERICAN CIVIL LIBERTIES UNION

Why is the Prosecution of 2 Live Crew Unwarranted?

In order to prosecute anything for obscenity, you have to show that it is without any artistic merit and that it appeals to prurient interest as determined by community standards. A record that has sold 1.7 million copies must have some artistic merit. And it seems absurd to suggest that any of this violates community standards when Andrew Dice Clay's

SOURCE: Reprinted with permission from *U.S. News & World Report*, June 25, 1990.

albums sell in local record stores, X-rated movies play in area theaters and *Penthouse* is available all over the place. If you wanted to arrest people for using this language, you could go to any schoolyard in Broward County.

Where Do We Draw the Line?

Nobody knows how. What strikes one person as offensive and obscene does not strike another person as such.

Don't These Lyrics Glorify Brutalization of Women?

The research does not show that people are more likely to go out and brutalize somebody after listening to such lyrics. This is a country that glorifies violence in all of our popular cultural forms, from Westerns to cop movies.

Does Racism Underlie the Prosecution of 2 Live Crew?

Those charges have some credence, when you look at similar stuff the officials have *not* gone after.

Should There Be Any Limits on Music Lyrics?

We don't think so. I don't think that there are any words in any song that have not appeared in books or in serious literature. The notion that you suddenly isolate this and decide it's a crime because somebody put it on a record doesn't make any sense. If I were living in Broward County, I would much prefer that the sheriff was going after real crime.

DISCUSSION QUESTIONS

1. The central argument here is a syllogism:
    > Song lyrics should be banned if they go beyond community standards.
    > 2 Live Crew lyrics go beyond community standards.
    > 2 Live Crew lyrics should be banned.

    Would either author object to the major premise? Where do they differ?
2. Contrast the evidence each offers in trying to define "community standards." Who decides what community standards are?
3. Governor Martinez says the law should prohibit obscene lyrics in order to protect children. How does Mr. Glasser answer this?
4. Because 2 Live Crew is a black group, Mr. Glasser suggests racism may be in issue in charges made against them. How does Governor Martinez answer this?
5. What is implicit in Mr. Glasser's statement that citizens of Broward County should like to see their sheriff going after real crimes?

Q: Why can't this veal calf walk?

A: He has only two feet.

Actually, <u>less</u> than two feet. Twenty two inches to be exact. His entire life is spent chained in a wooden box measuring only 22 inches wide and 56 inches long. The box is so small that the calf can't walk or even turn around.

Most people think animal abuse is illegal. It isn't. In veal factories, it's business as usual. "Milk-fed" veal is obtained by making a calf anemic. The calf is *not* fed mother's milk. He's fed an antibiotic laced formula that causes severe diarrhea. He must lie in his own excrement —choking on the ammonia gases. He's chained in a darkened building with hundreds of other baby calves suffering the same fate. They are immobilized, sick, and anemic.

Toxic Veal

The reckless use of oxytetracycline, mold inhibiting chemicals, chloramphenicol, neomycin, penicillin, and other drugs is not just bad for calves. It is toxic to you.

But doesn't the USDA prevent tainted veal from being sold? Absolutely not. The USDA itself admits that most veal is never checked for toxic residue.

Antibiotics in veal and other factory farm products create virulent strains of bacteria that wreak havoc on human health. *Salmonella* poisoning is reaching epidemic proportions.

Veal factories maximize profits for agribusiness drug companies because they are a breeding ground for disease. To keep calves alive under such torturous conditions, they are *continually* given drugs which can be passed on to customers.

It doesn't have to be this way. And with your help, it won't be. Please, don't buy veal!

Courtesy of the Humane Farming Association.

DISCUSSION QUESTIONS

1. The ad presents two deductive arguments. One relates to the treatment of animals; the other to the treatment of people. Establish the syllogisms.
2. How effective is the "cruelty to animals" argument? Is it helped or hurt by the ambiguity of the term "two feet"?
3. How effective is the "reckless use of chemicals" argument? Would additional evidence have helped the author's case?
4. On the mail-in coupon, the ad complains that factory farms are "destroying the American family farm." Is this just tacked on? Is it related to the rest of the argument?
5. Is there any evidence that more chemicals are injected into veal calves than to other animals raised for meat?
6. Do the photos in the ad make it more persuasive?

AMERICA NEEDS A
FLAG-PROTECTION AMENDMENT

Senator Bob Dole

On June 14, 1777, the Continental Congress adopted the Stars and Stripes as the official flag of the United States. After 213 years, it is long past time to give our flag the kind of protection the Founding Fathers expected, and the kind of protection the American people are demanding.

Unfortunately, the Supreme Court let the people down with a 5–4 vote to OK flag burning. Even worse, Congress has decided to ignore the overwhelming majority of Americans who favor a constitutional amendment to save Old Glory from the desecrators, those kooks who get their kicks burning, trampling or spitting on our flag.

Instead of listening to the American people, Congress hid behind a filibuster, fuzzing up the debate with three major misconceptions about the constitutional amendment and about those of us who support it.

Misconception One: We were trying to amend the Bill of Rights for the first time in history.

That is a hoax. The simple truth is, the flag amendment changes nothing in the Bill of Rights. The American people know that the first amendment—an amendment which states that "Congress Shall Make No Law Abridging The Freedom of Speech"—was never intended to protect the act of flag burning. That's why 48 states have already passed flag desecration statutes.

The simple fact is, flag burning is an act; it is conduct, malicious conduct. It is not speech.

Misconception Two: Congress should decide the flag burning issue.

This is also false. The people should decide. That is what the Founding Fathers wanted, and that is why they made the process to change the constitution so challenging: A two-thirds vote of Congress, and approval of 38 state legislatures. Unfortunately, the people may never get the chance to amend their constitution.

In the heartland of America, some folks just can't understand what Congress is up to. Frustrated by Congress' flag filibuster, the City Council in Douglass, Kan., has voted unanimously to make flag burning illegal. Mayor Ron Howard spoke for America when he said: "Down here, we believe in the flag. I'm no lawyer, but it's come to the point that we've got to do whatever we can to protect the flag."

Misconception Three: Supporters of the constitutional amendment are demagogues.

Another falsehood. I always thought the flag was something special. I always thought we had a right to stand up for the flag without being accused of being a "demagogue" by liberal journalists or political opportunists. Unfortunately, about all we heard from our opponents was a

SOURCE: Reprinted from the *Mobile Press Register*, July 4, 1990. Reprinted by permission of the author.

frenzy about their own campaigns and re-election prospects, about campaign commercials and the terror of facing the people out on the campaign trail.

The last time I looked, the American flag had 50 stars on it for 50 states of real people who will be cut out of Old Glory if Congress continues its stubborn refusal to approve a constitutional amendment. Remember, approval by Congress would send the flag amendment for final action to the state legislatures, representatives closer to the people. After all, the Constitution says, "We The People," Not "We The Congress."

Despite 58 percent support for the amendment in both houses of Congress, the flag filibuster won this time. But the flag's day will come.

I don't have much faith in Congress, but I have a whole lot of faith in The American people—people like George and Beverly Rhoades of Fond Du Lac, Wis.

Last week, the desecrators burned a flag stolen from the Rhoades' front yard where the family had proudly erected a homemade memorial to their son Louis, who was killed in Vietnam 22 years ago. Mrs. Rhoades doesn't know who desecrated her son's memorial. But she is absolutely determined to see this nation enact a flag protection amendment.

"We'll keep fighting," she said. "There's no patriotism in our country anymore for our young children to look up to."

DISCUSSION QUESTIONS

1. The prevailing law on flag-burning is based on a syllogism. It argues that citizens are entitled to freedom of speech and that flag-burning is an exercise of free speech. How does the author challenge this view?

2. Comment on other areas where speech and action become merged. If pro-life activists gather and block the entrance to an abortion clinic, is that free speech? If a girl dances on a barroom stage with little or no clothes, is that free speech?

3. The author rejects three misconceptions about efforts to pass a constitutional amendment. Are his three challenges equally persuasive?

4. The author speaks of the "American people," "real people," and the nation's "heartland." Whom is he talking about? Are the people who reject his view (the Supreme Court, congressional leaders, etc.) less than real Americans?

5. Identify the places where the author leaves factual talk to go into emotional, patriotic language. Is this a wise thing for him to do?

6. Why all the fuss about flag-burning? How many flags have been burned in your area during your lifetime? What seems to be the motive for all the effort to pass a constitutional amendment?

ARGUMENT
BY AUTHORITY

*"Thanks to the Buddha, I won
$10,000.00."*

—L. W., Fla.

Much of what you believe—or are asked to believe—must be accepted simply on the word of an expert. Your doctor says you have glaucoma. Your mechanic says the car needs a valve job. Your newspaper reviews the latest *Police Academy* film and calls it awful. Scientific authorities say the universe is expanding. In such instances, you are asked to accept a view on the basis of someone's authority.

It is reasonable to credit such testimony if it fulfills two conditions: (1) The speaker must be a genuine expert on the subject at hand, and (2) there must be no reasonable probability of bias. When Zsa Zsa Gabor, for example, turns from her show-business career to praise the effects of acupuncture, you can justly question her expertise in the area. When Tommy Lasorda appears on television praising the excellence of Ultra Slim-Fast, you know he is being paid for the advertisement and suspect a degree of bias.

Remember, however, that these unreliable arguments are not necessarily false. Zsa Zsa Gabor may be expressing an important truth about acupuncture, and Tommy Lasorda may be giving his honest opinion of Ultra Slim-Fast. Nevertheless, it would be unreasonable to accept an argument—or to build a persuasive essay—solely on the authority of such speakers. You should relate their views to other evidence and to the word of other authorities.

EXPERT TESTIMONY

Many arguments raise the question of genuine expertness. Authorities may be unnamed. (Advertisements for health products often print testimony from "Brazilian researchers" or "five New York doctors.") They may be unfamiliar. (*"Promise of Saccharin* is a provocative book—readable and profoundly informed."—Colonel Winston X. Montgomery, III.) They may be known largely by their degrees. (A Kansas medico, in recommending goat gland surgery to restore vitality, signed himself "John R. Brinkley, M.D., C.M., Dr.P.H., Sc.D. . . .") And they may appear with strange credentials. (A self-help book by Scott Reed describes him as "one of the nation's leading mind-power experts.") Persuaders always magnify the reputations of authorities who agree with them. A temperance circular quoting William Gladstone's condemnation of alcohol calls him "the greatest prime minister in English history."

Sometimes speakers of unquestioned authority express themselves in areas outside their competence. Actor Tony Randall praises Easy-Off Oven Pads. Actress Brooke Shields warns of the medical effects of cigarette smoking. Rural evangelists pinpoint weaknesses in evolutionary theory. And a U.S. Senate subcommittee (by a 3–1 vote) declares that human life begins at conception. You should judge such people on the quality of their evidence, not on their word as experts.

Religious Authority

Equally questionable as authorities are "God" and "everyone." Because the claim is not subject to verification with hard evidence, one can champion almost any opinion by saying it conforms to divine will. A correspondent to the *Mobile Press* once assured readers that West Coast earthquakes were God's punishment for California's sinful lifestyle. Another correspondent declared it would violate "Christ's plan for the world" if the United States gave up its holdings in Panama. And during the 1980 and 1984 elections, the Moral Majority (and pro-life organizations) insisted that Ronald Reagan was God's choice for president of the United States.

Christian writers routinely quote passages from the Bible to declare the will of God and thus open up a rich area of argument. As mentioned earlier, religious questions often do not lend themselves to meaningful discussion because people cannot agree on necessary definitions. Clearly, an argument involving biblical authority can be persuasive only when addressed to someone who already accepts the truth of scripture and who interprets it in the same way as the speaker. There are large differences between those who claim the Bible *is* the word of God, those who say it *contains* the word of God, those who enjoy it as an anthology of great literature, and those who reject it altogether.

Even when participants in a discussion agree on preliminary matters, problems remain. Because biblical texts were written by many authors over the course of 1300 years and include a wide variety of opinions, literary styles, and translations, persuaders can find a passage or two to support any argument they choose to make. (Bishop James Pike illustrated this by asking ironically, "How many persons have been reborn from meditating on the last line of Psalm 137: 'Blessed shall he be that taketh and dasheth the little ones against the stone'?") Consequently, when facing a scriptural argument, you should take time to trace the references. You will often find that authors quote passages out of context (they might be championing the superficial counsel of Job's friends) and quote passages inaccurately from memory. They may cite lines scarcely related to the issue at hand. ("Only God can save America now. See Chronicles 7:14.")

An interesting modern claim says, "Of course, God favors capital punishment; otherwise He wouldn't have used it as a means to save the world." The problem with this argument is that it also puts God on the side of betrayal of friends, unjust trials, torture, and other atrocities.

Mass Authority

The authority of "everyone" is claimed in statements beginning, "They say," "Everyone knows," or "All fair-minded people agree."

Such arguments can be convincing in instances where "they" (some notable majority) have demonstrably committed themselves on a matter they are competent to judge. Arguments announcing "More women choose Simplicity than any other pattern" and "Budweiser—Largest Selling Beer in the World" are genuinely impressive because, in these areas, the opinion of a mass audience is superior to that of any particular expert. (What renowned epicure is qualified to assure you that Old Style Lager is America's best-tasting beer?)

It is important to remember that America's democratic procedures and its jury system both rely on the expertness of "everyone."

But mass authority can be distorted in a number of ways. It can be claimed arbitrarily. ("Everyone knows that Jimmy Carter stole the 1976 election.") It can be coupled with ambiguous language. ("More men get more pleasure out of Roi-Tan than any other cigar at its price.") And it can be invoked in areas that call for technical information. (A Gallup poll reported that 41 percent of Americans believe that cigarette smoking is a cause of birth defects.) In such instances, "everyone" is a dubious authority. When you're having severe chest pains, it's no time to take a poll.

Still, mass opinion is worth listening to, especially when it becomes more or less unanimous. Remember the famous counsel, "If you can keep your head when all about you are losing theirs, probably you haven't grasped the situation."

Divided Authority

The word of a genuine expert will not, of course, settle every argument. Alexander Pope put the question best:

> Who shall decide when Doctors disagree.
> And soundest Casuists doubt, like you and me?

The plain fact is that many issues are complex, and experts hold opposing views. Legal authorities disagree over whether certain means of gathering evidence violate constitutional safeguards. (Was John DeLorean entrapped?) Eminent psychiatrists appear in court arguing the mental competence of particular defendants. (Was John Hinckley insane?) Medical experts do not agree on whether a month-old fetus is human. (Is abortion murder?)

Which authorities should you believe? In such cases, it's probably best to side with the majority of experts. However, when you hear a genuinely important authority voicing a minority view (for example, Rachel Carson on insecticides, or Linus Pauling on vitamin C), you would do well to withhold judgment altogether and await further evidence.

Critical Authority

You should recognize that some authorities have more established reputations than others. For example, many publications contain reviews of books, plays, and movies, but the reviews of the major New York newspapers, the television networks, and nationally circulated periodicals (*Time, Newsweek, Harper's,* and *Christian Science Monitor,* etc.) are generally thought more critically reliable.

If a book, movie, or play wins praise from critics writing in these publications, the reviews may be quoted in newspaper ads and on book jackets. If an advertisement quotes reviews from other sources, it strongly suggests that the work was not praised by the major critics. It may not be very good.

Of course, you can enjoy any book, play, or movie whatever the critics say, but you should recognize the varying standards of critical authorities. You should be warned, for example, when you see the cover of the paperback edition of Nancy Freeman's *Joshua Son of None* boasting rave reviews from the *El Paso Times,* the *San Gabriel Valley Tribune,* the *Macon Georgian,* and the *Oceanside Blade-Tribune.*

You should recognize these distinctions when writing a critical essay. If the book or movie you're championing is praised by the major critics, quote the reviews. If it found favor only with lesser authorities, you probably shouldn't mention the reviews at all.

BIASED TESTIMONY

Even when speakers are admitted experts in the field under discussion, an argument should be examined for the possibility of bias. An argument has a probable bias if the authority profits from expressing it or if it reflects the predictable loyalty or routine antagonism of a group. To dismiss the testimony of biased individuals does not mean calling them liars or even saying they are wrong; it means a condition exists that makes it unreasonable to accept a conclusion *solely* on their authority.

You don't ask a barber whether you need a haircut.

Rewarded Opinions

Experts profit from making an argument when it brings them money or prestige. The financial incentive is easy to recognize when Bill Cosby recommends Jell-O (or Kodak film), when Uri Geller proclaims his psychic powers on lecture tours, and when owners of outdoor movies protest the unnaturalness of daylight saving time.

Today many people earn money by convincing you of preposterous "facts." Tabloid advertisers boast incredible products that will let you grow new hair, develop a larger bust, win at the racetrack, lose 16 pounds in a week, and find true love by wearing Madame Zarina's talisman. Papers like the *Star* and the *National Enquirer* routinely carry stories of reincarnated housewives, arthritis cures, and space creatures that appeared in Canada. Recent best-selling books reveal that Errol Flynn was a Nazi spy, that Marilyn Monroe was murdered, that the Mafia killed President Kennedy, and that the Lindbergh baby is still alive. Such stories are fun to read, and there may be splinters of truth in some of them. But you can give no special belief to the authors of such tales. They are making money peddling their extravagant claims.

The effect of prestige is clear when individuals discuss their incomes, their reading habits, and their sex lives. In these areas, egos are threatened—and people lie.

The impact of money and prestige on an expert is sometimes difficult to establish. For example, few scientific authorities have affirmed the existence of Atlantis or of UFOs, but the few who do have won a level of recognition—along with television appearances, lecture tours, and book contracts—that they could never have won voicing more orthodox opinions. (You won't get on a talk show saying that fluoride prevents cavities.) These experts may be expressing their honest judgments, but you should remember all that acclaim when evaluating their testimony.

The 1987 revelations concerning TV evangelist Jim Bakker and church secretary Jessica Hahn illustrate problems relating to argument by authority. Both told of a sexual episode, though each remembered it differently. We know, however, that Bakker was trying to save his reputation as a religious leader. And we know Hahn changed her story twice when offered large amounts of money. In such a case, you have to rely on outside evidence. You can't be comfortable believing either authority.

Similarly, when you read current articles about AIDS, you should recall that a lot of people stand to profit by exaggerating the health danger. There are researchers who want a grant to build a new laboratory, evangelists who need to proclaim God's vengeance, reporters who are looking for a sensational headline, and politicians who want to appear in the news. When you see the dire warnings, ask yourself who is telling the story. (The place to get facts about AIDS is the Centers for Disease Control in Atlanta.)

In the mid-1980s, headlines warned that AIDS was spreading into the heterosexual community. Cases appeared among people who insisted they had no involvement with homosexuals or drugs. Medical experts later discovered that many of these people were lying to protect their reputations.

Predictable Judgments

An argument by authority is presumed to be biased if it is totally predictable—that is, when it reflects a traditional loyalty or antagonism. When you want to learn about the new Ford Escorts, you can't rely on the word of your Chevy dealer. You can't learn the truth about a woman's character by asking her ex-husband.

A classic example of a predictable and biased judgment occurred in 1977 when the University of Alabama's football team was ranked second in the final Associated Press and United Press International polls. Thereupon, the Alabama state legislature issued its own poll, and the Crimson Tide moved up to No. 1. Equally predictable are pamphlets on smoking and health distributed by the Tobacco Institute, articles on gun control and crime appearing in the *American Rifleman*, and the publicized study of pain relievers produced by the makers of Bayer aspirin.

In 1986, when Attorney General Edwin Meese appointed a commission to investigate the effects of pornography on the social order, he remembered that a 1970 commission appointed by President Nixon had found that pornography did not cause dangerous behavior. So Meese selected a commission that would bring in a different ruling. Most of the members he chose were well known as militant opponents of pornography. And they brought in a report recommending a repressive agenda for controlling sexual images and texts. There may be merit in these recommendations, but they came from a biased source.

This presumption of bias appears most notably in political argument. When any Democrat is nominated for president, the candidate and the party's platform will be praised in liberal periodicals (*Washington Post, St. Louis Post Dispatch, Commonweal, The Progressive*, etc.) and condemned in conservative publications (*Chicago Tribune, U.S. News & World Report, Los Angeles Times, National Review*, etc.). When any president finishes a State of the Union message, opposition speakers will call his program inadequate, wrongheaded, and potentially dangerous. You must judge these claims on specific evidence; such predictable views carry little authority.

DISTORTING QUOTATIONS

Besides a doubtful expert and a biased opinion, other misleading features attend argument by authority. Statements are sometimes abridged. (The advertisement for Kyle Onstott's *Mandingo* quotes a review from the *Dallas News*: ". . . like no other book ever written about the South. . . .") Claims may be irrelevant to the issue at hand. (The paperback edition of *Nightmare in Pink* prints Richard Condon's opinion that "John D. MacDonald is the great American story-teller.") Quotations can appear without a source. (See *Hand in Hand*—"The Most Widely Praised Picture of Them All!") And undated quotations can be impressive. (During his presidential campaigns, opponents printed statements Ronald Reagan had made years before when he was a Democrat.)

Exact quotations can be presented in a distorting context. Under the heading "How L.B.J. Would Remake America," *Common Sense* printed a sentence from President Johnson's State of the Union message: "We are going to try to take all the money that we think is unnecessarily being spent and take it from the 'haves' and give it to the 'have nots' that need it so much." As the context of the speech made clear, the president did not advocate taking from the rich to give to the poor; he proposed taking money from the more heavily funded federal programs and putting it into those with smaller appropriations.

For decades, conservative speakers quoted Nikita Khrushchev's line "We will bury you," interpreting it as a Soviet threat to destroy the United States. The sentence is lifted totally out of context. Actually, Khrushchev was saying that the communist economic system would outproduce the capitalist system, and thus survive it. The statement wasn't addressed to the United States.

In the same way, temperance advocates like to strengthen their argument by quoting lines from Chaucer ("Character and shame depart when wine comes in") and Shakespeare ("O thou invisible spirit of wine, if thou hast no name to be known by, let us call thee devil!") The lines, of course, are not direct expressions of these authors; they come from literary characters who are speaking in a dramatic context.

The hallmark of distorted quotations is the *Congressional Record*, which purports to be a record of what went on during House and Senate sessions. The periodical does record what the legislators said. But it also deletes what they said and reports what they wish they had said. It is a magnificently self-serving document and should be immediately questioned when quoted as an argumentative source.

Audiotaped and Videotaped Evidence

With the advent of tape and video recorders, a persuader can produce new kinds of distorted testimony. In the 1972 senatorial campaign in Alabama, opponents broadcast Senator John Sparkman's voice saying, "Will the cause of desegregation be served? If so, the busing is all right." The two sentences were spliced together from separate parts of a taped interview. President Nixon recorded his phone calls and office conversations and produced the tapes that eventually implicated him in the Watergate scandal. Noting that the president made totally contradictory statements on the tapes, Congressman Tip O'Neill speculated about Nixon's intention:

> Now that tells you what he was going to do with those tapes. He was going to take them with him when he left and spend years editing them, and then he could string together a record of his own which would show he was the greatest man ever to live. He'd be able to prove it with the tapes. You never would have known about any of the other tapes. That would have been thrown away. They would have only given you all these tapes with him making a hero of himself.

In the Abscam trials in the early 1980s, the FBI convicted government officials with the help of videotapes that showed them taking money and making incriminating promises to an agent posing as an Arab sheikh asking for favors. Here it is important to remember that the FBI agents had complete control of the situation. They could introduce topics, guide the conversation, stop it when convenient, tape some episodes, not tape others, and then choose which tapes they wanted to show in court. The

Abscam defendants may not have been faultless, but it is hard to imagine St. Francis of Assisi surviving such a test.

In 1984, a California jury saw films showing John DeLorean with quantities of illegal cocaine. They also saw a number of FBI agents who were taking part in the elaborate charade. The jury believed that DeLorean was a victim of entrapment. They found him not guilty.

In 1986, advocates produced a radio ad about cigarette companies and broadcast New York City Mayor Ed Koch's voice repeating, "They are selling death." In fact, Koch had said this not about tobacco but about New York City bathhouses, which he thought were spreading AIDS.

You must take great care in analyzing audio and video evidence. There is a lot to consider besides the words and pictures you see.

Lies

Expert testimony can lend itself to bald misstatement of fact on the part of authorities or of those who quote them. A national columnist accused author Quentin Reynolds of being a Communist and a war profiteer. A U.S. senator called newsman Drew Pearson a child molester. Many have circulated the story that three Pennsylvania students on LSD became blind from staring at the sun for several hours and that a Michigan schoolteacher took off all her clothes to demonstrate female anatomy to her coed sex education class. All these sensational claims were untrue.

Fictional quotations appear as evidence. For many years the statement "We shall force the United States to spend itself to destruction" was attributed to V. I. Lenin and used to ground conservative political argument. Lenin never said that or anything like it. More recently, liberal sources circulated a paragraph protesting the communist threat and concluding, "We need law and order"; they ascribed this to Adolf Hitler. The quotation is pure fiction. Several years ago a tabloid headlined the news that marijuana may cure cancer. The story quoted Dr. James H. Kostinger, director of research for the Pittsburgh Academy of Forensic Medicine, who had been conducting studies in this area for four years. Investigation later revealed that the academy did not exist and that no medical school in Pittsburgh had ever heard of Dr. Kostinger.

Although expert testimony can be misused by dishonest writers and speakers, it remains a forceful element of legitimate argument. When genuine authorities agree with you, quote them in your writing. Your case will be more persuasive.

EXERCISES

How reliable are these arguments from authority?

1. "I know UFOs are real because I've seen one."—Dennis Weaver
2. Baron Philippe de Rothschild's Mouton-Cadet—"Enjoyed more

by discerning people than any other bordeaux wine in the world."

3. "The most disadvantageous peace is better than the most just war."—Erasmus

4. *Shakespeare of London* by Marchette Chute: "The best biography of Shakespeare"—Bernadine Kielty, *Book-of-the-Month Club News*

5. "72% of men have had sex by age 19."—Tom Biacree, *How Do You Rate?*

6. The Mont Blanc Diplomat—"Many pen experts here and abroad consider the Diplomat to be the finest pen ever designed. It's Europe's most prized pen, unmatched in writing ease."

7. "Causes of Cancer Remain Unknown"—headline in the *Tobacco Observer*

8. "Adolf Hitler Is Alive!!!"—headline in the *National Examiner*

9. "More people will read this issue of *Parade* than there are Communists in the Soviet Union."

10. *Hitler's Daughter* by Gary Goss: "A brilliant academic satire"—Dennis Renault, *Sacramento Bee;* "A hilarious time"—Harry Cargas, *Buffalo Press;* "Raunchy and unfair"—Otto Tumiel, *Reading Intelligencer*

11. Pond's Cold Cream—"They say you can tell by a girl's complexion when she's in love."

12. "A bad peace is even worse than war."—Tacitus

13. "I might possibly be the Lindbergh child."—Harold Olson

14. Tareyton—"America's best-selling charcoal-filter cigarette."

15. "If I have a sore throat, or a rasp, or something that feels like laryngitis, I will visualize the color blue. Certain colors represent specific areas of the body, and blue is the color for the throat."—Shirley MacLaine

16. *Vampire's Kiss:* "Just about the most interesting film of the year so far"—Andy Klein, *L. A. Herald Examiner*

17. "There's never an uncomfortable moment with the Plus 90i from Bryant. That's what I call having the right stuff."—Chuck Yeager, USAF, Ret.

18. "WordFinder has changed my life. I never used to use a thesaurus."—William J. Buckley, Jr.

19. "President James Garfield was able to write Latin with one hand and Greek with the other—and at the same time."—Dave Dutton, *Weird and Wacky Facts about Famous Oddballs*

20. "Cast thy bread upon the waters: For thou shalt find it after many days."—Ecclesiastes

21. "Nick Bouniconti switched to Natural Light because he prefers the taste."—Beer advertisement

22. Model Tai Collins held a Washington press conference to announce she had had an affair with Senator Charles Robb (Dem., Va.). She insisted she was "not out to hurt him" and that the announcement was unrelated to the fact pictures of her were being sold in the current issue of *Playboy*.

ESSAY ASSIGNMENTS

Write an essay either affirming or opposing one of these statements. The arguments you encounter in your background reading will include expert testimony, and so should your essay.

1. Marijuana should be legalized.
2. Vitamin C pills are necessary for good health.
3. Speaking in tongues is a genuine spiritual gift.
4. Flying saucers are here.
5. Fluoridation of drinking water is dangerous.
6. A faith healer can help you.
7. Nuclear power is the answer.
8. To remain healthy, one should avoid X. (Fill in the X.)

ELVIS

IS ALIVE!

Patrick Cotter

Startling new evidence suggests that Elvis Presley's long-time manager, Col. Tom Parker, arranged for The King to fake his own death so he could lead a normal life, reveals a top author.

Since Elvis vanished from the scene ten years ago, there has been widespread speculation that he was alive. Now Gail Brewer-Giorgio, author of an amazingly prophetic novel, *Orion,* makes a series of stunning new revelations, indicating that the superstar's alleged death is an elaborate hoax.

In the book, published in 1979, the wily manager of an immensely popular rock n' roll superstar fakes his client's death to allow him to escape the prison of superstardom.

EVIDENCE

Now Brewer-Giorgio, of Marietta, Georgia, discloses that she is in possession of disturbing new evidence indicating that the novel was closer to fact than fiction.

But the veteran writer fears that releasing her most conclusive proof, a tape recording Elvis made four years after his "death," will ruin The King's new life as an ordinary man.

"I am in a terrible position," she told the *Examiner.* "It's the most incredible tape you'll ever hear. The whole thing has got to be handled delicately.

"Elvis feels that he made a mistake by hoaxing his own death. He said he has been recognized, but he knows no one will believe anyone who says they saw him."

The circumstances surrounding the publication of *Orion* lead Brewer-Giorgio to believe that Col. Tom Parker masterminded both Elvis' masquerade and the mysterious disappearance of her book from shelves all across the country.

At first the book, for which she was given a $60,000 advance, was well-received and well-promoted. But suddenly it simply vanished from the shelves of bookstores. Now *Orion* "is nowhere to be found," she says.

"It's fiction that was stopped because it got too close to the truth," adds Brewer-Giorgio. "It's very, very strange."

Shortly after she finished writing the book in 1978, a songwriter friend showed it to Mae Boren Axton, who wrote Elvis' first million seller hit, "Heartbreak Hotel," introduced The King to Col. Parker, and became Elvis' "second mother."

SOURCE: Reprinted by permission from the *National Examiner,* August 11, 1987.

ASTONISHED

Axton repeatedly told Brewer-Giorgio how astonished she was at how well the author had captured the soul of Elvis in the book—and marveled at her knowledge of events and traits that were known only to insiders.

By an eerie coincidence, Axton had been Brewer-Giorgio's eighth-grade English teacher.

Later, after the book was copyrighted but before it was published, TV reporter Geraldo Rivera did a story: "The Cover-Up On The Death Of Elvis Presley."

A short while after that, Brewer-Giorgio received a copy of the medical examiner's report on Elvis, a document that Rivera was unable to obtain for his show.

"The contents are astounding and, if correct, give evidence that Elvis indeed was not the subject of that particular report," says Brewer-Giorgio.

Axton suggested that Brewer-Giorgio allow one of the top literary agencies in the country to handle the sale of *Orion*. The president of the agency's office in Nashville, Tennessee, at the time, Bob Neal, was Elvis' first manager. Neal has since died.

Although Brewer-Giorgio was bowled over by the agency's eagerness to handle the book, she balked at their insistence on an exclusive three-year contract and gave *Orion* to another agent.

But shortly after being published, she says the book "mysteriously disappeared." The publisher said it simply wasn't selling well, said Brewer-Giorgio, but assured her she could keep the money they had given her.

" 'And please,' they urged," she adds, " 'do nothing or say nothing about Elvis Presley.' But I knew the book was doing fine. In fact I still get calls about it.'

Brewer-Giorgio asked a friend in the publishing business to investigate.

LAWSUIT

"The friend heard it was the Colonel that had gone to the head of the publishing house, threatening a lawsuit," adds the author. "But why? What had I unwittingly touched on? What had I uncovered?"

Brewer-Giorgio took no action at the time because she was trying to recover her reprint rights to her own book. Then, suddenly, they were given back, "out of the blue."

Shortly after that, she was given the tape by two strangers who insisted they remain anonymous.

"They know everything," she says. "I insisted on witnesses during their visit. I was presented with a tape and told I may do with it what I wish."

Brewer-Giorgio is now agonizing over whether to have the tape scientifically analyzed and compared to a known recording of The King's voice to determine if it is truly Elvis speaking.

The voice mentions the attempted assassination of President Reagan in 1981, proving the tape could not have been prepared beforehand.

"Elvis tells in his own words how he managed to fake his own death, how it seemed right at the time, and how he misses the music now.

"There are times when he says he would like to come back, but that he would be foolish to enter a life he tried so hard to escape."

DISCUSSION QUESTIONS

1. The author's argument is based on a number of authorities. How impressive are each of these?
   a. Gail Brewer-Giorgio
   b. *Orion*
   c. Elvis talking on the tape recording
   d. People who recognized Elvis but weren't believed
   e. Mae Boren Axton
   f. Geraldo Rivera
   g. The medical examiner's report
   h. The source who gave Brewer-Giorgio the report
   i. Bob Neal
   j. The publisher of *Orion*
   k. Brewer-Giorgio's "friend in the publishing business"
   l. Unnamed sources who talked to this friend
   m. Two strangers who provided the tape recording
   n. "Witnesses" who saw them do it
2. Why might you choose not to believe Brewer-Giorgio? Why might you choose not to believe *Orion?*
3. Is it unprecedented that a book "vanished from the shelves of bookstores"?
4. Could Colonel Parker (or *any* person in power) persuade a publisher to withdraw a book because it is too revealing or sensational?
5. Is this essay easy to read? Comment on the effect of the first paragraph, the language, the headings, the transitions, etc.

A man sets out to discover the origins of human time. To define mankind's presence in history.

An epic challenge. But one well-met by Richard Leakey. Definitive paleoanthropologist. Director of Kenya's National Museums. Author of the much acclaimed *Origins* and *The Making of Mankind*.

Some men merely make history. Mr. Leakey re-defines it.

His heralded finds at Lake Turkana in Kenya altered many previously unchallenged anthropological views.

Asia had been identified as the birthplace of modern humanity. Leakey unearthed evidence establishing Africa as its origin.

Richard Leakey and Rolex: linked by a reverence for the majesty of time.

From *Kenyapithecus* to *Homo sapiens*, a 14,000,000-year walk through time.

Human evolution was commonly considered an unbroken cord. His discoveries confirm more complex lines of descent.

Many focus on the violence in our species. He sees us as inherently cooperative, stressing our forebears made tools, not weapons.

This piecing together of the evolutionary mosaic demands much of the scientist. And no less of his Rolex. Whether foraging for fossils in desert scrub, or scrambling over rocky escarpments in search of them. Richard Leakey and his Rolex. The pairing is ordained by a shared vocation —the comprehension of time in the fullness of its majesty.

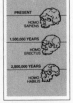

Leakey's outline of human evolution.

ROLEX

The Rolex Explorer II Oyster Perpetual Chronometer in stainless steel.
Write for brochure. Rolex Watch, U.S.A., Inc., Dept. 612, Rolex Building, 665 Fifth Avenue, New York, New York 10022-5383.
World headquarters in Geneva. Other offices in Canada and major countries around the world.

Explorer II. Oyster Perpetual are trademarks © Rolex 1985

Courtesy of Rolex Watch, U.S.A., Inc. Reprinted from *The New Yorker*.

DISCUSSION QUESTIONS

1. Look over this ad quickly. Does it impress you as handsome and probably effective? Would it persuade people to buy Rolex watches?
2. Who is the audience for this ad? Is it the ordinary man on the street?
3. What is the argument here? Are readers being told to buy a Rolex because Richard Leakey wears one?
4. Does Mr. Leakey recommend the Rolex? What does he say about his watch?
5. Is the watch useful to him in his scientific work? If so, what features of it are mentioned?
6. The last line says that Mr. Leakey and Rolex have a shared vocation: "the comprehension of time in the fulness of its majesty." What does this mean?
7. The ad uses short paragraphs, short sentences, and even some incomplete sentences. How do these affect your reading of the ad?

GOVERNMENT DOCUMENT REVEALS
CRASH OF THREE "FLYING SAUCERS"

Jane Hulse

Government officials may put down UFOs as science-fiction bunk, but a UFO researcher says they can't deny the contents of a top-secret memo sent to then-FBI Director J. Edgar Hoover in 1950.

The memo relates how the Air Force recovered three "so-called flying saucers" that crashed in New Mexico. Aboard each of the three crafts were "three bodies of human shape but only 3 feet tall," the memo states.

The memo is one of hundreds of secret government documents proving the existence of UFOs, according to Robert Hastings, an independent UFO researcher from Albuquerque. Hastings, 35, was in town to speak on the Arapahoe Community College campus Monday night, one stop on his national lecture circuit.

The documents, declassified under the Freedom of Information Act beginning in 1975, indicate a massive coverup by military and intelligence officials, Hastings says.

"The public has a right to know the facts," he said in an interview. He said the government is being "shortsighted to keep the public so totally in the dark regarding seemingly vital information that affects not only Americans, but the entire human race."

The 1950 memo is "frustratingly vague," Hastings said, but it's the most tantalizing key to the UFO mystery.

The memo describes the flying saucers as "circular in shape with raised centers, approximately 50 feet in diameter." The small bodies were dressed in "metallic cloth of a very fine texture." Each was "bandaged in a manner similar to the blackout suits used by speed flyers and test pilots."

The memo doesn't say where in New Mexico the crash occurred. But the crash is blamed on the government's "very high-powered radar setup in that area" that could have interfered with the "controlling mechanisms of the saucers."

The brief memo doesn't reveal what happened to the bodies or the flying saucers. Hastings, working with former National Security Agency employee W. Todd Zechel, is striving to end the mystery through investigation and by pressing for release of more secret documents.

The government documents released to Hastings refer to UFOs repeatedly nosing around nuclear weapons laboratories and ICBM sites. Others note attempted aerial interceptions of UFOs by military jet aircraft.

"Whoever is flying these things is highly interested in our nuclear weapons," Hastings said. UFO sightings increased after World War II, a fact Hastings links to the "birth of the nuclear age."

SOURCE: Reprinted by permission of Scripps Howard News Service. Reprinted from the *Mobile Register*, October 23, 1985.

Hastings speculates that the UFOs and their passengers may be "sending a signal to the government that they have the capacity to interfere with a nuclear launch."

Hastings says that military and intelligence officials are covering up the facts about UFOs because of the "potential for panic."

He says the public can handle the information and "it's just a matter of time before it all comes out anyway."

In 1977, *U.S. News & World Report* speculated that before the end of the year then-President Carter was "expected to make what are described as 'unsettling disclosures' about UFOs" based on CIA data.

That didn't happen, and now the public isn't any closer to knowing the truth about UFOs. The Reagan administration has "stonewalled" the issue, Hastings said, and made release of classified documents more difficult.

Hastings's interest in UFOs began as a "pure fluke" in 1967 when he was visiting an air traffic control tower on Malmstrom Air force Base, near Great Falls, Mont.

"Five UFOs were tracked on military radar," he said. "For a half-hour period they hovered over nearby ICBM silos, violating sensitive air space. Then they flew off at an estimated speed of 5,000 mph, far beyond the capability of any conventional aircraft."

Then 17 years old, Hastings was "scurried out of the room."

Hastings, a photographer and filmmaker, spends about four months a year on the lecture circuit to finance his UFO research. Aside from released government documents, he says his information comes from interviews with retired military personnel.

He shied away from speculation, preferring to talk instead about facts contained in government documents. But he did issue one assurance.

"They are benevolent," he said of the extraterrestrials. "There is nothing to indicate hostility. At some point they will make themselves known."

DISCUSSION QUESTIONS

1. Hastings refers to a number of authorities that seem to support his belief in UFOs.
   a. A memo to J. Edgar Hoover, director of the FBI
   b. "Hundreds of secret government documents"
   c. W. Todd Zechel, National Security Agency employee
   d. "More secret documents"
   e. *U.S. News & World Report*
   f. President Jimmy Carter
   g. People at the Malmstrom Air Force Base who tracked five UFOs in 1967
   h. Retired military personnel who were interviewed
   How persuasive is each of these?
2. Consider everything the essay tells you about Robert Hastings. Is he

a genuine expert in the areas under discussion? Is there any reason to suspect bias?

3. How can the Reagan administration and the military and intelligence communities continue to stonewall when Hastings has solid documentary evidence to refute them?

4. What do you know of the 1967 sighting at Malmstrom Air Force Base?

5. How persuasive is Hastings' speculation about the UFOs, their passengers, and their purpose?

WHAT JESUS SAID ABOUT HOMOSEXUALITY:

" "

WHAT THE VATICAN HAS TO SAY:
"INTRINSIC MORAL EVIL...
AN OBJECTIVE DISORDER...BEHAVIOR TO WHICH
NO ONE HAS ANY CONCEIVABLE RIGHT"[1]

WHAT IN THE WORLD IS GOING ON HERE?

What Dignity/USA says about homosexuality: After serious study of our spiritual heritage, we believe that lesbian and gay Catholics are numbered among the People of God, and that they can express their sexuality in a manner that is responsible, loving and consonant with Christ's message?[2]

For nearly 20 years, Dignity has been the national organization fighting for equal rights for lesbians and gay men in the Catholic Church. In over 100 chapters across America, Dignity sponsors the Mass and Sacraments, along with educational and social programs, and a Biennial Convention.

But now, Dignity chapters are under attack. Ultraconservative forces in the Vatican and in America are seeking to turn the clock back to pre-Vatican II days. They are forbidding us to worship on Church property. Priests are prohibited from ministering to us. A whole group of the faithful is being ignored, discarded and despised—because of its sexual orientation.

But the Church is more than a building or a small group of men. The Church is black and white, women and men, gay and straight. The Church is the whole People of God.

When an institution as powerful as the Catholic Church discriminates, all people suffer. You know someone who is gay or lesbian. We are your brothers and sisters, your sons and daughters. We are lay people and clergy. We, too, are the People of God.

Dignity calls on the National Conference of Catholic Bishops to speak out against the expulsion of Dignity chapters, and to dialogue with us on the pastoral care of lesbian and gay Catholics.

Oppressive measures strengthen Dignity. We will continue our struggle. We invite you to join us.

Please use the coupon below or write: Dignity/USA, Suite 11-T, 1500 Massachusetts Avenue, N.W., Washington, D.C. 20005. Help support our work by making a tax-deductible contribution or request more information. Make checks payable to Dignity/USA. Our mailing list and all inquiries are held in strict confidence.

[1] Vatican Congregation for the Doctrine of the Faith, "Letter to the Bishops of the Catholic Church on the Pastoral Care of Homosexual Persons," October 1, 1986.
[2] See Dignity/USA, "Statement of Position and Purpose."

☐ **YES!** I want to help Dignity. Here is my tax-deductible contribution:
 ☐ $15 ☐ $25 ☐ $50 ☐ $100 ☐ $500 ☐ Other: $_____
☐ Please send me more information.
☐ I want information about the Eighth Biennial Dignity Convention to be held in Miami, Florida, July 23–26, 1987.

Name _____

Address _____

City _____ State _____ Zip _____
Send to: Dignity/USA, Suite 11-T, 1500 Massachusetts Avenue, N.W., Washington, D.C. 20005. Make checks payable to Dignity/USA. Our mailing list and all inquiries are held in strict confidence.

Courtesy of Dignity/USA.

DISCUSSION QUESTIONS

1. The argument about homosexuality contrasts opinions of three authorities: (1) Jesus, (2) the Vatican, and (3) Dignity/USA. Evaluate these on the basis of their expertness and their freedom from bias.
2. How significant is it that Jesus made no statements rejecting gay people? Did he make any statements accepting gay people?
3. Why did the author limit quotations to those of Jesus in the gospels? Why didn't he quote Genesis and St. Paul? Are they equal authorities?
4. Are there many gay Catholics? Does the author emphasize the number of people involved in Dignity/USA? Why?
5. Under the situation the author claims, "Priests are prohibited from ministering to us." What is implicit in this statement?
6. The argument stresses that "The Church is the *whole* People of God." Who is it saying the Church is not?

VITAMIN E IN THE
HANDS OF CREATIVE PHYSICIANS

Ruth Adams and Frank Murray

Of all the substances in the medical researcher's pharmacopoeia, perhaps the most maligned, neglected and ignored is vitamin E. In spite of this apparent ostracism in the United States, however, some of the world's leading medical authorities are using alpha tocopherol—more commonly known as vitamin E—to successfully treat and cure a host of mankind's most notorious scourges.

For those medical researchers who are at work trying to treat and prevent heart attacks—our No. 1 killer—and to help many more thousands who are dying of related circulatory disorders, vitamin E is playing a major role. And for many athletes, vitamin E (in the form of wheat germ oil, specially formulated oils for stamina and endurance, vitamin E capsules and perles, etc.) has long been as indispensable as calisthenics.

"There are over 570,000 deaths from heart attacks each year," says a publication of the American Heart Association, "many thousands of them among people in the prime of life—and growing indications that heart disease may be a disease of prosperity."

In scientific minds, vitamin E may be related to fertility and reproduction, said an article in *Medical World News* for April 18, 1969. But a famous ball player, Bobby Bolin of the San Francisco Giants, credits the vitamin with keeping his pitching arm in condition. He developed a sore shoulder in 1966, resulting in a poor pitching season for two years. He began to take vitamin E. The article said that he expected to be a "regular starter" at the beginning of the 1969 season, and that vitamin E was responsible for the good news.

It isn't surprising that many athletes have discovered the benefits of taking vitamin E regularly. The vitamin is in short supply in most of our diets. Vitamin E is an essential part of the whole circulatory mechanism of the body, since it affects our use of oxygen. When you have plenty of vitamin E on hand, your cells can get along on less oxygen. This is surely an advantage for an athlete, who expends large quantities of oxygen. And, according to recent research at the Battelle Memorial Institute, which we will discuss in greater detail in a later section of this book, vitamin E, along with vitamin A, is important to anyone who lives in the midst of constant air pollution.

From *The Summary*, a scientific journal published by the Shute Institute in Canada, a publication we will frequently refer to, we learn additional facts about vitamin E. Dr. Evan Shute, who heads the clinic, and Dr. Wilfrid E. Shute, his brother, have pioneered in work with vitamin E for more than 20 years. *The Summary* condenses and abstracts for doctors and medical researchers some of the material on relevant subjects that has appeared in medical journals throughout the world.

SOURCE: Reprinted from *Vitamin E., Wonder Worker of the 70's.* New York: Larchmont Books, 1972.

For instance, a Hungarian doctor reports on the encouraging effects of vitamin E in children born with certain defects. Of all vitamin deficiencies, she believes that vitamin E is the most important in preventing such occurrences. She has given the vitamin with good results in quite large doses to children who would otherwise be almost incapacitated. Mothers, too.

She tells the story of a woman who had three deficient children, two of them with Down's Syndrome or mongolism. When she was pregnant for the fourth time, the physician sent her away for a rest—"tired, aging, torpid" as she was, with "a diet rich in proteins, liver, vegetables and fruit with large doses of vitamins, especially vitamin E, and thyroid hormone." She returned in six weeks to give birth to a perfectly healthy baby!

As for another insidious disorder—chronic phlebitis—Dr. Evan Shute says that most doctors have no idea of how common this condition is. It should be looked for in everyone, he says, certainly every adult woman. After describing the symptoms—a warm swollen foot and an ache in the leg or foot which is relieved by raising the feet higher than the head—he tells his physician readers, "Look for chronic phlebitis and you will be astounded how common it is. Treat it with vitamin E and you will be deluged with grateful patients who never found help before."

Describing a symposium on the subject of vitamins E, A and K, Dr. Shute tells us that speakers presented evidence that vitamin E is valuable in doses of 400 milligrams daily for treating claudication—a circulatory condition of the feet and legs—and that a similar dosage helps one kind of ulcer.

High dosage of vitamin E improves survival time of persons with hardening of the arteries and should always be given to such patients, according to Dr. Shute. He adds that there are some 21 articles in medical literature, aside from the many he himself has written, showing that vitamin E dilates blood vessels and develops collateral vessels—thus permitting more blood to go through, even though the vessel is narrowed by deposits on its walls.

An article that appeared in *Postgraduate Medicine* in 1968 by Dr. Alton Ochsner, a world-famous lung surgeon, states that he has used vitamin E on every surgical patient over the past 15 years and none has developed damaging or fatal blood clots.

Dr. Shute goes on to say that, at the Shute Clinic, all surgery patients are routinely given vitamin E both as a preventive and as a curative measure.

He quotes an article in *Annals of Internal Medicine*, saying that thrombosis or clot formation "has become the prime health hazard of the adult population of the Western world." Dr. Shute adds these comments: "Here is a real tragedy. Twenty years after we introduced a simple and safe clotting agent, alpha tocopherol, to the medical world, everything else is tried, including dangerous drugs and the anti-coagulants, and with all these the results are extremely unsatisfactory. When will the medical profession use vitamin E as it should be used for this condition?"

He quotes a statement from the *Journal of the American Medical Association* showing that the average teenage girl or housewife gets only about half the amount of iron she should have from her diet in the United States. Then Dr. Shute says, "Another nutritional defect in the best fed people on earth! In one issue the *JAMA* shows the average American is often deficient in iron and vitamin A. Now what about vitamin E?" He, of course, has pointed out many times that this vitamin is almost bound to be lacking in the average diet. As we mention elsewhere, up to 90% of the vitamin E content of various grains is lost during the flaking, shredding, puffing processes that are used to make breakfast cereals.

Dr. Shute then quotes a newsletter on the U.S. Department of Agriculture survey revealing that only half of all American diets could be called "good." He comments thusly, "One continually reads claptrap by nutritionists contending that the wealthiest country in the world feeds everybody well. This obviously isn't true. It is no wonder that deficiency of vitamin E is so common when even the diet recommended by the National Research Council of the U.S.A. contains something like 6 milligrams of vitamin E per day before it is cooked!"

In another issue of *The Summary*, we learn how two Brazilian researchers are working on heart studies done on rats that were made deficient in vitamin E. Of 26 rats, only six normal ones were found. All the rest showed some heart damage when they were tested with electrocardiograms and other devices.

Two German researchers report on the action of an emulsified vitamin E solution on the heart tissues of guinea pigs. They found that the vitamin protects the heart from damage by medication, and helps to prevent heart insufficiency. Dr. Shute adds that this paper indicates that vitamin E should be investigated further in hospital clinics.

Animals deficient in vitamin E produced young with gross and microscopic defects of the skeleton, muscles and nervous system. They had harelips, abdominal hernias, badly curved backs and many more defects. This was reported in *The Journal of Animal Science*, Volume 22, page 848, 1963.

Two American obstetricians report in the *American Journal of Obstetrics and Gynecology* that they know of no way to prevent serious damage and death for many premature infants. Dr. Shute comments, "These authors apparently have not seen our reports on the use of vitamin E in the prevention of prematurity." He goes on to say, "No comparable results have been reported."

A report in the journal, *Fertility and Sterility*, indicates that in six percent of patients studied, the cause of abortion and miscarriage lay in the father's deficient sperm, not in any deficit of the mother. The authors studied carefully the medical histories of many couples who had been married several times. Dr. Shute comments, "We have long advocated alpha tocopherol for poor sperm samples, especially in habitual abortion couples."

A Romanian farm journal reports that extremely large amounts of vitamin E, plus vitamin A, were given to 77 sterile cows. Within one to one-and-a-half months, their sexual cycles were restored and 70 percent of them conceived.

A German veterinarian reports in a 1960 issue of *Tierarztliche Umschau* that he uses vitamin E for treating animals with heart conditions. A one-year-old poodle with heart trouble regained complete health after

14 days on vitamin E. A three-year-old thoroughbred horse with acute heart failure was treated with vitamin E for two weeks, after which time its electrocardiogram showed only trivial changes even after exercise. The vet uses, he says, large doses of the vitamin.

And an Argentinian physician reports in *Semana Med.* that vitamin C is helpful in administering vitamin E. It works with the vitamin to retain it in body tissues. Dr. A. Del Guidice uses the two vitamins together in cases of cataracts, strabismus and myopias. He also noted that patients with convulsive diseases are much helped by vitamin E—massive doses of it—so that their doses of tranquilizers and sedatives can be lessened.

A letter from Dr. Del Guidice to Dr. Shute tells of his success in treating mongolism in children with vitamin E. For good results, he says, it must be given in large doses from the age of one month on. He continues his treatment for years sometimes, and claims that spectacular results can be achieved in this tragic disease.

Two Japanese scientists report in the *Journal of Vitaminology* that hair grew back faster on the shaven backs of rabbits when they applied vitamin E locally for 10 to 13 weeks.

And again from Argentina comes word of vitamin E given to 20 mentally defective children in large doses. In 75 percent, the intelligence quota was raised from 12 to 25 points, "with improved conduct and scholarly ability. Less attention fatigue was noted in 80 percent, and 90 percent had improved memory." A short experience with neurotic adults showed that vitamin E brought a definite reduction in phobias, tics, obsessions and other neurotic symptoms.

In one issue of *The Summary,* Dr. Shute prints a letter of his to the editor of the *British Medical Journal* (July 1966) urging this distinguished man to consider vitamin E as a treatment for pulmonary embolism. He says, "I have used nothing else for years and no longer even think of embolism (that is, blood clots) in my patients, even in those with records of previous phlebitis. Dosage is 800 International Units a day." He adds a PS to readers of *The Summary:* "The Editor could not find space for this letter unfortunately."

A *British Medical Journal* editorial comments on our present methods of treatment for blood clots in leg veins. Raising the foot off the bed, bandaging the legs and getting the patient on his feet doesn't seem to be very helpful, says the editor. Using anticoagulants seems to help some, but we should speedily develop some new methods of treatment. Dr. Shute comments that one would think that vitamin E has a clear field, since nothing else is very effective. It is easy to use, he goes on, safe and effective.

Each issue of *The Summary* contains many articles that have appeared in world medical literature on vitamin E and related subjects. In other countries, vitamin E is treated quite seriously in medical research, is routinely used in hospitals and clinics. In our country, such use is rare.

These are just a few of the case histories that Dr. Shute reports, at his own expense, in *The Summary.* The book is not available for nonmedical people, since it is written in highly technical terms. However, we suggest that you recommend these publications to your doctor, if you or someone you know is suffering from a disorder that might be treated successfully with vitamin E. The address is: Dr. Evan Shute, Shute Foundation for Medical Research, London, Ontario, Canada.

DISCUSSION QUESTIONS

1. The case for vitamin E is supported by reference to a range of authorities:
   a. A publication of the American Heart Association
   b. An article in *Medical World News*
   c. Bobby Bolin of the San Francisco Giants
   d. Many athletes
   e. Recent research at the Battelle Memorial Institute
   f. *The Summary*
   g. The Shute Institute in Canada
   h. Dr. Evan Shute
   i. Dr. Wilfred E. Shute
   j. A Hungarian doctor
   k. Speakers at a symposium on the subject of vitamin E
   l. 21 articles in medical literature
   m. An article in *Postgraduate Medicine*
   n. Dr. Alton Ochsner
   o. An article in *Annals of Internal Medicine*
   p. A statement in the *Journal of the American Medical Association*
   q. A U.S. Department of Agriculture survey
   r. The National Research Council of the United States
   s. Two Brazilian researchers
   t. Two German researchers
   u. The *Journal of Animal Science*
   v. Two American obstetricians
   w. The *American Journal of Obstetrics and Gynecology*
   x. A Romanian farm journal
   y. A German veterinarian
   z. *Tierarztliche Umschau*
   aa. An Argentinian physician
   bb. *Semana Med.*
   cc. Dr. A. Del Guidice
   dd. Two Japanese scientists
   ee. The *Journal of Vitaminology*
   ff. An editorial in the *British Medical Journal*
   Evaluate the relative authority of these.
2. A number of consecutive paragraphs give quotations from respected medical journals along with Dr. Shute's commentary. Do these usually say the same thing?
3. The authors begin by noting that vitamin E has been "maligned, neglected and ignored" by American doctors. How can this occur if the vitamin has been so successful in tests and studies?

4. Studies do show that animals and humans deficient in vitamin E improve significantly when given the vitamin. Does this prove that vitamin E should be added to most people's diet?
5. Who publishes *The Summary*?
6. How successful was Bobby Bolin as a pitcher in 1969?
7. Make a list of the maladies that vitamin E is said to cure. Do these wide-ranging claims for the vitamin make the case for it more persuasive?

DR. DURANT DEMONSTRATES PSYCHOKINESIS

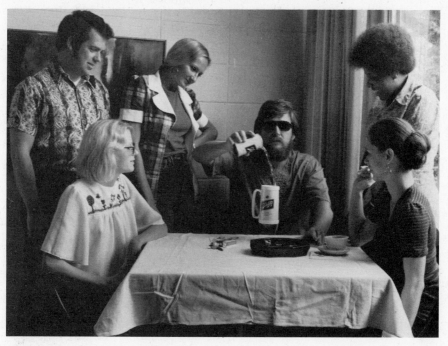

Dr. James Durant, Professor of Psychology at Millburn University, demonstrates his
celebrated powers of psychokinesis to officers of the Student Government Association. The
photograph was taken at the Faculty Club before a group of faculty and students. The
event was supervised by Dr. Xavier Crosert, Dean of the College of Arts and Sciences.
Courtesy of Redstone Wire Service.

DISCUSSION QUESTIONS

1. To establish the credibility of this argument, you must consider the photograph itself as well as the many references and sources mentioned. How reliable as authorities are each of these:
   a. Dr. James Durant
   b. Professor of Psychology
   c. Millburn University
   d. Officers of the Student Government Association
   e. A group of students and faculty
   f. Dr. Xavier Crosert
   g. Dean
   h. College of Arts and Sciences
   i. Redstone Wire Service
   j. Daniel McDonald
   k. University of South Alabama
   l. HarperCollins, Publishers
2. If your investigation found all these sources to be reliable, might you still have reason to doubt the existence of psychokinesis?

"THERE IS
NO SAFE SEX"

Robert C. Noble

The other night on the evening news, there was a piece about condoms. Someone wanted to provide free condoms to high-school students. A perky, fresh-faced teenage girl interviewed said everyone her
age was having sex, so what was the big deal about giving out condoms? Her principal replied that giving out condoms set a bad example.
Then two experts commented. One was a lady who sat very straight in
her chair, white hair in a tight perm, and, in a prudish voice, declared
that condoms didn't work very well; teenagers shouldn't be having sex
anyway. The other expert, a young, attractive woman, said that since
teenagers were sexually active, they shouldn't be denied the protection
that condoms afforded. I found myself agreeing with the prude.

What do I know about all this? I'm an infectious-diseases physician
and an AIDS doctor to the poor. Passing out condoms to teenagers is
like issuing them squirt guns for a four-alarm blaze. Condoms just don't
hack it. We should stop kidding ourselves.

I'm taking care of a 21-year-old boy with AIDS. He could have been
the model for Donatello's David, androgynous, deep blue eyes, long
blond hair, as sweet and gentle as he can be. His mom's in shock. He
called her the other day and gave her two messages. I'm gay. I've got
AIDS. His lover looks like a fellow you'd see in Sunday school; he
works in a bank. He's had sex with only one person, my patient (*his*
second partner), and they've been together for more than a year. These
fellows aren't dummies. They read newspapers. You think condoms
would have saved them?

Smart people don't wear condoms. I read a study about the sexual
habits of college women. In 1975, 12 percent of college women used
condoms when they had sexual intercourse. In 1989, the percentage had
risen to only 41 percent. Why don't college women and their partners
use condoms? They know about herpes. They know about genital warts
and cervical cancer. All the public-health messages of the past 15 years
have been sent, and only 41 percent of the college women use condoms.
Maybe your brain has to be working to use one. In the heat of passion,
the brain shuts down. You have to use a condom every time. *Every time.*
That's hard to do.

I can't say I'm comforted reading a government pamphlet called
"Condoms and Sexually Transmitted Diseases Especially AIDS." "Condoms are not 100 percent safe," it says, "but if used properly will reduce
the risk of sexually transmitted diseases, including AIDS." *Reduce* the
risk of a disease that is 100 percent fatal! That's all that's available between us and death? How much do condoms reduce the risk? They
don't say. So much for Safe Sex. Safe Sex was a dumb idea anyway. I've
noticed that the catchword now is "Safer Sex." So much for truth in

SOURCE: Reprinted from *Newsweek*, April 1, 1991. Reprinted by permission of the author.

advertising. Other nuggets of advice: "If you know your partner is infected, the best rule is to avoid intercourse (including oral sex). If you do decide to have sex with an infected partner, you should *always* be sure a condom is used from start to finish, every time." Seems reasonable, but is it really helpful? Most folks don't know when their partner is infected. It's not as if their nose is purple. Lots of men and women with herpes and wart-virus infections are having sex right now lying their heads off to their sexual partners—that is, to those who ask. At our place we are taking care of a guy with AIDS who is back visiting the bars and having sex. "Well, did your partner use a condom?" I ask. "Did you tell him that you're infected with the virus?" "Oh, no, Dr. Noble," he replies. "it would have broken the mood." You bet it would have broken the mood. It's not only the mood that gets broken. "Condoms may be more likely to break during anal intercourse than during other types of sex . . ." Condoms also break in heterosexual sex; one study shows a 4 percent breakage rate. "Government testing can *not* guarantee that condoms will always prevent the spread of sexually transmitted diseases." That's what the pamphlet says. Condoms are all we've got.

Nobody these days lobbies for abstinence, virginity or single lifetime sexual partners. That would be boring. *Abstinence and sexual intercourse with one mutually faithful uninfected partner are the only totally effective prevention strategies.* That's from another recently published government report.

MEDIA MESSAGES

What am I going to tell my daughters? I'm going to tell them that condoms give a false sense of security and that having sex is dangerous. *Reducing* the risk is not the same as *eliminating* the risk. My message will fly in the face of all other media messages they receive. In the movie "The Tall Guy," a nurse goes to bed with the "Guy" character on their first date, boasting that she likes to get the sex thing out of the way at the beginning of the relationship. His roommate is a nymphomaniac who is always in bed with one or more men. This was supposed to be cute. "Pretty Woman" says you can find happiness with a prostitute. Who are the people that write this stuff? Have the '80s passed and everyone forgotten sexually transmitted diseases? Syphilis is on the rise. Gonorrhea is harder to treat and increasing among black teenagers and adults. Ectopic pregnancies and infertility from sexually transmitted diseases are mounting every year. Giving condoms to high-school kids isn't going to reverse all this.

That prim little old lady on TV had it right. Unmarried people shouldn't be having sex. Few people have the courage to say this publicly. In the context of our culture, they sound like cranks. Doctors can't fix most of the things you can catch out there. There's no cure for AIDS. There's no cure for herpes or genital warts. Gonorrhea and chlamydial infection can ruin your chances of ever getting pregnant and can harm your baby if you do. That afternoon in the motel may leave you with an infection that you'll have to explain to your spouse. Your doctor can't cover up for you. Your spouse's lawyer may sue him if he tries. There is no safe sex. Condoms aren't going to make a dent in the sexual epidemics that we are facing. If the condom breaks, you may die.

DISCUSSION QUESTIONS

1. What are Dr. Noble's credentials? Is he competent to talk on this issue? Is he speaking as a moral or religious authority?
2. How impressive are the other authorities mentioned in the essay? Consider each of these:
   a. "Two experts" speaking on the evening news
   b. "A study" about the sexual habits of college women
   c. A government pamphlet "Condoms and Sexually Transmitted Diseases Especially AIDS"
   d. Dr. Noble's patients: "a 21-year-old boy with AIDS" and "a guy with AIDS"
   e. "One study" on the breakage rate of condoms
   f. A "recently published government report"
   g. Two movies: *The Tall Guy* and *Pretty Woman*
3. How threatening are the diseases Dr. Noble mentions? How does he emphasize the problems involved?
4. What is the difference between "safe sex" and "safer sex"?
5. The author mentions half a dozen reasons why "Condoms just don't hack it." What are these?
6. Dr. Noble says, "Condoms just don't hack it" and "Safe sex was a dumb idea anyway." Is this appropriate language for a physician writing on a serious medical subject?
7. Did you find the article easy to read? Is Dr. Noble an effective writer?

SEMANTIC
ARGUMENT

"Buick Electra. The name alone speaks volumes."

Semantic argument tries to make a persuasive point by using impressive language rather than by presenting or arranging evidence. It should convince no one.

Semantic argument always sounds good. Its effectiveness derives from the nature of words. A word can have two levels of meaning: a denotative meaning—that is, some specific thing or condition to which it refers *(paper, swim, beige)*, and a connotative meaning—that is, certain emotional responses that it arouses. Connotations can be affirmative *(national leader, negotiation, right of unlimited debate)* or negative *(politician, deal, filibuster)*. Semantic argument uses connotative words to characterize an issue or to enhance the tone of a discussion.

SNARL AND PURR WORDS

Connotative words (sometimes called purr words and snarl words) do not prove anything; they just call something good or bad. American politicians of both parties regularly run for office, for example, on a program favoring *obedience to God, family, and country; adherence to law and order; separation of powers; fiscal responsibility; personal integrity; economic progress without inflation;* and *faith in the American dream.* They oppose *absenteeism, wasteful spending, communism, anarchy, economic floundering,* and *stagnation.* The essence of such an argument is its vagueness—and its usefulness. When asked for an opinion on a controversial issue like busing, for instance, a candidate can resort to language:

> First, let me put this issue in perspective. My record shows I have always fought for the cause of education and for our children, who are the hope of this great nation. I recognize the profound complexities in this area and the honest differences presently existing between good men. I assure you I will work for a positive, fair, and democratic solution. Trust me.

What is the speaker's view on busing? You can't even guess.

This kind of argument can praise any entity—a party platform, a current novel, a union demand—as *authentic, just, reasonable, natural,* and *realistic* or condemn it as *irresponsible, asinine, phony, dangerous,* and *superficial.* It can celebrate one citizen as a *Samaritan,* a *patriot,* and an *independent thinker* and reject another as a *do-gooder,* a *reactionary,* and a *pseudo-intellectual.* (One person's *terrorist* is another person's *freedom fighter.*) Such terms have little specific meaning. A rich collection highlights every election. In Alabama, Fob James, a little-known candidate, won the governorship with a campaign that affirmed "the politics of compassion and a renaissance of common sense." In the 1988 national campaign, George Bush assured us that American was sustained by "a thousand points of light."

Semantic language depends on its emotional associations. An automobile is more appealing when named an *Eagle SX/4;* a bill, when called a *right-to-work law:* and a military settlement, when termed *peace with honor.* In successful argument, much depends on finding the right words. It is easy to champion *baseball, hot dogs, apple pie, and Chevrolet,* and it is hard to attack a position bulwarked with powerful language. How can anyone oppose *fair-trade* laws, the *right-to-life* movement, or a *clean air* act? Who can question the importance of the *miracle nutrient coenzyme Q10?*

Currently a favorite advertising word is *nature.* A laxative is called "Nature's Remedy"; a shoe, "The Naturalizer"; and Rheingold, "the natural beer." L.A. Beer was particularly celebrated. It boasted that "a special natural brewing process along with the finest natural ingredients and slow, natural aging produce a beer with less alcohol, that tastes as good as a regular beer." Beer hardly seems to qualify as natural, since it takes a chemist to make it. Still, if you look at things in a broad perspective, every process and ingredient can be called natural.

The word *light* is equally popular, and equally chancy. Sometimes it means a product has significantly fewer calories; sometimes it doesn't. The Wesson Oil that's called "light and natural" has the same calories as regular Wesson Oil—it's just paler in color. While most light beers have 50 to 80 fewer calories than regular beer, Michelob Light has shed only 15.

Another word to watch for is *best.* Some products—like gasoline, aspirin, and toothpaste—are called parity products. This means all brands are about the same. None can claim to be *better* without offering a body of evidence. But because none is superior to the rest, all can claim to be *best.* Every one of them. Remember this when you hear "Nestlé makes the very best," or "Gillette—the best a man can get," or "Minute Maid—the best there is." Such products are indeed the best, just like their competitors are.

There is a special group of words you should look out for—words like *helps, virtually, up to,* and *relatively.* These modify any claim they appear with. You've seen the promises. Product A *helps* control dandruff, Product B leaves dishes *virtually* spotless, Product C lets you lose *up to* 15 pounds in a week, and Product D is *relatively* inexpensive.

Advertisers have called up an impressive range of associations to offer Blue Cross, Lemon-fresh Joy, Cashmere Bouquet, Old Grand-Dad, and Lincoln Continental Mark VII LSC—plus Obsession, Canadian Mist, 280-ZX, Triumph Spitfire, English Leather, and Brut 33 by Fabergé. Such names often make the difference. Millions of dollars have been earned and lost as Carnation Slender won the market from Metrecal, as DieHard outsold the J. C. Penney battery, and as Taster's Choice defeated Maxim instant coffee. For years, the best-selling perfume in the world was called Charlie.

Names make a difference. A weight-loss book titled *The New Dimensions II Bio-Imagery Programming Figure Enhancement System* has a lot going for it (perhaps too much). Products like Algemarin soap, Mr. Turkey luncheon meats, Jhirmack shampoo, Hyundai Scoupe, and Volkswagen Facade seem to labor under a handicap. But a creative persuader can do wonders. Who can forget the jam advertisement "With a name like Smucker's, it has to be good"?

Recent administrations have done wonders with semantic argument. Did President Reagan order the Army, Marines, and Air Force to invade Grenada? No, the "Caribbean Peace Keeping Forces" made a "pre-dawn vertical insertion" into Grenada. Did President Bush order a military attack on Iraq? No, he announced "Operation Desert Storm."

Names

Even people's names carry associations. In comic fiction, you know immediately that Mary Worth is good and that Snidely Whiplash is bad. Real-life examples demonstrate the American rejection of vague or foreign-sounding names. For years Hollywood hired performers like Charles Buchinsky and Doris von Kappelhoff and made them stars as Charles Bronson and Doris Day. For a long time, Household Finance Corporation presented loan officers to the public as "friendly Bob Adams." Currently, men with mild names like Scott Simpson, Robert Remus, and Jim Harris appear on the professional wrestling circuit as "Nikita Kiloff," "Sergeant Slaughter," and "Kamala, the Ugandan Giant." Sylvester Ritter wrestles as "the Junkyard Dog."

Names are important in politics. John Varick Tunney had always been called Varick until he chose to run for office. After Opinion Research of California polled citizen response to the name Varick, he reverted to his unused first name and became Senator John Tunney. It is noteworthy that the serious candidates for the presidency in 1976 (Senators Udall and Jackson, President Ford, Governors Reagan and Carter) were introduced as Mo, Scoop, Jerry, Ron, and Jimmy. In the 1980 race, the candidates were Jimmy, Ted, Ron, George, Bob, John, and Big John. Only Senator Baker (Howard) had a name that needed work.

In 1984, the candidates were Ron and Walter (called Fritz), though much attention was given to Jesse (a fine biblical name for a minister) and to Gary Hart (formerly Gary Hartpence). Jesse ran again in 1988, as did a number of candidates with safe names—George, Bob, Al, Jack, Pat, Paul, Joe, Bill, Pete, and Sam. However, the American public also faced more complicated ethnic names like Mario Cuomo and Mike Dukakis. (His close friends called him Michael.)

INDIRECT STATEMENT

Semantic argument can also work indirectly; that is, in a particular context, a purr word expressed is also a snarl word implied. To advertise "Oil Heat Is Safe," for example, is to imply that gas and electric heat are dangerous. To describe a movie as "not recommended for immature audiences" is to boast that it is impressively sexual or violent. When Tampax was advertised as a "natural cotton" product, it was reminding readers that it was not one of the sponge tampons that had been associated with toxic shock syndrome and several deaths.

In the years before things became explicit, commercial advertisers used many indirect attacks. Diners Club said, "Why go abroad with a credit card you've outgrown?" Playtex asked, "Are you still using the same brand of tampons they invented for your grandmother?" And Scope mouthwash boasted it was "Minty-fresh, not mediciney."

Such argument produces rich paradoxes. The ad for *Valley of the Dolls* reported that "Any similarity between any person, living or dead, and the characters portrayed in this film is purely coincidental and not intended"; this told moviegoers that the film was about real-life Hollywood stars. Another ad declared that the "United States Supreme Court has ruled that *Carnal Knowledge* is NOT OBSCENE," which meant that it was.

When George Wallace ran for governor of Alabama in 1980, his two opponents in the Democratic primary could not tastefully point out that he had recently married a country singer and that he was crippled. So one opponent produced television ads showing his own elegant wife and saying "When you elect a governor, you elect a first lady." The other opponent was less subtle. His TV ads showed him running up the steps of the statehouse.

Sometimes, semantic claims are not meant to be penetrated. This is especially true when impressive language is used to mask a negative admission. For example, when government economists announce that the inflation rate is "slowing down," they wish to communicate optimistic reassurance rather than what the words really say, that prices are still high and still climbing. When manufacturers label a garment "shrink-resistant," they want to suggest that it will not shrink, not what the term literally says, that the garment will resist shrinking, and thus that shrinkage will certainly occur. Advertisers for an inexpensive portable radio wish to imply that it is powerful and can pull in signals from distant stations, but what they say is, "You can take it anywhere."

You have to admire the creative language that public relations experts use to mask problems. When the Reagan administration admitted giving the media false stories about Libyan unrest, it called the stories "disinformation." One corporation specified a large sum of money on its annual balance-sheet and declared it a "negative investment increment." You know what that means.

PERSUASIVE STYLE

The attempt to communicate more than is literally said also occurs when persuaders use impressive language to add character to an argument. Couching their views in religious allusions, folksy talk, or esoteric jargon, they argue more with style than with facts. In a letter to the *Saturday Review,* for example, Gelett Burgess maintained that Shakespeare did not write the plays attributed to him. His language was intellectual:

> Sir:
> My recent communication relative to Oxford-is-Shakespeare elicited responses which evince and hypostatize the bigoted renitency usual in orthodox addicts. For the Stratfordian mythology has engendered a strange nympholepsy like a fanatical religion which is not amenable to reason or logic and abrogates all scientific methods.

As a contrast, consider the tone of this fund-raising letter sent out by Senator Jesse Helms:

> Dear Friend:
> Will you do me a personal favor and place the enclosed bumper sticker on your car today?
>
> And, will you use the enclosed form to let me know if I can send you a Reagan for President button to wear?
>
> I'll be deeply gratified if I could hear from you immediately. . . .
>
> Won't you please, please dig down deep and give as you have never given before?
>
> Whether Ronald Regan wins or loses is up to folks like you and me. The decision rests in our hands.
>
> I pray that you will answer this call for help. God bless you.

The senator tried to make his message more persuasive by speaking as a Christian Southern gentleman.

You should, of course, judge an argument solely on the evidence brought forward to support a conclusion, not on the effect of connotative language. Similarly, in writing argument, fight the temptation to overuse snarl and purr words. Avoid pedantic language and high-sounding phrases. Your reader will think, perhaps rightly, that you are compensating for weaknesses in your case.

Connotative language defies meaningful analysis. Is it true that "Education without God produces a nation without freedom," that Nike running shoes are "faster than the fastest feet," that Fleishmann's Gin is "Clean . . . Clean . . . Clean"? Who can say? Until the claims are clarified and documented, such vague language can produce only empty and repetitive argument. Fleishmann advertisements, it should be noted, once offered to explain "What do they mean CLEAN . . . CLEAN . . . CLEAN?" The answer: "They mean the crispest, brightest drinks under the sun are made with clean-tasting Fleishmann's Gin." This is about as meaningful as semantic argument gets.

EXERCISES

How effective are these semantic arguments?

1. I want to distinguish my program from that of Senator Williams. My position has been firm where his has been pig-headed. My actions have been energetic and creative where his have been manic and bizarre. I am much concerned in these areas where he is obsessive.
2. "At Ford, Quality is Job 1"; "Nobody sweats the details like GM."
3. I oppose the bleeding-heart radicals who are opposing President Reagan's peace efforts in Central America. All he's trying to do is destabilize unfriendly governments and neutralize the terrorists.
4. The human organism is a homeostatic mechanism; that is, all behavior is an attempt to preserve organismic integrity by homeostatic restoration of equilibrium, as that equilibrium is disturbed by biologically significant organizations of energies in the external or internal environments of the organism.
5. Macho cologne—"It's b-a-a-a-d."
6. I can't decide which car to buy. I'm choosing between a Dodge St. Regis, a Honda Accord SE-i, an Olds Cutlass Salon, a Toronado Troféo, a Caprice Silver Classic, a Thunderbird, a Chevelle Malibu Classic Estate, a Geo Prizm, an Isuzu Trooper, and a Continental Mark VII Bill Blass.
7. Night Repair was scientifically formulated in Estée Lauder's U.S. laboratories as part of the Swiss Age-Controlling Skincare Program. Although only nature controls the aging process, this program helps control the signs of aging and encourages skin to look and feel younger.
8. When a correspondent wrote to *Personality Parade* asking whether Elvis Presley had learned to act, columnist Walter Scott responded, "Mr. Presley has always been good to his mother."
9. Christian Dior's Eau Sauvage—"Virile. Discreet. Refreshing. Uncompromising. A fragrance of masculine refinement."
10. We guarantee our product will reduce your waist by up to three inches in the first two weeks or double your money back.
11. The abortion issue comes down to this: Should a baby be mutilated for the convenience of its mother?
12. Try Naturade Conditioning Mascara with National Protein. (Contains stearic acid, PUP, butylene glycol, sorbitan sesquioleate, triethanolamine, imidazolidinyl urea, methylparaben, and propylparaben.)

13. Don Siegelman believes we need an Attorney General tough enough to fight the drug dealers, drunk drivers, career criminals, and anyone else who would harm our families.
14. Miller beer. Made the American way.
15. As a resident of this city for some time, I have become accustomed to the pathetic whining your paper is prone to whenever city government fails to apishly follow your always myopic and generally self-defeating plans for civic "betterment." Tolerating such infantile and retrograde twaddle was the price, I told myself, of a free and unshackled press.
16. A problematic of canon-formation, in contradistinction to an ideology of tradition, must assimilate the concept of tradition within an objective history, as an effect of monumentalization by which a canon of works confronts an author over against the contemporary social conditions of literary production, as simply given.
17. Fahrvernügen—It's what makes a car a Volkswagen.
18. You may now acquire directly from the National Historic Mint a first-edition Statue of Liberty Commemorative—the authentic "Double Eagle" Series "L"—honoring the 100th anniversary of one of America's most honored national treasures.
19. I can't decide which brand to smoke. I'm choosing between Barclay, Benson & Hedges, Carlton, Cambridge, Kent, Parliament, Tareyton, Montclair, and Winston.
20. "Part of the great pleasure one gets from Dewar's 'White Label' Scotch is the reassuring knowledge that you have chosen something authentic."

ESSAY ASSIGNMENTS

Write an essay either affirming or opposing one of these statements. The material you encounter in your background reading will include a good deal of semantic argument, and so may your essay.

1. Abortion is murder.
2. Feminist organizations want to destroy the American family.
3. Who needs poetry?
4. Capital punishment is necessary.
5. The publishers of *Hustler* and *Penthouse* should be sent to jail.
6. America needs some old-fashioned patriotism.
7. We should make "America the Beautiful" our national anthem.
8. X should be abolished. (Fill in the X.)

PSYCHOMETRY

David St. Clair

That fancy ten-dollar word means holding something in your hand and getting the vibrations from it—no more than that.

After a while, all objects take on the personality of their owner, and just as fingerprints cling to a drinking glass, your psychic print remains on things you wear and touch. Don't ask me why, because I don't know. This phenomenon, like so many others in this field, has yet to be investigated scientifically.

Quite often a good medium will be able to give you a reading just by holding an object belonging to you. Again, like the radio set, she tunes out the world around her—especially her own thoughts—and tunes in to what the object is transmitting. Then she reports what is coming through to her. If she is right, you should tell her so and she'll know she has tuned in to your particular vibrations. Then the reading will continue with ease and (one hopes) with accuracy.

In Los Angeles there is one well-known medium, the Baroness Lotta von Strahl, who has helped the Los Angeles police solve innumerable cases by the exclusive use of psychometry.

One of her most famous cases was that of the Manson killings. The day after they found the bodies of Sharon Tate and her friends in all that blood and gore, the police came (secretly, of course!) knocking at Lotta's door. They had objects that belonged to the victims and also a knife or two that they were sure must have been dropped by the killers. What could she see?

Lotta took the objects and began to have horrible pains. She felt the stabbings in her back and stomach and, a few times, was tempted to ask the police to go away and not force her to go through this torment. But she kept on. She said that she picked up the name "Mason" or "Maxon," and that the man was small, with piercing dark eyes. She also said that the killers were not just men but that there were women with them, and young girls at that. She was puzzled when she kept getting "the same last name. You know," she told the officers, "it's almost as if they were all members of the same *family*." Then she saw something that puzzled her. It was an old town in the days of the Wild West but "nobody lives there. It's strange, but the doors are open and the houses have no substance."

Of course, when Charles Manson was finally caught, he did have several girls with him who formed his "family." They had been living at a ranch that served as a location for shooting Western films. What Lotta had seen was the empty false fronts of the movie set.

Another case involved a violent murder at a Mexican-American wedding. The groom had been stabbed and the bride was wounded. The police had arrested several suspects, but none of them admitted commit-

SOURCE: Reprinted by permission. From *David St. Clair's Lessons in Instant ESP*. New York: New American Library (Signet Books), 1978.

ting the crime. The police gave Lotta the dead man's shirt, all torn and brown with dried blood, and she picked up something about a man with a birthmark on his upper-right shoulder. The police had photographs of the corpse. No, he didn't have such a mark. "Then," said the medium, "the murderer has such a mark. If you find the man with this birthmark, he will confess."

The police called in all the suspects and asked them to remove their shirts. One had a birthmark just where Lotta had said it would be. He denied killing the bridegroom, but when the police told him about Lotta and what she had seen, he began to scream about witchcraft, broke down, and confessed.

Psychometry is easy, especially if you practice and if you—what's the magic word?—*listen*.

Here it is terribly important to *listen* to the information you get from the object. Don't hesitate to say something because *you* don't feel it applies. *You must stay out of it.* It is vitally important for your success that you keep *yourself* out of it as much as possible. Once again, you are only the radio receiving the message—and radios don't think or decide what they will broadcast.

The first time I ever tried psychometry, I was interviewing two wonderful mediums in San Jose, California: Marcia Warzek and Norma Dart, for my book *The Psychic World of California.* Both women had been doing psychometry for a large audience that afternoon, going from row to row and telling people things about themselves no stranger could possibly have known. The audience was amazed and, I'll confess, I was impressed. Later that evening I said to Norma, "That must be very difficult to do, isn't it?"

"Not at all," she said, and promptly took off her bracelet and handed it to me. "Just relax, close your eyes, and tell me the first thing that comes to your mind. Don't force it and don't try to analyze it. Just let the images come and I'll tell you if you're right or not."

I took that bracelet (a little self-consciously, for after all, they were the psychics, not I!) and as I held it, I started to smile.

"What's so funny?" Norma asked.

"I've got a dumb picture here," I said with some embarrassment. "It couldn't possibly mean anything, because it doesn't have anything to do with you."

"Well, what is it? You let me decide if it's for me or not."

"I see a large sailing ship," I said, "with its sails unfurled, and it's going across choppy water." I opened my eyes and handed her the bracelet. "See? That meant nothing at all."

"Oh no?" Norma got up and went out of the room. In a few minutes she was back with a book in her hand. "When my husband died recently, I decided to take all his books and incorporate them into my own library. I wanted to have the same bookplate in them that I had in my own books. I've been combing San Jose for the past month trying to find that bookplate. Look!" She opened her book and pointed to the bookplate. It was a picture of a ship, its sails unfurled, going against a rough sea.

After that, I did psychometry for my family and acquaintances, even saved a friend of mine a few dollars on the purchase of an antique

Chinese vase. She was anxious to have it, but the dealer wanted $500 for it. She took me with her to help her make up her mind. I know quite a bit about American and English antiques but nothing about Oriental art. Yet as I picked up the vase I decided to do some psychometry on it. The first words I got were "not old."

"Should I buy it?" she asked me, with the dealer standing right there.

"No," I said with great authority. "It's not old. It's a fake."

The dealer looked thunderstruck. "What do you know about the Ming period?" he asked haughtily.

"A great deal," I lied, "and this vase is not more than thirty years old and not worth more than fifty dollars."

He was sure I was from the police and began to apologize for having tried to sell us something that wasn't genuine. We walked out in righteous indignation and had a good laugh about it in a nearby bar. My friend bought the drinks with some of the $500 I had saved her.

One of the first times I ever did psychometry in public was in Dallas, Texas. I was lecturing on various aspects of psychic phenomena and when I mentioned that it was possible to get information from inanimate objects, a lady in the front row got up and handed me a very expensive diamond wristwatch. "Let's see what you can get from that," she said.

I held the watch and looked at the lady. She was superbly dressed in the very latest fashion—Gucci shoes, diamond necklace, Louis Vuitton handbag, the works. There I stood before over four hundred people and what did I get? A tumbledown shack, an old Ford up on cinder blocks, and two or three small children running around with bare feet, dirty clothes, and ratted hair.

"Well?" she said.

I gulped, trying to get out of this public fiasco and wondering if Texans still used guns to run charlatans out of town. I decided to play it honest. "What I get can't have anything to do with you. There is a shack, an old Ford, and some dirty half-naked children playing around it."

"Oh yes," she beamed. "That does mean something to me. That was the way we lived until Daddy struck oil!"

I repeat: Keep *yourself* out of the reading!

The longer an object has been worn, the stronger the vibrations will be. When giving a reading, ask for something the person has carried with him for a while. A key ring bought just a few days ago won't tell you anything, but a pair of glasses worn for five years will be an encyclopedia of information.

Also make sure that the object has had only one owner. If someone gives you a ring that has also been worn by her mother or her sister, you may well get conflicting vibrations. Often I've been telling someone things and she'll say, "No, that doesn't mean a thing," and *then* she'll tell me that she bought that object in a secondhand store or antique shop. I have no way, then, of knowing *who* the vibrations belong to.

When you are giving a reading, insist that the person be entirely honest with you. If you say that he drives a green car, and he drives a brown car, tell him to say so. Many people will want to please you, and they will stretch the truth (or just plain lie) to "help" you along. They are only confusing things because until you start getting the truthful "Yes, that makes sense" answers, you have no idea whether you have tuned in to that person or not. Insist that people be honest with you; it'll help you give them a better reading.

Every now and then, you'll find yourself telling someone things, they'll go along and admit that you are absolutely right, and then you'll hit one item and they'll balk: "No. That isn't me. I don't know what you're talking about." If the image in question fades away and doesn't repeat itself in the reading, then most likely you were wrong. But if it *keeps* returning or won't go away, and the person keeps denying it, it is almost 100 percent certain that this person doesn't know or doesn't remember what he or she is talking about.

I've had people tell me, as much as a month later, that I had been correct and they just hadn't realized it then. I remember with one woman I kept getting the name Sarah. No, she didn't know any Sarah. The name came back and wouldn't go away. "I have the impression that this Sarah is in spirit and is guiding you, protecting you," I said. No, she had never had a Sarah in her life. I must be wrong.

Then, about three months later, I got a letter from the woman. She had gone back to visit her aged mother and had told her of the reading. When she mentioned the name Sarah, her mother almost fainted. The first child the mother had ever had was named Sarah, but she was born with a severe deformity and only lived a few days. The mother had never told any of the children that came after Sarah that they had had a sister who died.

The information may be given to you in many different ways. You may get names, dates, places, and so on—by "get" I mean you'll *hear* them inside your head or else you'll *see* them written out in your mind's eye.

You may get colors, or heat or cold. You may get symbols. You may see an eagle, for example, and know this person doesn't keep eagles as pets or shoot eagles on her days off, so the big bird must be symbolic of something. Don't try to interpret the eagle symbol *unless* the interpretation is given to you immediately after the image. If all you get is the bird, then give her the bird and let her interpret it to her own satisfaction.

One last thing that is *very important. Never* give someone a reading who doesn't want it! It will only end in disaster, with you looking like the main candidate for the Nobel Prize for Jerks. If someone says that he doesn't want to have anything psychometrized, then *don't* insist. You will get no cooperation from this negative soul but be blocked at every level by his negativity. Don't say I didn't warn you!

Any further questions, dear students? Good. Let's get to *work*. Find yourself someone (the less well you know them, the better) who has an object and wants a reading. Have that person take off the object and hold it in her hands. Tell her to close her eyes and imagine currents of electricity running down both her arms into her palms. Have her recharge the object to put even more of herself into it. Then, when you feel ready to begin, ask her to hand it to you.

Say whatever comes into your head. You may start to get words or names even before the object touches your own hands. Fine—say what you get. Keep asking for confirmation of your facts. Make the person say yes or no or maybe, but get her confirmation in some way or else you won't know if you're on the right track.

If you don't get anything at all, ask for another object and hold *both* those objects together. You can pass the objects from one hand to another if you choose, press them against your forehead, do anything with them (within reason!) to make you closer and more in touch with their vibrations.

If you still don't get anything, pass the objects back. Either ask for another item to hold or forget the whole thing with that particular person. And remember, just because you bomb out with one person doesn't mean you'll do it with another. Maybe you just couldn't find that first person's wavelength.

Keep at it until you get it right . . . and you will.

Okay, you may say, this is all very nice but what *good* is it? Why bother to learn this spooky stuff with the long name?

Good question! I've already cited two of the reasons: to help track down a murderer and to decide if something, like the fake antique vase, is really worth the price.

But there are other reasons. You are about to sign a contract, say. You hold it for a few minutes and "something" just doesn't feel right to you. You ask to take it home and study it overnight. Then, in the calmness of your own study, you read the small print at the bottom! No way do you agree with those terms!

You get a letter from a friend. He is saying one thing but by holding his letter and "listening," you get what he was *thinking* as he was writing— and that was something completely different. I'm not suggesting that you'll get his exact words, but you'll get his mood and his emotions, and you'll be able to judge for yourself whether or not to take his letter at face value.

On being introduced to someone, you reach out and take his hand. Blaaahhh! comes back the response in quick psychometric fashion. Uh-huh, you say to yourself, I'd better *watch* this fellow.

I've had students who were collectors of various and sundry things use their psychometry to cut through all the muddle at flea markets and head straight for the items they would be interested in. It saves a lot of time and shoe leather.

I myself like to collect occult and psychic books, especially those written before 1940. I've gotten so that I can go directly to such books in the most jumbled shop and my hand will reach for the interesting ones first. Furthermore, if the book has been signed by the author, I *know* the signature is in there before I open the cover.

There are many ways psychometry can be used in your daily life. After all, that's why you are taking this course, correct?

DISCUSSION QUESTIONS

1. What biographical facts does this essay tell you about David St. Clair? Does he seem to be someone you'd like to know? Do you feel you can trust him?

2. What does the writing style tell you about the author? Does he use many big words, many long sentences? Does he seem concerned about communicating with *you?*

3. If you wanted to verify the story of Baroness Lotta von Strahl's helping the police solve the two crimes, how could you do it?

4. What keeps you from being too impressed by the fact the Baroness guessed the name "Maxon" and knew of Charles Manson's eyes and his family? When are you learning about these facts?

5. What advantages does a psychic have because of these features of psychometry?
   a. The subject hands the psychic an object.
   b. The subject comments about right and wrong facts as the reading progresses.
   c. Some images can be interpreted either literally or symbolically.
   d. Some subjects try to help the psychic by lying or by exaggerating things about themselves.
   e. One should never do a reading for a "negative" person.

6. If you tried a psychometry exercise and a psychic saw a ship on a choppy sea and the name "Sarah," could you find a way to tie these into your life story?

7. If you tried to do a reading on some other member of your class, what advantages (besides psychic power) would you have to help you make correct statements?

BILL HAYS.
A CITIZEN'S APPROACH
TO COUNTY GOVERNMENT.

When Bill Hays was called upon to serve in local government, he came to public office not as a politician, but as a private citizen.

Because he entered office mid-term, he inherited numerous county-wide problems. But through hard work and clear vision of a better Mobile, he is steadily putting county government back on the right track.

It's this calm sincerity and dedication that sets Bill Hays apart from the loud rhetoric of some politicians.

His intelligent, non-political approach to solving problems is making our community vital again, not just for a few, but for the good of all.

Bill Hays is working for Mobile, independently, as a responsible citizen. Without fear or favor to any special interest group or individual. His is a responsible voice that leads with courage and integrity.

This election, let's rise above politics.
Vote Bill Hays.

Hays
COUNTY COMMISSION · DISTRICT TWO
A RESPONSIBLE VOICE

DISCUSSION QUESTIONS

1. The main argument here is that Bill Hays is running for office not as a "politician," but as a "citizen." What is the denotative meaning of these words? What is the connotative meaning?
2. The argument boasts that Hays was never elected to the office he now holds; he was "called upon to serve." What does this tell you?
3. What other associations attend the idea of being "called"?
4. Beginning with "hard work" and "clear vision," list the vague political words and phrases. How many of these have a specific definition?
5. Does the candidate give you any idea of what he plans to do if elected? What are his plans for schools, roads, taxes, etc.?
6. Is this the kind of language a candidate should use?

THE INFANTILE MINDS
OF ANTI-SMOKERS

Carol Thompson

Throughout history, there have been inquisitions, persecutions and repressions ("Snuff Out the Collusion," Vol. 15, No. 30). And every single one of them was caused by garbage just like the anti-smokers. Hysteria, credulity, sanctimonious poop-spouting and sophistries are the hallmarks of their type.

"Smoking is the leading preventable cause of death," like, if you don't smoke, you won't die. And as if when you remove one leading cause of death, another doesn't immediately take its place, until, by this process, you have eliminated all freedom and are demanding that people live like puritanical insects to serve bureaucrats' statistics.

The way their infantile minds are arranged, they actually believe that it is only the other people that are supposed to be judged according to how well they serve bureaucrats' statistics, while their own pleasures must not be interfered with out of such considerations. They'd self-righteously denounce smoking and then go hang-gliding. They assume that it's the sheer relative numbers of people smoking versus hang-gliding that makes smoking worthy of attack, as if virtue consists of denying the pleasure of the greatest number of people.

At least half of the deaths attributed to smoking are known to be falsely claimed. The anti-smokers are so morally corrupt they don't even care whether the things they say are true or not. They think that if they repeat a lie often enough, people will believe it, and that makes it truth.

Bill Lueders claims that smoking kills "195 times as many as the current demon drug, cocaine." This is directly comparing deaths of old people with deaths of young ones, from something used by a few million people at most with something used by over 50 million, and used for only a few years versus several decades. You'd have to have the IQ of a baboon to believe this. And the only way garbage like that can persist is when the lie spreaders refuse to allow the people to refute them, as Lueders and his fellow anti-smokers have done.

Anti-smoker ethics consist of demanding that they be held above moral judgment while they lynch their victims. They live in a make-believe world where they pretend they are white knights courageously battling evil tobacco companies. Smokers are dehumanized and reduced to passive nonentities, with anti-smokers posing as their self-appointed guardians.

It is not a coincidence that the anti-smoking movement comes at a time when the American people are renowned as the stupidest beings on the planet earth. If people in the old days didn't fall for their crap, it's not because they were stupid or ignorant or amoral. They had actual working minds which were capable of seeing through it.

SOURCE: Reprinted from *Isthmus*, September 14–20, 1990. Reprinted by permission of the author.

They stand in the <u>wreckage</u> of every noble ideal, and <u>yammer</u> that the greatest thing they can teach your children is not to smoke. This is a generation of <u>vermin</u> and it's about time somebody had the guts to say so.

DISCUSSION QUESTIONS

1. Count the number of snarl words in this letter. How many do you get?
2. What does such language tell you about the author's belief, her emotional commitment, her creativity?
3. Does this barrage of snarl words make the argument more interesting? More persuasive?
4. How does she handle the statistical argument comparing tobacco deaths with cocaine deaths? Is her answer effective?
5. She talks of "smokers," "anti-smokers," and "people in the old days." Whom is she talking about? How do such generalizations affect her argument?
6. Is there any reason to suspect the author is biased? Why did she write this essay?
7. Is the author a good writer? Can you hear her voice in her prose?

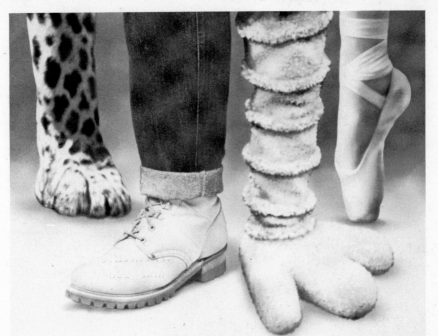

Who Else Can Fill These Shoes!

Only your Public Television station consistently brings you quality programs that inspire, entertain and inform. Programs like THE CIVIL WAR, SESAME STREET and NOVA.

It's television you can trust. With educational programs you want your children to watch. And programs your whole family can enjoy together.

You can depend on Public Television. For analysis, perspective and an in-depth look at controversial issues. Programs that respect your curiosity and intelligence.

Your Public TV station depends on you, too! The programs you love are made possible through the loyal, financial support of viewers like you. It's a proud partnership that helps enrich the quality of life for all Americans.

Public TV is TV Worth Watching

PBS

Courtesy of Public Broadcasting Service.

DISCUSSION QUESTIONS

1. The central message of the ad is that "Public TV is TV Worth Watching." What does this say about commercial TV?
2. Go through the four paragraphs of the text and locate other examples of indirect statement. What do these say about commercial TV?
3. Why the specific reference to *The Civil War* and *Sesame Street* and *Nova*? Why these three?
4. Explain the shoes in the picture. What do they tell you about the shows on public TV? (Clue: the second from the right refers to a *Sesame Street* character.)
5. Whom is this ad addressed to?

PAVE THE
STUPID RAIN FORESTS!

Ed Anger

I'm madder than a monkey with a rotten banana over all this hulla-baloo about saving the stupid rain forests in South America.

Wimpy environmentalists are crying big fat tears because a bunch of headhunters in Brazil are chopping down some trees to make a little extra spending money.

These fruitcake Chicken Littles believe if we chop up jungles there won't be any more air and we'll all die.

Hogwash! They can PAVE the darn rain forests for all I care.

Let's face it. The first thing our Founding Fathers did when they landed on America's shores was start cutting down trees.

George Washington and Thomas Jefferson were farsighted enough to know that you can't build shopping malls in the woods, for crying out loud.

Our great nation doesn't have one single rain forest and I'm breathing just fine, thank you.

If the rain forests are so healthy, then why in hell are all the people who live there trying to come here?

And another thing. The nuclear plant protesters who scream doom and gloom about the rain forests are the same nut cases who believe in this ozone stuff.

You know, there's supposed to be a hole in the ozone layer over the North Pole or something, and we're all supposed to get cancer and die because it lets too much sunshine in. Phooey!

It's supposed to be caused by all those cans of spray paint we've used to make America more beautiful. So let's just put ozone in spray cans and sell it to these scaredy-cat environmentalists.

These yellow bellies could just spray it into the air and patch the hole over the North Pole in no time flat.

I mean, how difficult can it be to put ozone in a can?

And while I'm on the subject, I'll tell you another thing. These bleeding-heart nature freaks say they want to save the rain forests and all that stuff for our children. That's a crock.

Ask any red-blooded American teenager where he'd rather be—in a nice air-conditioned shopping mall playing video games or slapping mosquitoes in some godforsaken jungle?

DISCUSSION QUESTIONS

1. What can you infer when an author named Ed Anger begins his essay "I'm madder than a monkey . . ."?

SOURCE: Reprinted with permission from *Weekly World News*, August 7, 1990.

2. Do you think the author is genuinely angry about this issue? Why is he writing this article?
3. What evidence is there that Anger is more than an ignorant loud-mouth?
4. Whom is this article addressed to?
5. Why does he invoke patriotic language: "our Founding Fathers," "Washington," "Jefferson," "Our great nation"?
6. Do his arguments against environmentalists seem genuine? How reasonable is his plan to patch the ozone layer?
7. Is the author a good writer?

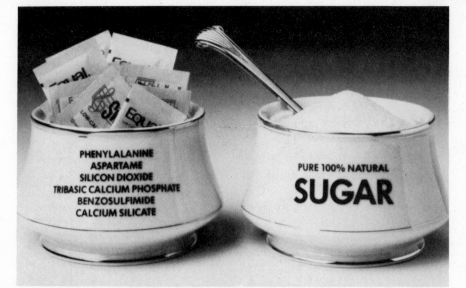

PHENYLALANINE
ASPARTAME
SILICON DIOXIDE
TRIBASIC CALCIUM PHOSPHATE
BENZOSULFIMIDE
CALCIUM SILICATE

PURE 100% NATURAL
SUGAR

WHICH WOULD YOU RATHER PUT ON YOUR KIDS' CEREAL?

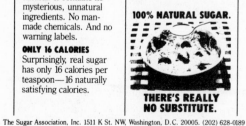

The decision is in your hands. But before you make it, here are some things to think about.

SUGAR IS SAFE
Unlike any artificial sweetener, sugar is on the government's FDA GRAS list (Generally Recognized As Safe).

100% NATURAL
Sugar is pure and 100% natural. It contains no mysterious, unnatural ingredients. No man-made chemicals. And no warning labels.

ONLY 16 CALORIES
Surprisingly, real sugar has only 16 calories per teaspoon—16 naturally satisfying calories.

SUGAR TASTES BEST
In a recent taste test, sugar was preferred nearly 3 to 1 over the leading artificial sweetener.

So if you want your kids to have a low calorie sweetener that's 100% natural and perfectly safe, give them real sugar. After all, don't they deserve to have it as good as you did?

100% NATURAL SUGAR.

THERE'S REALLY NO SUBSTITUTE.

The Sugar Association, Inc. 1511 K St. NW, Washington, D.C. 20005. (202) 628-0189

Courtesy of the Sugar Association, Inc.

DISCUSSION QUESTIONS

1. The advertisement attacks chemicals with long names, calling them "artificial" and "man-made." Can it be argued that these are natural products?

2. Is sugar a natural product? Does one dig it out of a mine and bring it to the table?

3. Why does the author attack "tribasic calcium phosphate" rather than "NutraSweet"?

4. What is the effect of the modifiers "pure," "100%," and "natural"?

5. Who is the author addressing? Is the ad making a rational or an emotional argument?

6. How effective are the picture and the lines in bold print? How many readers would read down into the small print?

CONGRESSMAN HYDE AND "INCONVENIENT" PREGNANCIES

James J. Kilpatrick

It was a little after 12:30 on the afternoon of Oct. 11 when Henry Hyde of Illinois went to the well of the House. He had come to oppose—most eloquently to oppose—what became known as the Boxer amendment.

The amendment would permit poor women and girl children to obtain abortions through Medicaid if they become pregnant by reason of rape or incest. Hyde lost. The amendment carried by 216 to 206, and true conservatives will applaud that outcome.

Hyde's concern—very nearly his total concern—was for "the unwanted, innocently inconvenient unborn." He liked that phrase so much that he repeated it: Pregnancy resulting from rape or incest is an "inconvenient" matter. Yes, the gentleman acknowledged that a woman thus victimized "has serious human problems." He agreed that rape and incest are "tragedies." But after he had concluded these ritual remarks, he was back to his theme. Public funds must not be used for abortions for the poor. This is because abortion "is a public matter."

Hyde is a fine, stout Republican on many issues, but on this issue his position is indefensible. Perhaps he does not grasp his own inconsistency. Hyde does not object to abortion with private funds; he suggested during debate that if the Playboy Foundation, or Planned Parenthood, or Stewart Mott will pay for such abortions for the poor, OK by him. If the victim of rape or incest will report promptly to a hospital, when she may or may not have conceived, let her be curetted then. Nothing wrong with that. But once a poor woman becomes pregnant, too bad.

The three foremost opponents of the Boxer amendment were Hyde, Bill Natcher of Kentucky and Silvio Conte of Massachusetts. All three have fathered daughters. It would be interesting to ask them to look into their hearts—really to look into their hearts—and ask them a blunt question: If your daughter had become pregnant as a result of rape, would you honestly insist that she carry the despised infant to term? Would you then claim the child as your grandchild? Would you regard this as a mere "inconvenience"? How would the gentlemen respond?

I speak with some emotion on this subject. My godchild Julie was raped last April. A masked intruder forced his way into her apartment, put a pistol to her naval, made her submit to sodomy, then raped her. Six months later she relives the experience in her nightmares. She will never recover fully. No victim of rape ever does. The humiliation, the horror, the degradation, the invasion of her most private self—these will dwell with her. The gentleman from Illinois is unmoved. He says only that if she had become pregnant, how "inconvenient" it would have been.

SOURCE: Reprinted from the *Mobile Register*, October 20, 1989. Reprinted by permission of the Universal Press Syndicate.

Inconvenient! What a jolly little word! Madam finds it inconvenient to play bridge on Tuesday. Would it also be inconvenient to have tea on Friday? Dear me, says the gentleman from Illinois, what an inconvenience it is to have inconvenient things happen. The gentleman cannot imagine a woman's living for nine months with the product of hate and brutality growing in her womb. He would spare the well-to-do such an inconvenience. Their right to obtain an abortion would not be disturbed. It is only the poor woman, dependent upon Medicaid, who would effectively be compelled to undergo this ordeal. Sweet Henry! Fair Henry! He weeps for the innocent embryo; he has no tears left for the innocent woman.

Abortion is not a "public matter." A more intensely private matter could not be imagined. And this is the curious thing about "conservatives," including such conservatives as George Bush. The president has threatened to veto the bill if the Boxer amendment remains in it. If there is one basic tenet of the conservative philosophy, it is that government must not interfere with the private lives of a free people. I find it unconscionable that conservatives should defend this ultimate denial of a woman's freedom over her own reproductive organs. Barbara Boxer of California carried the day. She had help from other women in the House, notably Louise Slaughter of New York and Marge Roukema of New Jersey. Jim McDermott of Washington added a knowledgeable word of support; as a psychiatrist he has treated victims of rape. Don Edwards of California warned that the American public "is tired of listening to judges and legislatures telling them how to make the most personal decisions of their lives." The gentleman will never speak a truer word.

DISCUSSION QUESTIONS

1. The author, a known conservative spokesman, is opposing a pro-life position on abortion. Is this a paradox?
2. Do you like the author? Are you drawn to him because of his language, his way of arguing, and his point of view?
3. Does it help his case that he doesn't become hostile and resort to snarl words?
4. How do the references to his godchild Julie influence his argument? How do you respond to them?
5. The author says the Boxer Amendment would prevent poor women (and no one else) from having abortions. Will *any* abortion law do more than that? (What would happen in your state if tomorrow morning the legislature passed a strong antiabortion law?)
6. Comment on the author's use of gentle mockery. How does he play on the word "inconvenient"?
7. Contrast the places where the author writes in a colloquial style with where he writes more formal prose. Do the two styles fit well together?

FALLACIES

*"How to Tune Up Your
Marriage—Just Like a Car"*
—Essay by Priscilla Kroger

Certain forms of misleading argument are so common they have been
specifically labeled. Although most could be analyzed as faulty induction,
deduction, and so on, they are treated separately here because the terms
describing them should be familiar to you. You will meet them often; they
are part of the language of argument.

FALSE ANALOGY

To argue by analogy is to compare two things known to be alike in one
or more features and suggest that they will be alike in other features as
well. This is reasonable argument if the compared elements are genuinely
similar. (Josh Woodward is an outstanding player and coach; he'll make a
fine manager.) It is fallacious if the features are essentially different. (You
have *fruit* for breakfast; why not try *Jell-O* for breakfast?)

You test an analogy by asking whether the comparison statement (if
there is one) is true and whether the elements compared are sufficiently
alike. A comparison statement is particularly questionable if it is simply
an adage. Reelection campaigns regularly submit, for example, that "you
wouldn't change horses in the middle of the stream." But even the smallest
consideration will remind you of situations where you would be eager to
change horses. Equally vulnerable are arguments insisting that "you can
lead a horse to water but you can't make it drink" (meaning some people
are unteachable) and that "where there's smoke, there's fire" (meaning
some gossip is true). Hearing these analogies, you might want to point
out that scientists (with brain probes) can make a horse drink itself sick
and that where there's smoke, there could be dry ice.

More often, you reject an analogy by showing a fundamental difference between the things compared. A common argument insists, "We
have pure food and drug laws. Why can't we have laws to keep movie-
makers from giving us filth?" Here you must examine the definitions
relating to "pure" and "filth." Food is called "impure" when the person
eating it gets physically sick. Because the individual who devours X-rated
movies doesn't get sick, there is no comparable definition of pornographic

"filth." Thus the analogy fails. Similarly, facing the argument, "We should no more teach communism in the schools than we should teach safecracking," you can respond that knowing a thing is not practicing it and that, unlike safecracking, being a communist is not a crime.

The poster saying "I Don't Spit in Your Face—Please Don't Blow Smoke in Mine" seems excessive. The two actions aren't equally offensive.

Analogies can be dangerous. In recent years, the Ayatollah Khomeini has executed prostitutes, adulterers, and homosexuals. His argument: Iran is like a human body, and these people are an infectious gangrene. They must be destroyed to preserve the health of the state.

Some analogies are complex. Here is an argument that has appeared in many temperance campaigns: "There are 10,000 deaths from alcohol poisoning to 1 from mad-dog bites in this country. In spite of this, we license liquor but shoot the dogs." Because it is desirable to get rid of any dogs or any liquor that proves deadly, this analogy seems persuasive. The argument, however, recommends that *all* liquor be outlawed. This is reasonable only if you are willing to pursue the comparison and shoot all dogs. Similarly, you should scrutinize popular arguments that compare independent nations with dominoes and federal deficit spending with a family budget.

In argument, analogies can be an effective way to make a point. Justice Byron White, rejecting a sweeping law restricting dial-a-porn, said "It is another case of burning the house down to roast the pig."

In writing persuasive essays, you will find such analogies useful. But be careful. The comparison may make your subject seem trivial. (Evangelist David Noebel wrote that "Sex education without morals is like breakfast without orange juice.") Or it may add strange dimensions of meaning. (Author Jessamyn West praised the book *Four Cats Make One Pride* by saying, "It is about cats in the same way that *Huckleberry Finn* is about boys and *Madame Bovary* is about women.")

Keep your analogies simple and direct. Elaborate comparisons are never effective as argument.

PRESUMED CAUSE–EFFECT

Relating an event to its cause can lead to three different fallacies.

Argument in a Circle

Circular argument occurs when speakers offer a restatement of their assertion as a reason for accepting it. They make a claim, add "because," then repeat the claim in different words. They say, "Smoking is injurious because it harms the human body," or "One phone is not enough in the modern home because modern homes have plenty of phones."

Sometimes the expression is more oblique, with the "because" implied rather than stated. William Jennings Bryan once declared, "There is only one argument that can be made to one who rejects the authority of the

Bible, namely, that the Bible is true." It is hardly persuasive to argue that a thing is true because it is true. <u>Repetition is not evidence.</u>

Today, circular argument appears regularly in discussions of pornography. Definitions of obscenity never get beyond the one given by Supreme Court Justice William Brennan in *Roth v. United States:* "Obscene material is material which deals with sex in a manner appealing to prurient interest." This says that obscene material is obscene material.

The issue was not clarified in 1989 when the Supreme Court rejected the congressional effort to shut down the dial-a-porn industry. The Court specified that "indecent" messages could not be outlawed, only those that were "obscene."

Post Hoc Ergo Propter Hoc

<u>The post hoc fallacy</u> ("After this, therefore because of this") occurs when a person mentions two past events and insists that because one happened first, it necessarily caused the second. Using such evidence, people have argued that Martin Luther left the Catholic priesthood to get married, that President Herbert Hoover caused the Great Depression, and that young people rioted during the 1960s because they were brought up under the permissive theories of Dr. Benjamin Spock. Such logic can make much of coincidence. *Christian Crusade* compared crime statistics for two six-week periods and headlined "Murder Rate Jumps 93 Percent in Oklahoma Following Death Penalty Ban." The cause-effect relationship was, it said, "self-evident."

Nothing illustrates the weakness of the post hoc fallacy better than Stephen J. Gould's example. He noted solemnly that as Halley's Comet approached the earth, the price of ice cream cones in Boston rose regularly.

<u>Post hoc reasoning is fallacious because it ignores more complex factors that contribute to an event.</u> A Smith-Corona advertisement proclaimed that "Students Who Type Usually Receive Better Grades" and suggested that buying a child a typewriter will improve his or her schoolwork. The fallacy here is the implication that simply owning a typewriter makes the difference. Other factors seem more likely to account for the higher grades. Parents who buy their child a typewriter are concerned about the youngster's education, take pains to see that the child studies, and can afford to provide other cultural advantages as well. The typewriter alone gives no one higher grades.

<u>Recognizing the post hoc fallacy will keep you from jumping to unwarranted conclusions.</u> No one can deny, for example, that some people who wear copper bracelets suffer no arthritis pain; that some heroin addicts have significantly fewer accidents than other drivers; that some patients who took the antidepressant Prozac have become homicidal, and that some individuals who witnessed John Kennedy's assassination have died in dramatic ways. Nevertheless, these cases do not justify sensational cause-effect conclusions. A post hoc judgment would ignore the range of other factors involved.

Another example: A 1985 study by Emory University psychologists reported that women who read romantic historical novels have sex 74 percent more often than those who don't. Here it is hard to establish what is cause and what is effect.

The post hoc fallacy is used particularly by people who write about curses. Many books describe the tragic events that occurred in the Romanov, Hapsburg, and Kennedy families after they were put under a curse. Stories tell the horrible fate of people who owned the Hope diamond. Magazine articles appear regularly reporting that every person who was involved in breaking open King Tut's tomb is now either dead or sadly crippled. When reading such stories, you should remember Darrell Huff's wonderful line: "Post hoc rides again!"

Non Sequitur

Non sequitur means "it does not follow." This fallacy occurs when a person submits that a given fact has led or must inevitably lead to a particular consequence. One can take a fact ("Governor Clinton was unfaithful to his wife") and project a conclusion ("He would make a poor president"). Or one can take an anticipated fact ("If the Equal Rights Amendment becomes a law") and spell out the consequences ("American family life is doomed"). The reasonable objection, of course, is that the conclusion does not necessarily follow.

The term non sequitur is widely used. It lends itself to describing arguments with multiple causes ("The more you know—the more you do—the more you tax your nerves—the more important it is to relax tired nerves. Try safe, nonhabit-forming Sedquilin") or arguments so extreme that they fall outside the usual categories ("Of course Jehovah's Witnesses are communists; otherwise there wouldn't be so many of them"). But the term is of little value in defining general argument; almost any kind of fallacious reasoning is a non sequitur.

Still it's useful to know the term when you read the ad for Emeraude perfume: "I love only one man. I wear only one fragrance."

BEGGING THE QUESTION

People beg the question by assuming something it is their responsibility to prove. They build their argument on an undemonstrated claim. Generally it takes the form of a question. ("Have you stopped beating your wife?" or "Is it true blondes have more fun?") But it can appear as a declaration. ("Busing is no more the law of the land than any other communist doctrine.")

Another form of begging the question is to make a charge and then insist that someone else disprove it. ("How do you know that flying saucers haven't been visiting the earth for centuries?" or "If Jeane Dixon doesn't have psychic powers, how could she predict the assassination of President Kennedy?") In all argument, the burden of proof is on the person making the assertion. Never let yourself be put in a position where you have to disprove a claim that was never proved in the first place. One of the most common instances of begging the question today is the anti-abortionist's charge: "How can you approve of slaughtering babies?"

IGNORING THE QUESTION

People can ignore a question in different ways: They can leave the subject to attack their opponent, or they can leave the subject to discuss a different topic.

Ad Hominem Argument

An ad hominem argument attacks the opposing arguer rather than the question at issue. ("Senator Thurmond favors resumption of the draft because he is too old to have to serve," or "District Attorney Phillips wants to become famous prosecuting my client so he can run for governor.") Here, nothing is said of the main issue; the speaker ignores the question by attacking an adversary.

It should be noted, to avoid confusion, that an argument about a particular individual—a candidate, a defendant—is probably not ad hominem argument. In such a case, the person *is* the issue.

The fallacy often takes this form: "Of course you believe that—you're a woman" (or a Jew, Catholic, Southerner, business executive, etc.) It also can involve snarl words: "I expected this from a bleeding-heart liberal" (or a wild-eyed environmentalist, Bible-thumping fanatic, labor-union radical, simple-minded bastard, etc.).

A good rule: *Never make an ad hominem argument.* Attacking your opponent is an admission that your case is weak. If you have a substantial argument and want people to know it, a good policy is to flatter your adversary.

Extension

The fallacy of extension has the same effect as an ad hominem argument. Here persuaders "extend" the question until they are arguing a different issue altogether. When a convict's execution is stayed, people ask, "What about the rights of the victim?" When women are admitted to medical schools under a quota system, the cry goes up, "What about the rights of men?" In both cases, the question is reasonable, but it moves the argument to a new topic.

"Some of the best examples of extension appear on bumper stickers. You see "Register Communists, Not Guns." And "America: Love It or Leave It."

Either–Or

The either–or fallacy is a form of extension. Here partisans distort an issue by insisting that only two alternatives exist: their recommendation and something much worse. They describe a temperance election as a choice between Christianity and debauchery. They depict abortion as a choice between American family life and murder. Should you question any feature of American foreign policy, they challenge, "Which side are you on, anyway?"

To all such examples of ignoring the question, the reasonable response is "Let's get back to the issue."

FALLACIES IN OTHER FORMS

Most of the fallacies mentioned in this chapter could be analyzed as examples of induction, deduction, semantic argument, and so on. A false analogy, for example, is a deduction with invalid form; a post hoc error is induction with an insufficient sample; and any bad argument can be called a non sequitur. But special terms do exist for these fallacies, and it may be valuable to have two ways of looking at them.

Unless you are championing a particularly weak cause, keep these fallacies out of your writing.

EXERCISES

Identify the fallacies in these arguments.

1. Okay, if you think psychokinesis isn't possible, explain to me how Uri Geller can bend keys just by looking at them. *post hoc*
2. Of course you oppose no-fault auto insurance. You're a lawyer.
3. "I'm tired of being called a racist. I'm not a racist. The racists today are Jesse Jackson and the NAACP."—Rush Limbaugh
4. Of course, the Bible is true. St. Paul says, "All scripture is given by inspiration of God."
5. I don't like the idea of abortion either, but I think it's better than having some poor woman kill herself trying to raise 11 or 12 children.
6. "Just two days after Liz Taylor announced plans to wed Larry Fortensky, her ex-husband Eddie Fisher took an overdose of painkillers and was rushed to a hospital in a life-and-death crisis."—*National Enquirer* story
7. Arguing from the principle that a person is sick "when he fails to function in his appropriate gender identification," Dr. Charles Socarides, a New York psychoanalyst, concludes that homosexuality is a form of mental illness.
8. I oppose public smoking laws. If the government can make smokers stay in restricted places, can't they do the same for other groups: garlic eaters, children, gum chewers, crippled people, whistlers, and so on? *slippery slope*
9. If evolution is true, why has it stopped?
10. Guilt is a terrible thing. Studies show that women who are promiscuous suffer feelings of low self-esteem.

11. I pay for my college education just the way I pay for my groceries in a supermarket. Why does the administration think it can tell me what courses I have to take?

12. Gay people are essentially criminal. Look at the homosexuality that goes on in prison. post hoc

13. My father smoked a pack of Camels every day for 40 years. Then he died of lung cancer. I'm going to sue R.J. Reynolds for $5 million. post hoc

14. Jim and Tammy Bakker are suffering right now, just like Job and his wife. And like Job, they will rise to new prosperity and happiness.

15. After receiving the Lourdes medal, this cash-starved women received a $75,000 miracle.

16. Creationism in the public schools? Pretty soon we'll have to give equal time to the stork theory. Slippery Slope

17. For over a century, every American president elected in a year ending in "0" died in office. But Ronald Reagan didn't. Astrologer Joan Quigley says her forecasts saved him.

18. "You'll love the Meat Lovers Pizza if you like meat and you like pizza."—Pizza Hut ad

19. It's not right to end the life of a terminally ill loved-one. St. Paul wrote, "If we are to live like Christ, we must die like Christ."

20. Sure, veterans should have a G.I. bill to give them breaks getting a job or an education. But mothers who stayed home to raise their young children deserve a G.I. bill too.

21. You have to get excited over something. Why not Kellogg's Corn Flakes?

22. "Millions of people are misnamed at birth, causing them problems and unhappiness throughout their lives."—Krishna Ram-Davi

---

ESSAY ASSIGNMENTS

Write an essay either affirming or opposing one of these statements. The arguments you encounter in your background reading may well include logical fallacies. Your essay should have none, or at least none you didn't intend.

1. We should never have deserted our allies in Vietnam.
2. A massive conspiracy led to the assassination of President Kennedy.
3. Prostitution should not be considered a crime; there is no victim.
4. Daylight saving time is unnatural.
5. If I had a different name, I'd be more successful.
6. America's space program is a waste of money.
7. The Hope diamond put a genuine curse on all those who owned it.
8. X causes crime. (Fill in the X.)

BILINGUALISM: DO WE
WANT QUEBEC HERE?

Howard Banks

"The one absolutely certain way of bringing this nation to ruin, of preventing all possibility of its continuing to be a nation at all, would be to permit it to become a tangle of squabbling nationalities." So warned Teddy Roosevelt in 1915.

We have avoided that danger here—which Canada clearly has not. We have avoided it in part because of the common use of English by all of the immigrants that make up America: Adopting the English language has always been part of becoming American. Relative ease of communication in a single language has provided a kind of national glue, a common thread to the creation and development of a nation that is spread over a wide area and harbors diverse interests, beliefs and national origins.

But a threat to that thread is emerging in the increasingly strident political campaign for separate Spanish teaching. Fortunately, most Hispanic-Americans don't support the idea. A loud minority of Hispanic politicians and leftish liberals do.

"There are obvious differences (with Canada), but the parallels are clear enough," says Kathryn Bricker, executive director of U.S. English. This is the organization founded by former Senator S. I. Hayakawa to pursue his idea of a constitutional amendment that would make English the official language of the U.S.

Bilingual teaching began as an offshoot of the civil rights movement in the 1960s. It was at first intended to help so-called LEP kids (for limited-English-proficient) get into the mainstream of economic life by teaching them English. But it has turned into a monster born out of a loosely worded 1974 decision from the Supreme Court (Lau v. Nichols). This concerned a complaint by a Chinese that his children were not being taught English adequately in the local public schools. One possible remedy listed by Justice William Douglas was teaching the children in Chinese.

And then the predictable happened. The Department of Education was established in the Carter era and was looking for something to do. Why not promote bilingualism? There would be jobs and money in it. So it didn't take the bureaucrats long to launch a vast, federally funded bilingual education program. Because by far the largest number of immigrants today come from Spanish-speaking countries, Spanish was the logical co-language.

In many areas of the country where there are concentrations of Spanish-speaking kids, bilingual education has in practice turned into mostly Spanish teaching. "If it is measured against the original intent, to teach English to disadvantaged children, it's a failure. If it had been

SOURCE: Reprinted with permission from *Forbes*, June 11, 1990.

intended to teach Spanish, it would have been a tremendous success," says Bricker.

The clearest indication of failure is the high dropout rate of Hispanic high school kids. Since the early 1970s, the dropout rate for white children has been tending down slightly. The dropout rate for black kids has more or less halved and is now roughly the same as for whites. The exception is for Hispanics. Their dropout rate is stubbornly high, roughly double that for the other groups, and the trend, if anything, has recently been rising slightly. Yet—and here's an apparent paradox— Spanish-speaking Americans have a lower unemployment rate than blacks and slightly higher average earnings. How come?

A survey by the Civil Rights Commission has found that when the differences in educational attainment, and especially for proficiency in English, are eliminated, what emerges is that Hispanics do as well as the rest of the population. A logical conclusion is that the poor language proficiency of many Hispanics is dragging down their average economic performance.

The issue of Spanish-language teaching of Hispanics is emotion-charged. Merely raising questions about the efficiency of the so-called bilingual program often leads to accusations of racism. Such noises come mainly from those that benefit most from these programs—Hispanic politicians, bureaucrats whose careers depend on the programs, the providers of textbooks in Spanish and, maybe, some teachers who retain their jobs (and sometimes get a bonus) because they speak Spanish.

It's a big economic issue, too, for these groups. A guesstimate by the Education Department suggests that when the $160 million cost of the Bilingual Education Act, 1974, is added to other programs involved in bilingual education, the cost reaches $1.5 billion a year. Each child in bilingual education is "worth" around $350 a year to a school. But "once they become fluent in English, the school district loses its bilingual funding," explains Sally Peterson, a teacher for 26 years at Glenwood Elementary School, Sun Valley, Calif., and founder of the 20,000-member Learning English Advocates Drive.

The crying shame is how badly that money serves those it is intended to help. As jobs tend away from assembly-line work, where little language is involved, to computer screens, pay and working conditions depend on educational and English attainment. Today's anti-English bias, it seems, sentences too many minority school leavers, particularly Hispanics, to a second-class economic life.

Typically, the pols' response is to call for yet more money to be poured into a failed program. Fortunately, most Hispanic-Americans don't buy those arguments. A government survey asked Hispanic parents to rank 70 items in importance to their children's education. Teaching them English was third; teaching them Spanish was third, too, but from the bottom. A recent poll by the *San Francisco Chronicle* showed that 69% of Hispanics approved of English being the official state language in California.

But the proponents of bilingualism tend to be types who know what is best for other people, even if the majority doesn't agree.

So, would a constitutional amendment, as proposed by ex-Senator

Hayakawa and now by Representative William Emerson (R–Mo.), solve the problem? It wouldn't hurt.

To oppose bilingualism is not the same thing as opposing the teaching of foreign languages. It is merely to insist that to be American one should understand English—a not very onerous requirement. In any case, some 23 states, from Arizona to Virginia, have passed or have pending legislation to make English the official language.

Bilingualism undermines the very basis on which this country has been built: assimilation of diverse nationalities into a new nationality. Many intellectuals scorn what this country represents, and for them bilingualism is a handy tool. It is a handy tool, too, for those looking for ways to pry money out of the taxpayer. But, as Canadians have learned, it is not a good way to create a national identity or preserve national unity.

DISCUSSION QUESTIONS

1. What practical effect would an English Language amendment have? What do you infer when the best the author can say is "It wouldn't hurt"?

2. Making his case, the author refers to "glue," a "thread," "an off-shoot," and the effort to "launch" a program. How effective is his use of figurative language?

3. The author says that bilingual programs are favored by "leftist liberals" and were instituted by the Department of Education, which "was looking for something to do." What fallacy does this illustrate?

4. School administrators would say they are using a bilingual teaching approach because it is the best way to help Hispanics master English. Why does the author say they do it? Name the fallacy.

5. How does he answer the charge that people who hold his position are racist?

6. Many Hispanics who come through bilingual programs later drop out of school and take low-paying jobs. Is it self-evident that bilingual teaching causes this?

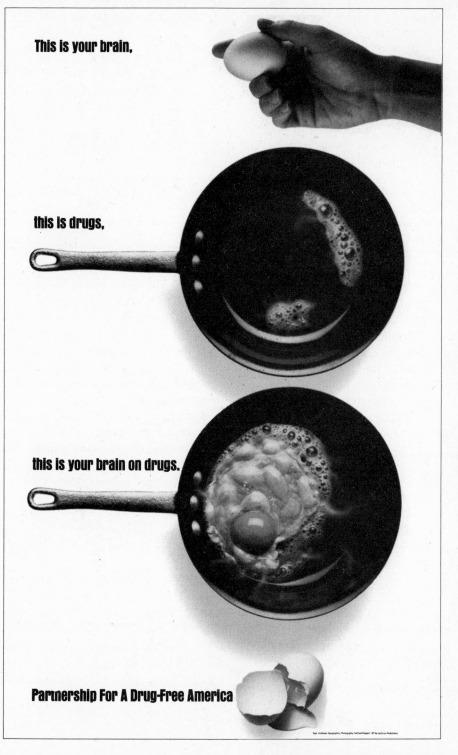

This is your brain,

this is drugs,

this is your brain on drugs.

Partnership For A Drug-Free America

Courtesy of Keye, Donna, Pearlstein.

DISCUSSION QUESTIONS

1. How accurate is this argument by analogy:
    a. Is your brain like a raw egg?
    b. Are drugs like a hot frying-pan?
    c. Will drugs change your brain the way a frying pan changes an egg?
2. Is this an effective ad? Why do you think so?
3. Talk about comparable examples of argument by analogy:
    a. Marriage is like . . .
    b. A weekend at the Gulf is like . . . .
    c. Learning to use the computer is like . . .
    d. Legalizing abortion is like . . .
    Do the comparisons have to be point-by-point true to be generally true?
4. Who is the audience for this ad?

DIARY OF
AN UNBORN CHILD

October 5
Today my life began. My parents do not know it yet, I am as small as a
seed of an apple, but it is I already. And I am to be a girl. I shall have
blond hair and blue eyes. Just about everything is settled though, even
the fact that I shall love flowers.

October 19
Some say that I am not a real person yet, that only my mother exists.
But I am a real person, just as a small crumb of bread is yet truly bread.
My mother is. And I am.

October 23
My mouth is just beginning to open now. Just think, in a year or so I
shall be laughing and later talking. I know what my first word will be:
MAMA.

October 25
My heart began to beat today all by itself. From now on it shall gently
beat for the rest of my life without ever stopping to rest! And after
many years it will tire. It will stop, and then I shall die.

November 2
I am growing a bit every day. My arms and legs are beginning to take
shape. But I have to wait a long time yet before those little legs will
raise me to my mother's arms, before these little arms will be able to
gather flowers and embrace my father.

November 12
Tiny fingers are beginning to form on my hands. Funny how small they
are! I'll be able to stroke my mother's hair with them.

November 20
It wasn't until today that the doctor told mom I am living here under
her heart. Oh, how happy she must be! Are you happy, mom?

November 25
My mom and dad are probably thinking about a name for me. But they
don't even know that I am a little girl. I want to be called Kathy. I am
getting so big already.

December 10
My hair is growing. It is smooth and bright and shiny. I wonder what
kind of hair mom has.

SOURCE: Reprinted from the *Mobile Press*.

December 13
I am just about able to see. It is dark around me. When mom brings me into the world, it will be full of sunshine and flowers. But what I want more than anything is to see my mom. How do you look, mom?

December 24
I wonder if mom hears the whispering of my heart? Some children come into the world a little sick. But my heart is strong and healthy. It beats so evenly: tup-tup, tup-tup. You'll have a healthy little daughter, mom!

December 28
Today my mother killed me.

DISCUSSION QUESTIONS

1.   The argument about abortion hinges on the issue of whether a fetus in its early stages is a human person or a collection of cells. What evidence is offered here that the fetus is a person?
2.   Consider all the things this fetus knows. It talks of sunshine, flowers, a mother, a father, a female name, death, the relative health of some fetuses, and the intellectual debate about personhood. What fallacy is illustrated here?
3.   "I am a real person, just as a small crumb of bread is yet truly bread." How reasonable is this analogy?
4.   Comment on the problems of definition that exist when an entity with no brain or brain cells says, ". . . . it is I already."
5.   Who is saying, "Today my mother killed me"?

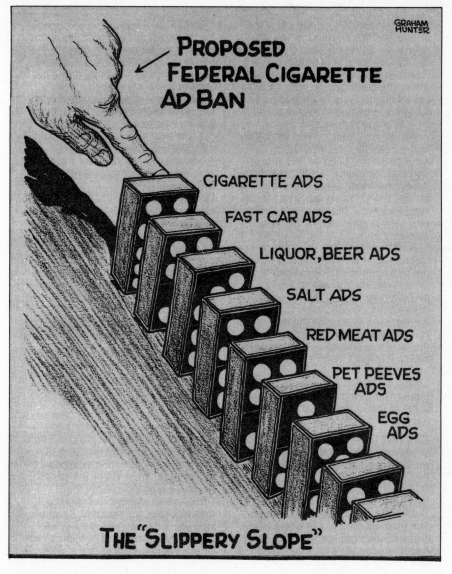

Courtesy of Graham Hunter and the *Tobacco Observer*. From the *Tobacco Observer*, May 1987.

DISCUSSION QUESTIONS

1. This is a kind of argument by analogy. Is it fair to say the health concern that would ban cigarette advertising could also ban ads for fast cars, liquor, beer, salt, red meat, and eggs?
2. Are these products roughly equal as threats to American health?
3. The cartoon also says that if cigarette ads are banned now, ads for the other products will be banned before long. Name this fallacy.
4. What is suggested by the image of "the slippery slope"?

DEADLY KING TUT
CURSE STRIKES AGAIN

Ron Caylor and Gordon Gregor

A horrifying chain of death and suffering has struck a British Royal Air Force flight crew who defied the legendary curse of King Tut's tomb.

The 3,000-year-old curse damns anyone who disturbs the Pharaoh—and all seven members of the RAF crew have been stalked by tragedy since transporting Tutankhamen's death mask and other priceless relics to London for a 1972 exhibition.

Here's what has happened to the seven, according to crew members and their families.

- The pilot and flight engineer have died of heart attacks—although military physical exams had showed them to be in perfect health.
- A crew member who playfully kicked the crate containing Tut's mask later shattered the very same foot in 18 places.
- The flight steward has been plagued by ill health and tragedies within his family.
- The navigator's home was gutted by fire.
- The co-pilot narrowly escaped being crushed in an accident, and his marriage has broken up.
- The only female member of the crew has had to undergo a serious head operation.

"Tutankhamen's curse killed my husband—I'm convinced of that!" declared Mrs. Dolores Laurie, the widow of pilot Rick Laurie. "And there is no telling who will be next.

"Make no mistake, this curse is very real. It is not a legend. It is horrifying—a deadly, diabolic curse that is not to be played with."

The world first learned of the curse in 1922 when archaeologists discovered King Tut's tomb near Cairo, Egypt, according to writer Philipp Vandenberg, author of "The Curse of the Pharaohs."

He said a hieroglyphic-laden clay tablet found in the tomb read: "Death will slay with his wings whoever disturbs the peace of the Pharaoh."

Since then the curse has claimed the lives of more than 30 people, among them scientists, archaeologists and scholars, said Vandenberg.

Surviving members of the RAF flight crew admit they knew about the curse when they flew to Cairo in 1972 to transport Tut's artifacts—valued at hundreds of millions of dollars—back to the British Museum.

"But we didn't take it seriously," recalled flight steward Brian Rounsfull. "In fact, we took turns sitting on the box containing the death mask, and we laughed and joked about it. We weren't being disrespectful—it was just a bit of fun."

SOURCE: Reprinted with permission from the *National Enquirer*, October 17, 1978.

And on the flight returning to England, the crewmen even played cards on top of the crates containing Tut's sacred objects—and ground engineer Ian Landsdowne once even playfully kicked the case containing the death mask, joking that he was kicking the most valuable thing in the world.

Recalled co-pilot John Tate: "We joshed each other about being the first to go (die), but none of us took it seriously. I didn't believe a word. I just didn't accept that a curse could work." But then things began happening—and suddenly the curse was no longer a joke.

In December 1972 a mysterious fire struck the home of navigator Jim Webb in Oxfordshire, England, and destroyed nearly everything the family owned.

"It wasn't like an ordinary house fire—it was just a mass of flames which consumed everything," said Dolores Laurie, who watched the blaze. "It was frightening."

Then, in May of 1974, Mrs. Laurie's husband Rick, 40, suddenly keeled over dead—the victim of a heart attack.

"It was mind-numbing," said the widow. "Rick had never spent a day in the hospital in 17 years we were married, and he'd passed all his annual medical checkups to insure his fitness for flying. He was in the best of health. I believe the curse of King Tut is to blame. It is a very powerful curse."

Shortly after Laurie's death, while flying the very same route the ill-fated flight crew had taken three years before, flight engineer Ken Parkinson suffered a heart attack and had to be hospitalized.

Three more attacks followed—and the last one killed him.

"The doctors were totally unable to find anything wrong with his heart," remembered Parkinson's puzzled widow, Ida. "They couldn't understand why he'd had an attack."

Meanwhile, catastrophe also was striking the other members of that ill-fated crew.

Crewman Landsdowne, who had kicked the crate containing Tut's golden death mask, fell 15 feet off a ladder in September of 1975 and broke his left foot in 18 places. "It wasn't until three weeks later that someone reminded me of the curse," he said. "It was then I remembered I'd kicked the case with this very same foot!"

Then, said co-pilot Tate, came the news that the crew's only female member, Pat Horne, "had an operation on her head."

Multiple tragedies hit flight steward Rounsfull. Twice severe chest pains sent him into a hospital's intensive care unit. Next, his brother-in-law died of a heart attack. Then his father-in-law fell down a flight of stairs and fractured his skull.

"Since the King Tutankhamen flight I've suffered a period of very bad luck," admitted Rounsfull. "I thought I was too sensible to believe in legends, but I do believe it could be the curse which has affected my life and those of other people."

For Tate, tragedy came in the form of a shattering breakup with his wife. He said he also was almost crushed recently when he raised a heavy garage door and it jumped its tracks, narrowly missing him.

"I'd like to believe that there isn't really anything to it (the curse), but it's difficult," he told The ENQUIRER.

Tate is convinced even worse things are in store for him. "I'm the last one, so I've got to be the next victim," he said. "I know I'm a marked man."

DISCUSSION QUESTIONS

1. King Tut's curse reads, "Death will slay with his wings whoever disturbs the peace of the Pharaoh." How many of the seven members of the RAF crew died? How many will die in the future?
2. Since the world learned of the curse in 1922, "more than 30 people, among them scientists, archaeologists and scholars" have died. Can these deaths be explained in any other way than as the result of the curse?
3. Is it more than an impressive coincidence that Ian Landsdowne later broke the "very same foot" he had used to kick the crate bearing Tut's mask? How many feet might he have broken?
4. How amazing is it that over a period of six years, a crew of seven people have experienced heart attacks, a fire, accidents, near accidents, injuries to relatives, divorce, and surgery?
5. Pat Horne had a "serious head operation." Why the vagueness here, especially after the vivid description of Landsdowne's broken foot? What might a "serious head operation" refer to?
6. Is there any reason to question the reliability of Dolores Laurie and of John Tate when they gave the *National Enquirer* dramatic statements about Tut's curse?
7. What common fallacy is illustrated by this essay?

How would you like the police to investigate your miscarriage?

So-called "pro-lifers" think nothing of invading women's privacy and jeopardizing their health. Their national campaign of violence and intimidation attracts plenty of media attention.

But the outrages they commit now are nothing compared to what would happen if they win.

Their Human Life Amendment to the Constitution treats the fetus as an independent human being from the very instant of fertilization. Abortion would be called murder under all circumstances. So would many effective birth control methods. And every miscarriage could be suspect.

While some anti-choice activists declare that only health professionals who assist with an abortion should be charged

with murder, countless women could be caught up in police investigations and prosecutions even if they are never arraigned.

If the right to choose abortion is limited or eliminated, women who can afford to travel could probably evade the law.

Poor women and teenagers with no resources would be forced to induce their own abortions, or subject themselves to an illicit, dangerous back-alley procedure.

And thousands of them would be brutalized, maimed and killed.

How do we know what will happen if the extremists win? Because that's the way it was before abortion was made legal and safe in 1973. The choice they present isn't whether abortion should be stopped.

Prohibition never worked.

The choice is privacy...or punishment. Safety for women...or terrible danger. It's really not a choice we need to make again.

Make time to save your right to choose. Before the so-called "pro-lifers" start making your choices for you.

Take action! Here's my urgent contribution to support Planned Parenthood's Campaign to Keep Abortion Safe and Legal:

NAME _____

ADDRESS _____

CITY _____ STATE _____ ZIP _____

Don't wait until women are dying again.   Ⓟ Planned Parenthood®

Courtesy of Planned Parenthood.

DISCUSSION QUESTIONS

1. The author speaks of women being "brutalized, maimed and killed." Identify other examples of emotional language in this ad. Is the language appropriate for the message?
2. Does the ad speak of those opposing abortion as "pro-life"? What are they called?
3. "The choice is privacy . . . or punishment. Safety for women . . . or terrible danger." Is this an example of the either–or fallacy?
4. Do pro-life advocates really intend that police investigate miscarriages? Is this a likely prospect under any legal situation? What fallacy is illustrated here?

THE *READER'S DIGEST:*
THERE IT GOES AGAIN

James M. Wall

The *Reader's Digest* has struck again. Check the table in your doctor's office (which is where I know I can always find the latest copy) or, if they still give away copies to shape young minds, ask your junior-high-age child to bring you the December issue. It's worth a look, because once again the *Digest,* house organ of the old-guard political right, takes the usual potshots at mainline Protestants and the National Council of Churches. John S. Tompkins's "Look What They've Done to My Songs" repeats the attack the *Digest* made at greater length in 1983, only this time it doesn't have the support of CBS's "Sixty Minutes."

The hook this time is the tired, old complaint that mainline churches are coming out with new hymnals that eliminate warlike, sexist hymns like "Onward Christian Soldiers," "The Battle Hymn of the Republic," "God Rest You Merry, Gentlemen" and "Faith of Our Fathers." Tompkins's specific target is the new hymnal of the Presbyterian Church (U.S.A.); this one also deprives him of "Stand Up, Stand Up for Jesus," which, you'll recall, asks "soldiers of the cross" to do the standing.

After lamenting the elimination of some of his childhood favorites, Tompkins gets down to his real purpose: badmouthing mainliners with the usual suspect complaints—about an Episcopal sex manual, a "witch" lecturing at a seminary, the NCC's critique of the Columbus anniversary, and United Methodists' support for Clergy and Laity Concerned, "a group dedicated to protesting American military presence in the world." (CLC couldn't begin to afford the publicity that plug provides its fund-raising efforts.)

Tompkins concludes that mainline denominations are losing members because they aren't giving folks the old-time religion (the same thesis the *Digest* and "60 Minutes" presented seven years ago). If it was good enough for Paul and Silas, it is still good enough for the *Reader's Digest.* A political leftward drift among mainliners is the cause of the decline in membership, Tompkins says: "congregations have responded to the endless politicking in dramatic fashion—by voting with their feet."

Statistical decline is undeniable, but one must begin with some right-wing presuppositions to conclude that the cause is liberal politics. There is by now a considerable body of literature on mainline membership figures—including Wade Clark Roof and William McKinney's *American Mainline Religion*—and it is clear from the data that the main reasons for declining membership have to do with low birth rates and aging members. In any case, there's little evidence that large numbers of people are leaving mainline churches in search of the old-time religion. In fact, liberal churches pick up a higher percentage of their members from more conservative churches than conservative churches do from more liberal ones.

SOURCE: Reprinted by permission from *Christian Century,* December 12, 1990.

It doesn't take a rocket scientist to figure our where Tompkins is coming from when he suggests that those who have become disenchanted with their church's focus should "join a renewal group." What organization does he suggest as a handy clearinghouse for such groups as the United Methodist Good News, the Presbyterian Lay Committee, the Episcopal Renewal Ministries and others? Why, none other than our old friend the Institute of Religion and Democracy, that neoconservative group that sprang into existence at the beginning of the Reagan era with sizable financial support from right-wing foundations. As the church lady says, "How convenient." The IRD (address given in the *Reader's Digest,* but you won't find it here) was created in those heady days when Ronald Reagan came into office promising to eradicate "the evil empire" with history's largest military buildup. Since that propitious start, IRD has indeed served as a clearinghouse for anyone disenchanted with mainline Protestantism, and may have fostered some of that disenchantment with its constant call to arms against mainliners and the NCC.

It was not criticism offered in a spirit of corrective Christian love coming from IRD headquarters a short distance from the Reagan White House. What IRD did with its literature and its special awards for contra-oriented churchpeople was to promote its own set of political causes, all of which bear a remarkable resemblance to the anticommunist policies of the Reagan–Bush administrations. Under the guise of lamenting the absence of spiritual concern among mainliners, IRD has been as guilty of political advocacy as the most rabid church supporters of left-wing causes. When the *Digest* tells churches "to live up to their billing as houses of worship," it is really saying: stay out of politics unless you are willing to support the political line favored by followers of the old-time religion who know the right way to travel in the jungles of Central America.

The churches do need to improve the quality of their work at the intersection of religion and society. Far too many partisan positions are taken by denominational and ecumenical groups, and social justice concerns have outstripped the development of a theological base. People with more impressive theological credentials than the *Reader's Digest* are reminding us that we need a solid theological response to the growth of evangelical churches. There is work to be done, and no one knows this any better than those religious leaders on the front lines who were confronting spiritual hunger in their congregations long before the IRD and the *Digest* wrapped religiosity in the Reagan banner. But it need not be assumed that statistics are the final word on the spiritual health of a religious institution.

So when someone comes up to you waving the December issue of the *Digest,* crying, "Look what they've done to my songs," just say you've heard it all before, and then suggest that together you sing a few verses of "Stand up, Stand up for Jesus, ye lovers of the Lord."

DISCUSSION QUESTIONS

1. The title and opening lines of the essay say, "There It Goes Again" and "The *Reader's Digest* has struck again." How do these establish

the tone of the article? What kind of analysis do they lead you to expect?

2. "The old-guard political right," "mainline Protestants," "the old-time religion," etc. Comment on examples of purr and snarl words used in this essay.

3. "If it was good enough for Paul and Silas, it is still good enough for the *Reader's Digest.*" What is the danger in using religious and literary allusions?

4. The *Digest* article says people are leaving mainline churches because they want old-time religion and hymns with military references. The author is dismissing this as a logical fallacy. What fallacy is it?

5. Why the emphasis on "corrective Christian love" and "ye lovers of the Lord"?

STATISTICS

*"I'll remember this as the night
Michael Jordan and I combined to
score 70 points."*

—Stacy King, Chicago Bulls

There are a number of ways in which statistics can be used to distort argument. Persuaders can cite impressive averages, irrelevant totals, and homemade figures. They can offer a number in a context that makes it appear larger or smaller, according to their wish.

AVERAGES

A common fallacy involves the use of so-called average figures: average income, average price, average audience size, and so on. It is easy to argue from such statistics because the word *average* can mean three things.

What, for example, is the average if a group of 15 homemakers, responding to a poll question, say they watch television 48, 40, 30, 26, 22, 18, 12, 10, 9, 8, 5, 5, 5, 1, and 0 hours a week? From these numbers, one can claim the group watches television an average of 15.933 hours a week, or 10 hours a week, or 5 hours a week. The 15.933 figure is the *mean* (the total number of hours watched divided by the number of viewers); the 10 figure is the *median* (the middle number in the series); and the 5 figure is the *mode* (the number that appears most frequently).

Each kind of average has its value, depending on the type of material being measured. But all three are available to the persuader who wants to manipulate an argument.

QUESTIONABLE FIGURES

Vague statistics can produce impressive averages. Numbers derived from memory, guesswork, and exaggeration can be averaged with amazing precision. (In the preceding paragraph, the 15.933 average was computed after 15 homemakers made rough guesses of their television viewing time.) Dr Kinsey interviewed American men and reported that those without a high school education averaged 3.21 sexual experiences a week. The annual FBI report *Crime in the United States*, which compiles material from police departments across the country, showed that Baltimore in one year had suffered a crime increase of 71 percent. But police departments report crimes differently and with different degrees of accuracy. The sensational Baltimore figure wasn't caused by a crime wave; it came from more accurate police reporting in the second year.

This kind of computation often derives from a biased source. Recently, divorce lawyer Michael Minton estimated the monetary values of 22 separate jobs and argued that a wife is worth $46,219.16 a year.

Similarly, amazing claims can be drawn from a small or partial sample. Some years ago a survey reported that 33.3 percent of all coeds at Johns Hopkins University had married faculty members. Johns Hopkins had three women students at the time. Advocates of extrasensory perception thrive on partial samples. They like to report cases of a gifted individual (Hubert Pearce, Basil Shakleton, or another) who has produced laboratory results for which the odds are 10,000,000 to 1 against chance being the explanation. Commonly, those who bother to question such claims discover that the individual cases were part of a longer series of tests and that the results of the entire experiment were not given.

Odd comparisons can produce misleading statistics. Commentators note that, in a given year, two million Americans get married, and one million get divorced. Then they claim that half of U.S. marriages are failing. (Actually, the marriages are a one-year statistic; the divorces involve people who wed during the previous 40 years.) Similarly, because of a dated norm, every state in the nation now reports its public-school students score "above the national average." (This has been called "the Lake Wobegon effect.")

IRRELEVANT NUMBERS

An argument can be bolstered with irrelevant statistics. Some years ago tobacco companies responded to evidence that smoking may cause cancer by counting filter traps. Viceroy boasted 20,000 filters ("twice as many as the other two largest-selling brands") until Parliament began claiming 30,000, and Hit Parade overwhelmed both with 400,000. (That was an average figure. The testing lab reported that one Hit Parade filter had 597,000 filter traps.) These were impressive numbers, but they were meaningless. There was no evidence that *any* filter protected a person from the effects of smoking. And no one had defined "filter trap."

Many arguments assign numbers to undefined objects. When you're told that Americans reported 550 UFOs last month, you wonder what these people saw. When you face the sensational headline "Asthma Deaths in U.S. Double in Seven Years," you read on and see the reason: Authorities have changed the definition of "asthma."

Advertisers take the practice a step further and employ numbers without references. You see a travel ad for Martinique offering "Four times the pleasure" and one for Montreal boasting "It's four times better." Better than what? Don't ask.

Cigarette advertisements offer precise numbers and irrelevant statistics. One ad boasts "Carlton is lowest." Another says Now is "lowest in tar and nicotine." These claims are possible because Carlton is referring to its King Size Soft Pack, and Now to its Soft Pack 100's. Neither ad shows how the figures make any difference to the average smoker.

Even when counting clearly defined items, speakers can offer irrelevant numbers. Responding to a demonstrated statistical relationship between cigarette smoking and an increased incidence of lung cancer, they can observe that the vast majority of smokers do not get cancer. As violent crimes increase, they can oppose gun control laws by calculating that only 0.0034 percent of American handguns are involved in homicides.

Equally creative computations goes into the unemployment figures produced by the U.S. Bureau of Labor Statistics. Because any administration can be faulted if unemployment is too high, the Bureau uses polling techniques that systematically underestimate the economic hardship within the labor force. A person is not "unemployed" unless he or she has actively looked for work in the preceding month. This method of counting eliminates people who have been sick, who have been forced into early retirement, and who have looked for months and have given up in despair.

However, a person can be looking regularly for work and still not be "unemployed." If an out-of-work longshoreman mows lawns two afternoons a month, he counts as being fully employed. If he helps out his brother in a family business and works for nothing, he is fully employed. If his daughter works an hour a month as a baby-sitter, she is just as employed (in administration figures) as a chemist who works 60 hours a week at Monsanto.

In an inspired move, the Reagan administration chose to enlarge the work force to include people in military service. Because all those added had jobs, the percentage of Americans who were unemployed dropped significantly. One can visualize a future day when an administration decides that the only Americans truly unemployed are Puerto Rican teamsters out of work in Cleveland. Then it will celebrate a grand era of full employment.

A rich example of irrelevant statistics occurred in 1985 when corporate officers at the Coca-Cola Company changed the taste of Coke. They had 200,000 tests demonstrating that the public preferred the taste of the new Coke to the old Coke and preferred it to Pepsi. Still, the change produced a nationwide protest that forced them to bring back the old Coke. Nobody cared about 200,000 tests. As one critic said, "It's like they redesigned the flag."

There is a kind of irrelevance in statistics derived from a singular example. Hollywood Bread, for example, advertised that it had fewer calories per slice than other breads; this was true because its slices were thinner. Carlton cigarettes boasted that it had been tested as the lowest in "tar" of all filter kings; one reason was that it had a longer filter than other cigarettes of the same length and therefore contained less tobacco. Television personality Hugh Downs announced that he got 28.3 miles per

gallon while driving a Mustang II from Phoenix to Los Angeles. The trip
is largely downhill.

HOMEMADE STATISTICS

The preceding examples indicate that people don't have to make up statistics to create a misleading argument. But, of course, they can make up
statistics if they want to. For example, the temperance advocate who built
an analogy on the claim that there were 10,000 deaths from alcohol poisoning to 1 death from mad-dog bites was using figures that exist nowhere
else.

Homemade statistics usually relate to things that have not been measured or are impossible to measure. Authorities can be suspiciously precise
about events too trivial to have been counted. (Dr. Joyce Brothers reported
that the "American girl kisses an average of 79 men before getting married." A Lane cedar chest advertisement warned that moths destroy
$400,000,000 worth of goods each year.) They can be glibly confident about
obscure facts. (A *Nation* article said that there were 9,000,000 rats in New
York City; Massachusetts Congressman Paul White, introducing a bill to
make swearing illegal, announced that Americans curse 700,000 times a
second.)

Imaginary numbers like these usually relate to areas in which it is
impossible to get real figures. To make an impressive argument, advocates
may want to specify the number of HIV-positive people in America today—or the number of pot smokers or abused wives. They may want to
report how much money was spent on pornography last year—or on
welfare fraud. The writers can find some information in these areas, but
because exact counts remain unavailable, they are strongly tempted to
produce a number that supports the case they are trying to make. Many
give in. Remember this the next time you see headlines announcing that
a rail strike in Chicago is costing the city $2,000,000 a day.

Even in instances where a measure of scientific computation occurred,
resulting statistics often seem singularly creative. Consider these examples, taken from recent news stories:

1. Seventeen percent of the babies born to near-affluent parents are
   unwanted.
2. Americans eat 38,000,000,000 hamburgers a year.
3. Up to 30 percent of American coeds are harassed by their professors.
4. Five percent of Americans dream in color.
5. Men aged 35 to 50 average one sexual thought every 25 minutes.
6. Every five seconds a women is beaten in the United States.
7. Fifty percent of people don't ask for help from a librarian.

Maybe you saw the Planned Parenthood ad that appeared in leading
newspapers. It said, "They did it 9,000 times on television last year. How

come nobody got pregnant?" Or maybe you saw the ad as it appeared later in *USA Today*. It began, "They did it 20,000 times on television last year."

With a little practice, you can identify homemade statistics with the naked eye.

ENHANCING A STATISTIC

With careful presentation, people can make any number seem bigger or smaller, as their argument requires. For example, many newspapers reported an Oberlin College poll that claimed that 40 percent of the unmarried coeds had engaged in sex, that 1 in 13 of these women became pregnant, and that 80 percent of the pregnancies were terminated by abortion. The "80 percent" figure seems startling until you ask, "80 percent of what?" Relatively modest statistics appear sensational when given as percentages of percentages of percentages.

More commonly, persuaders change the character of a statistic by simple comparison. They relate it to a smaller number to make it seem large or to a larger number to make it seem small. The contrasting number need have no relevance aside from offering an advantageous comparison.

In presidential primaries, candidates routinely predict weak results. They point out that the contest is not in their strongest state, that other duties have limited their public appearances, and that, all in all, they will do well to win 8 percent of the vote. Then when they win 11 percent, their followers announce, "He did well. His vote exceeded expectations." One reverses the process to dwarf a statistic. When Governor George Wallace—a law and order spokesman—had to face the fact that Alabama had the highest murder rate of any state in the nation (11.4 murders per 100,000 people), his office explained that this figure was not nearly so high as that for Detroit, Los Angeles, and other major cities.

In a summary statement on statistical manipulation, Darrell Huff (*How to Lie with Statistics*, New York, Norton, 1954) counseled the business community:

> There are often many ways of expressing any figure. You can, for instance, express exactly the same fact by calling it a one percent return on sales, a fifteen percent return on investment, a ten-million-dollar profit, an increase of profits of forty percent (compared with 1935–39 average), and a decrease of sixty percent from last year. The method is to choose which one sounds best for the purpose at hand and trust that few who read it will recognize how imperfectly it reflects the situation.

In a society subject to political controversy, social argument, and Madison Avenue rhetoric, such argument is common.

You should recognize examples of distorted statistics and avoid them as much as possible in your writing.

Of course you won't want to use specific numbers when they hurt the case you are making. Consider the diamond-industry ad urging the purchase of an expensive engagement ring: "Is two months' salary too much to spend for something that will last forever?" (One might answer, "Is $4000 too much to spend on a marriage that will last two months?")

Even when numbers favor your case, do not use them too extensively. A mass audience is rarely persuaded by a body of statistics. This explains why they are used so infrequently in the antismoking campaigns of the American Cancer Society and the American Heart Association.

You should remember, finally, that a number by itself means little or nothing. If in a particular year Montreal's baseball team leads the major leagues with 179 double plays, what does that mean? That it has a fine second baseman? That it has poor pitchers? That its home park has an Astroturf infield? Who knows? When 46 of 100 beer drinkers who "regularly drink Budweiser" preferred an unmarked mug of Schlitz (in a 1980 New Orleans test), what did that prove? Probably that most drinkers can't tell one beer from another. What can you conclude about an $21,000 annual salary, a 150-word poem, a $9.95 meal? Not much. An important quality of statistical argument was expressed in a scene in the film *Annie Hall:* The lovers, played by Diane Keaton and Woody Allen, are asked by their psychiatrists how often they have sex. She responds, "All the time. Three times a week." And he says, "Hardly at all. Three times a week."

EXERCISES

How reliable are these statistical arguments?

1. "There are 53 vampires in America today."—Headline in *The Sun*
2. If you begin having your hair styled, are people going to think you've gone soft? Half the Los Angeles Rams' line has their hair styled. If you want to laugh at them, go ahead. We don't.
3. Listening mistakes in the United States cost $10 billion a year.
4. Listerine Antiseptic stops bad breath four times better than toothpaste.
5. According to Rodale Press, cigarette smoking costs Americans $50 billion a year.
6. On Solidarity Day (September 19, 1981), thousands of union workers massed in Washington to protest the Reagan administration's economic policies. United States park police estimated the crowd at 260,000. AFL-CIO sources called it half a million.
7. "One out of six college women will be sexually assaulted this year."—Rape Treatment Center, Santa Monica Hospital

8. Using a simple cipher (A = 6, B = 12, C = 18, etc.), the words KISSIN-GER and COMPUTER both total 666, the number of the Antichrist. Certainly this proves something.

9. Leo Guild's book *What Are the Odds?* reports that a young man with a broken engagement behind him is "75 percent as happy" as one who has never been engaged.

10. It is estimated that each year some 10 million wise Americans spend $500 million on essential life-building food supplements and vitamin capsules. Can 10 million Americans be wrong?

11. "27 million Americans can't read a bedtime story to a child."

12. Mennen Speed Stick offers "110 percent protection." hyperbole

13. "Banging your head against a wall burns 150 calories an hour."— *National Enquirer* (July 15, 1986).

14. "Over 10 million men suffer impotence problems in the U.S. to-day."—Ken Druck

15. In her heyday, Clara Bow received more mail per week than the average town of 5000.

16. Studies show that therapy which includes an aspirin a day reduces heart attacks as much as 50 percent for some people. Aspirin, com-bined with exercise and the right foods, could save as many as 50,000 lives a year.

17. "1 in 10 have psychic power."—Uri Geller

18. The Government Accounting Office, urged on by Senator William Proxmire, calculated that the 1985 Presidential inaugural events cost the nation $15,512,339.59.

19. "With 200,000,000 of us, God had something good in mind."—Pos-ter displayed at a Gay Rights demonstration, New York.

20. There's something wrong here. The average sentence for a murderer in this country is 20.4 years. A rapist gets 9.4 years. An arsonist, 6.7 years. But Jim Bakker came before U.S. District Judge Robert Potter (known as "Maximum Bob") and was sentenced to 45 years in prison.

21. "You can smoke fewer cigarettes by smoking longer ones."—Ad for Max 120s

22. Rush Limbaugh—"Documented to be right 97.9 percent of the time."

ESSAY ASSIGNMENTS

Write an essay either affirming or opposing one of these statements. The material you encounter in your background reading will include statisti-cal argument, and so should your essay.

1. American industry is fighting pollution.
2. We need gun control laws to curtail crime.

3. Sex education leads to promiscuity, pregnancy, and disease.
4. It's proved: Cigarette smoking causes lung cancer.
5. IQ tests do not prove anything.
6. American income tax laws should be revised.
7. Laetrile is an effective treatment for cancer.
8. Statistics prove that X is a mistake. (Fill in the X.)

100,000 BEER COMMERCIALS?

Anheuser-Busch Companies

Have you heard the one about the average 18-year-old and the 100,000 beer commercials?

We'd almost be surprised if you hadn't. Since they first made the accusation in 1987, critics of the beer industry have repeated again and again that by the time the average American turns 18, he or she has seen 100,000 beer commercials on television. By now, no doubt, many people believe it. After all, spokesmen for such groups as the Center for Science in the Public Interest, which are widely perceived as interested only in the truth, have said it. Congress has heard witnesses testify to it. And reputable newspapers and magazines have reported it as gospel. So why shouldn't people believe it?

For just one reason. It isn't true.

We'd like to set the record straight. We'd like to explain how ridiculous the "100,000 beer commercials" accusation happens to be. And while we're at it, we'd like to raise some questions about the whole climate in which serious public issues are debated in this country. Specifically, we'd like to show how readily misinformation can achieve wide distribution—and ultimately, win acceptance by the public—if it suits some group's political agenda.

The origin of the "100,000 beer commercials" accusation is "Myths, Men & Beer," a lengthy and highly critical report on 40 beer commercials that appeared on network television in 1987. Athough written by four university faculty members, "Myths, Men & Beer" was published and paid for by the American Automobile Association Foundation for Traffic Study in Falls Church, Va. It did not receive academic peer review, nor was it ever published in a professional journal.

"Myths, Men & Beer" alleges that beer advertising presents a "powerful, distorted, and dangerous message . . . to young people." It urges that "the policy permitting the televising of commercials for beer be revised to prohibit such commercials."

The authors, of course, have a right to their opinion. They should, however, stick to the facts in arriving at their opinions. And that's where we take issue.

Let's think for a moment about the authors' assertion: "Between the ages of 2 and 18, American children see something like 100,000 television commercials for beer." Let's analyze this claim—for which, we hasten to point out, not one shred of evidence is provided in the report.

Sixteen years lie between a child's 2nd and 18th birthday. Sixteen years represents about 5,844 days, give or take a few for the vagaries of leap year. To see 100,000 beer commercials in that time, a young person would have to see an average of more than 17 beer commercials a day.

SOURCE: Courtesy of Anheuser-Busch.

We say that's ridiculous on the face of it. But let's walk it through to prove how absurd it is.

On average, beer commercials represent about 3.4 percent of the total number of commercials aired in any given market, according to figures supplied by the Arbitron Co., the authoritative source on the subject. So if 17 beer commercials a day represents 3.4 percent of the total, it takes only a little arithmetic to show that the average viewer is seeing a total of 503 commercials a day. Actually, that's a conservative figure, because children tend to watch less TV at the times when beer commercials are scheduled. But we'll use the most conservative figures to make our point all the stronger.

How much daily viewing would 503 commercials require? Well, the average network commercial runs about 23 to 25 seconds. Given that local commercials are often a bit shorter, we'll use 20 seconds as a conservative, low estimate of the length of the average TV commercial. We'll multiply 503 by 20 and then divide by 60 to get the number of minutes of commercials our kids are allegedly seeing each day: 168 minutes.

We suspect we've already made our point, but indulge us, please, to the end. How much TV would someone have to see in a day, on average, to witness 168 minutes of commercials? The answer can be calculated from this information:

A conservative—in this case, high—estimate of the number of minutes of commercials shown each hour on TV is 12. Dividing 168 by 12 gives the answer: 14 hours per day—on average for 16 years.

Now we know our children watch a lot of TV. And we know that a lot of them don't get their proper rest. But most of them, we are convinced, still sleep several hours a night. Many, we're quite certain, also attend school. Our own powers of observation also disclose the following: Many children still go outside and play, and whole flocks of them visit shopping malls.

Emboldened by this skepticism, we checked with A.C. Neilsen Co., which we consider a credible authority on these matters. And what do you know—they reported that average **weekly** TV viewing by 2- to 17-year-olds in 1988 was a little more than 23.5 hours, or less than 3.5 hours per day.

Pardon our sarcasm: the fact is, there are even more problems with the authors' claim. Nowhere, for example, is there any indication that the authors have taken into account **when children are watching TV, or what they're seeing.** (As we mentioned, we haven't either—but only to be conservative and give the authors a better chance to prove their claim.) The reality is, beer is advertised primarily during evenings and sporting events—and never on "Pee-Wees' Playhouse" or the "Wonderful World of Disney." The authors of "Myths, Men & Beer" don't seem to be aware, or care.

One more note along these lines. As we've noted, sporting events are a focus for beer advertising. But, in a typical major league baseball game, 11 is a high estimate of the number of beer commercials that might be shown. So according to the authors of "Myths, Men & Beer," the average child is seeing—on a daily basis for 16 years—the equivalent of about one and one-half baseball games worth of beer commercials.

And that's on top of the viewing this child is doing of shows without beer advertisements.

In short, the "100,000 beer commercials" charge is not just wrong; it's absurd and shoddy. It is, you'll excuse the expression, false advertising.

Now let's go on to the deeper issues. Why is it that an accusation as patently false as the one relating to 100,000 beer commercials gets levelled? And why does it then get repeated again and again and again—by people who obviously don't bother to check it—until it takes on the mantle of conventional wisdom?

The answer relates to the fact that alcohol-related issues are emotional ones that are heavily freighted with value judgments. In the minds of its critics, beer industry advertising is bad. Therefore, any information that would reflect negatively on this advertising—information, for instance, that would suggest that young people are being inundated and corrupted by it—gains an eager reception.

In saying this, we don't question the sincerity of the critics. We do, however, object to the way in which their deeply held views seem to interfere with their research and analysis—the way, in other words, in which their views seem to affect their intellectual standards. And we do question the willingness of some of our critics to leap enthusiastically upon such obviously flawed research if it advances their political agenda.

It's well known that if falsehood is repeated often enough, many people will believe it. But in this country, a strong media often puts the lie to would-be propagandists' claims. It's therefore also important to ask—why hasn't the media exposed the "100,000 commercials" canard for what it is?

In our view, it's because groups like Remove Intoxicated Drivers and the Center for Science in the Public Interest enjoy so much credibility with the public. Groups like RID are widely perceived as noble champions of good causes: Who wouldn't fight against drunk driving? (The beer industry certainly opposes it, but that fact can be easily overlooked.) Groups like the Center for Science in the Public Interest, meanwhile, are seen as above-the-battle guardians of society's broader concerns. (How many people understand that the CSPI has a minimal scientific staff and is essentially a political organization?) The upshot is that most people believe whatever these groups say.

In the end, it all boils down to a simple chain of events: Sloppy research, compromised by an underlying political agenda, produces a simple, quotable "fact" that meets the political needs of organizations which enjoy a wide public and journalistic following. The "fact" is repeated and repeated until, in short order, everybody "knows" it—even though it happens not to be true.

We could give many more examples, but we'll confine ourselves to a few that are central to the overall issue: specifically, to the critics' contention that advertising results in higher levels of beer consumption, underage drinking, and abuse.

In 1985, the Federal Trade Commission investigated these allegations in response to a petition by the CSPI and other parties. The FTC subsequently reported: "Our staffs' review of the literature regarding the

quantitative effect of alcohol advertising on consumption and abuse
found no reliable basis to conclude that alcohol advertising significantly
affects consumption, let alone abuse." At a Senate hearing just last year,
the FTC reiterated its position.

The FTC's findings shouldn't have come as too much of a surprise
to at least one of the groups seeking advertising restrictions. In its petition to the FTC, the CSPI conceded that "the available literature does
not demonstrate a causal connection between advertising and harm."

In effect, the FTC inquiry—and a similar one conducted in 1985 by
the U.S. Senate's Subcommittee on Alcoholism and Drug Abuse—gave
support to our view: Beer advertising doesn't significantly affect consumption, underage drinking, or abuse. It affects market share.

Ironically, this is a fact that even the authors of "Myths, Men &
Beer" acknowledge. In their report, they write: "It would be a grave
error to believe, for example, that advertising causes the people of a
culture to behave as they do, in any but trivial ways (selecting Brand X,
perhaps, over Brand Y.)"

Hurrah—sort of. Allow us to add that the "trivial ways" to which
the authors refer are the difference between success and failure to us. In
the beer industry, each point of market share is worth about $440 million
at the retail level. That's the whole reason members of the industry
spend as much as they do on advertising—to try to win market share.

Let us add, too, that while beer advertising rose in the 1980s, per
capita consumption of beer actually declined 2.5 percent between 1980
and 1988, the last year for which figures are available; that the number
of people killed in drunk driving accidents fell 9 percent between 1982
and 1988; and that the beer industry has played a substantial part in the
public awareness and education campaigns that are apparently helping
to reduce the abuse of alcohol.

In short, let us observe that reality is more complicated—and in
many cases quite different—from what our critics would have us all believe.

Alcohol abuse is a serious problem in this country, inflicting substantial damage on individuals and society. How we deal with alcohol abuse
also raises serious issues—involving such matters as commercial free
speech, individual freedoms versus society's interest in self-protection,
and appropriate assignments of responsibility for individual conduct.

To resolve these questions rationally will require all the intelligence
and solid information we can muster. Flawed information, fueled by
emotion and exploited for political ends, will make news. It may even
shape policy.

But it won't help.

DISCUSSION QUESTIONS

1. At one point in challenging the "100,000 commercials" claim, the
   author writes, "We suspect we've already made our point, but in-

dulge us, please, to the end." Why such an exhaustive analysis of the claim?

2. Does the argument make effective use of authorities? What does it say about each of these:
   a. Center for Science in the Public Interest
   b. American Automobile Association Foundation for Traffic Study
   c. Arbitron Company
   d. A. C. Neilsen Company
   e. Remove Intoxicated Drivers
   f. Federal Trade Commission
   g. U.S. Senate's Subcommittee on Alcoholism and Drug Abuse
3. Is the author angry at beer-industry critics? What is the tone of the essay. Does this tone help the argument?
4. How does the argument challenge the view that beer ads lead young people to drink dangerously? Is the argument persuasive?
5. How formal is this essay? What is the effect of lines like "Hurrah— sort of" and "But it won't help"?
6. Is the author an effective writer? Why do you think so?

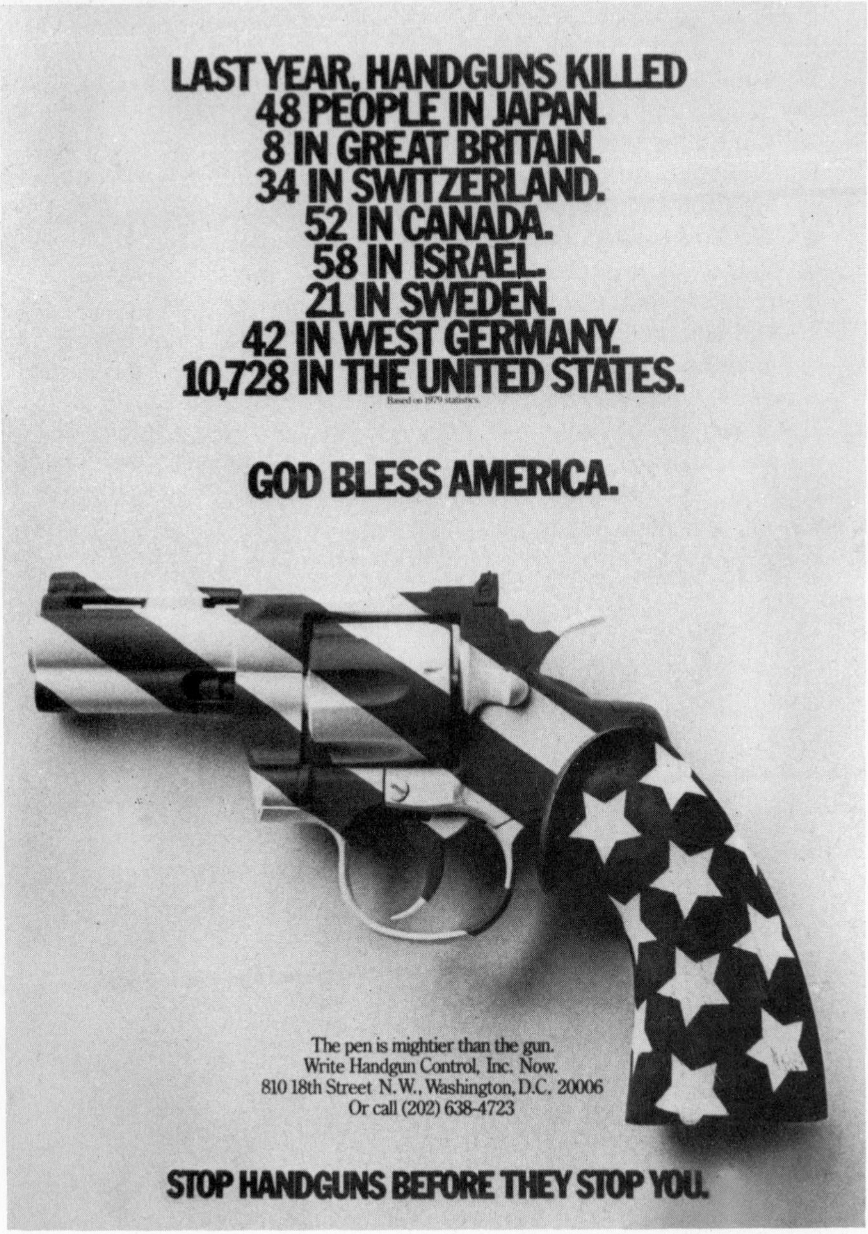

Courtesy of Handgun Control, Inc.

DISCUSSION QUESTIONS

1. What is the unstated conclusion of this ad? What is the author advocating?
2. Is the argument persuasive?
3. Would the argument be less persuasive if you were told the number of stabbings in Britain, the number of bombings in Ireland, the number of fatal beatings in West Germany, and so on?
4. If the sale of handguns was made illegal tomorrow, do you think the figures on the ad would be significantly different a year from now? Why or why not?

HYSTERIA ABOUT DIOXIN

Richard Phillips

To the Editor:

Kathy Ferchaud is to be complimented for her thorough and technically accurate reporting in the Jan. 2 edition on the latest scientific research on the risk to humans posed by the chemical dioxin. Much unwarranted hysteria on this subject has been promoted in the past, and it is gratifying to see your newspaper bring some objectivity to the issue.

Over 17,000 scientific publications have been written on the subject of dioxin, representing a research investment of over $500 million. From this body of literature, responsible scientists draw only one conclusion: No evidence exists that any human has ever died or had their life shortened due to dioxin.

Greenpeace would have the public believe that the thousands of scientists who performed that work are all on the payroll of big business. Let's test that:

Dr. Vernon Houck is Assistant Surgeon General and Director for Environmental Health and Injury Control for the United States Center for Disease Control. In 1989 testimony before the Georgia Department of Natural Resources, Dr. Houck concluded that a level of dioxin over 400 times that deemed by EPA to be safe would be fully protective of human health.

Dr. Renate Kimbrough is Toxicology and Risk Evaluation Advisor for the United States Environmental Protection Agency. On May 31, 1990, Dr. Kimbrough told the Washington Post: "The present levels (of dioxin) we're exposed to should not be of particular concern."

Dr. Robert Squire is a Johns Hopkins University School of Medicine research scientist. Dr. Squire performed the original analysis of the animal data 10 years ago as a consultant for the EPA. It was Dr. Squire's 1980 analysis that gives rise to the dramatic, but untrue, statement that "dioxin is the most toxic synthetic chemical known to science." In 1990, the state of Maine Scientific Advisory Panel asked Dr. Squire to re-examine the original animal tissue slides in the light of 1990 tumor science rather than the vastly less-precise procedures employed in 1980. Dr. Squire concluded, and stated in a May 24, 1990, letter to EPA: "based on all the biological evidence, I do not believe that dioxin poses a cancer risk to humans at any anticipated levels of exposure."

Greenpeace would have the public believe that the lowest doses of dioxin tested on laboratory animals (already 1,000 times the amount of dioxin that humans normally ingest through the food chain) led to significant abnormalities. In fact, the low dose of dioxin administered to the rats actually decreased the overall formation of tumors and other abnormalities. Further, this effect is of sufficient interest that the National In-

SOURCE: Letter to the *Mobile Register*, January 23, 1991. Reprinted by permission of the author.

stitute of Health has allocated funds to study the effect in more detail to develop dioxin analogs for possible clinical use in the treatment of breast cancer.

Greenpeace would have the public believe that "European countries began cutting back the amounts of dioxin that could be released." In fact, the Federal Republic of Germany analog to the U.S. FDA extensively and publicly reviewed their position on dioxin potency in October, 1990, and concluded by reaffirming their historic level of acceptable exposure (a level 166 times higher than the U.S. EPA, which has the most conservative view of any agency in the world). Based on the Banbury Conference on dioxin that Ms. Ferchaud reported, the head of the Netherlands National Institute of Health indicated his agency would recommend a new dioxin standard 1,666 times that of EPA.

The most notable finding that the dioxin conference reported was scientific consensus that dioxin does not act as a direct initiator of cancer; therefore, there exists some level (known as a "threshold") below which there is no increased cancer risk to humans. This threshold level was agreed to be on the order of 1,000 times the level currently accepted by EPA.

The dioxin issue is technically complex, but the multi-million dollar research effort is moving at a very rapid pace to a firm conclusion: Dioxin in the amounts we encounter in the environment simply does not represent a human health hazard.

I would be pleased to provide references and/or additional information on any and all of the points made above.

DISCUSSION QUESTIONS

1. The author makes continued use of numbers ("17,000 scientific publications"), particularly comparative numbers: "400 times" a certain level, "1,000 times," "166 times," "1,000 times," "1,660 times," and "1,000 times." Do such numbers have a strong impact?
2. How impressive is the use of authorities: Dr. Houck, Dr. Kimbrough, and Dr. Squire? What is particularly notable about Dr. Squire's testimony?
3. How effective are references to the Federal Republic of Germany, the Banbury Conference on dioxin, and the Netherlands National Institute on Health?
4. Why is Greenpeace so hostile to dioxin?
5. What is the author's attitude toward Greenpeace? Is he angry?
6. Who is Richard Phillips? What can you infer from his offer to provide information to interested readers?

Let's get mental illness out of the closet.

The disease no one wants to talk about is breaking our hearts and homes, filling our hospitals and streets. But there is hope--if we recognize it, name it, find out enough about it.

Exactly what is mental illness?

Mental illness, which affects almost 40 million men and women of all ages, causes severe disturbances in thinking, feeling and relating. The two most prevalent and devasting forms are schizophrenia and depression. *More than 1 out of 8 Americans will suffer a major depressive episode at some time in their lives.*

Every dollar goes directly to research

A fortune in care, pennies for research

Direct care for schizophrenia and depression costs about 35 *billion* dollars a year. Yet the total spent on research for these diseases, is about 1.1% of that spent on muscular dystrophy.

Needed: millions of dollars for a cure

We must get mental illness out of the closet, talk about it, dig into the causes and cures. And that takes dollars, so doctors and scientists can use advanced technology to improve diagnosis and treatment.

A major fund drive has been initiated, by the National Alliance for Research on Schizophrenia and Depression (NARSAD), to find the causes, cures and treatment of mental illness.

Who can help?

We need financial assistance from caring individuals, philanthropic foundations and concerned corporations.

Help fling open that door. Every dollar you send opens it a little more. Even just sending for information can open it a crack. *Let's hear from you.*

NARSAD Research Fund
60 Cutter Mill Road - Suite 200
Great Neck, New York 11021

Yes, I agree that more research must be funded now.
Enclosed is my tax deductible donation:

☐ $1000 ☐ $500 ☐ $250 ☐ $100 ☐ $50 ☐ Other
☐ Please send me more information about mental illness.

Name _____
Address _____
City _____ State _____ Zip _____

Courtesy of NARSAD.

DISCUSSION QUESTIONS

1. How effective is the author's use of statistics:
    a. "40 million men and women"
    b. "more than 1 out of 8 Americans"
    c. "35 *billion* dollars"
2. The amount spent on mental health research "is about 1.1% of that spent on muscular dystrophy." Why the comparison to muscular dystrophy? Is the author suggesting too much is spent on muscular dystrophy?
3. Why the continuing reference to "we" and "our"?
4. How effective is the "closet" reference? Is it possible this could weaken the author's argument?
5. The coupon at the bottom indicates sums a reader might send in to help NARSAD. What effect do these have?
6. How impressive is the photograph? Do you think it is more or less persuasive than the statistical argument?

SHOCKING TRUTH
ABOUT THE HOMELESS

John Blosser

Homeless Americans have been portrayed as pathetic victims of society, ordinary people down on their luck—but most of them are really alcoholics, drug abusers, criminals or are mentally ill, experts say.

A recent 27-city survey by the U.S. Conference of Mayors found that 76 percent of homeless people are unemployed, 43 percent are alcohol and drug abusers, and 25 percent are mentally ill, according to Michael Brown, a spokesman for the conference.

"We keep seeing TV shows and newspaper and magazine articles portraying the homeless as ordinary working people who have been victimized by an uncaring society. This just isn't true," said Dr. Robert Lichter, codirector of the Center for Media and Public Affairs in Washington, D.C.

"The reality is that the majority of the homeless have problems, such as drugs or mental instability, that aren't society's fault."

Margaret Beckham, a public affairs specialist with the Urban Institute in Washington, a "think-tank" that has published a book entitled "America's Homeless," said her organization discovered:

- 60 percent of homeless single men and 22 percent of homeless single women have spent more than three days in a county jail.
- 29 percent of homeless single men have served time in prison.
- 43 percent of homeless adults have been in institutions for mental illness or for drug or alcohol abuse.

Dr. Luis Marcos, a psychiatrist and vice president for mental health of New York City's Health and Hospitals Corporation, told The ENQUIRER:

"These homeless people are not Ozzie and Harriet temporarily down on their luck. The hard-core population of homeless is very troubled from a psychological, medical and social point of view.

"I estimate 80 percent have serious drug, alcohol or mental problems. Many of them are involved in crime.

"In Middle America, because of the media, people think the homeless are real families, helplessly homeless through economic reasons or disasters.

"In New York, we know differently. We see them lying in the streets or begging, being aggressive and pushy and dangerous. Before they could have a home or a job, they would need to be rehabilitated from drugs, alcohol or mental illness.

"Even if the housing was there, even if the jobs were there, these people would still be homeless."

SOURCE: Reprinted with permission from *National Enquirer*, March 13, 1990.

DISCUSSION QUESTIONS

1. The opening sentence denies that the homeless are "pathetic victims of society." It says they are really "alcoholics, drug abusers, criminals or . . . mentally ill." Is this an either–or judgment? Couldn't they be both?
2. The second paragraph reports that large percentages of the homeless are unemployed, alcohol or drug abusers, and mentally ill. What do these statistics prove? What is cause and what is effect?
3. Dr. Lichter suggests the homeless are in large measure responsible for their unhappy state. Dr. Marcos concludes these people are "very troubled." Are these authorities looking at the same set of statistics? What does this tell you about statistics?
4. Whom is this article addressed to? What seems to be the purpose of the essay?
5. Would the audience enjoy reading this article? Why or why not?
6. Is the article well written? Did you find it easy to read?

IN THE U.S., CRIME PAYS BECAUSE CRIMINALS DON'T!

IN OTHER COUNTRIES THEY DO.

IN ISRAEL:
MANDATORY LIFE IMPRISONMENT FOR MURDER; NO BAIL FOR MURDER SUSPECTS.

IN CANADA:
COMPULSORY LIFE IMPRISONMENT FOR MURDER; 80.6% HOMICIDE CONVICTION RATE.

IN GREAT BRITAIN:
83.5% HOMICIDE CONVICTION RATE; 87.9% ROBBERY CONVICTION RATE; 100% LIFE SENTENCES FOR MURDER.

IN JAPAN:
99.5% VIOLENT CRIME CONVICTION RATE; 98% RECEIVE JAIL TIME; NO PLEA BARGAINING.

IN NEW YORK CITY ALONE:
"THE CHANCE OF A GIVEN FELONY ARREST ENDING IN A PRISON SENTENCE . . . ONE OUT OF 108."
— From the New York Times

NATIONWIDE:
". . . FOR EVERY 500 SERIOUS CRIMES, JUST 20 ADULTS AND 5 JUVENILES ARE SENT TO JAIL."
— From U.S. News & World Report

GOD HELP AMERICA.

DEMAND PUNISHMENT FOR CRIMINAL BEHAVIOR. JAIL TIME FOR REPEAT OFFENDERS DETERS CRIME.

National Rifle Association, 1600 Rhode Island Ave., N.W., Washington, D.C. 20036.

Courtesy of the National Rifle Association of America.

DISCUSSION QUESTIONS

1. This ad was written to answer the argument on page 160. Is this an effective response?
2. What does this ad say about the sale of handguns in the United States?
3. What did the argument on page 160 say about high and low conviction rates and about compulsory sentences?
4. Name the fallacy illustrated by this argument.
5. Why should the National Rifle Association be so concerned about conviction rates and compulsory sentences?

NO, VIRGINIA, THERE

ISN'T A SANTA CLAUS!

Bruce Handy

Do you believe in Santa Claus?

This is a complex theological question that each child must decide
for him- or herself. Until now, that is. With the aid of computers, SPY JR.
has conducted a rigorous **statistical** investigation into the question of
Santa's existence. Be forewarned: you may not like our conclusions.

We begin our investigation by assuming that Santa Claus really does
exist. Now, if you've learned anything about human nature, you know
it's highly unlikely that a normal man would choose, for no particular
reason, to devote his life to making toys and delivering them to boys
and girls the world over. But this is an **objective** inquiry, and questions
of motivation aren't relevant. We want only to know whether such a
man could accomplish his mission.

Santa's first obstacle is that *no known species of reindeer can fly*. However, scientists estimate that out of the earth's roughly 2 million species
of living organisms, 300,000 or so have yet to be classified. So, even
though most of these undiscovered species are insects and germs, we
can't rule out the slight possibility that a species of flying reindeer does,
in fact, exist. And that no one besides Santa has ever seen one.

A bigger obstacle for Santa is that there are 2 billion children under
the age of 18 in the world. The good news is that he needs to deliver
presents only to *Christian* children, of whom there are approximately 378
million (according to figures provided by the Population Reference Bureau). Let's assume that 15 percent of these Christian children have been
bad and are thus—like Muslim, Hindu, Jewish and Buddhist children—
ineligible for gift getting. Still, at an average rate of 3.5 children per
household, Santa has a backbreaking 91.8 million homes to visit on any
given Christmas Eve.

Fortunately, Santa has 31 hours of Christmas Eve darkness to visit
all these homes if he travels from east to west, thanks to the rotation of
the earth. Unfortunately, this still works out to 822.6 visits per second.
So, for each Christian household with good children, Santa has just over
a thousandth of a second to land, hop out of his sleigh, jump down the
chimney, fill the stockings, distribute the rest of the presents under the
tree, eat whatever snacks have been left out, get back up the chimney,
climb back into his sleigh, take off and fly to the next house.

How fast is Santa moving? Assuming all 91.8 million stops are
spread evenly over the earth's landmass, Santa must travel 0.79 miles
per household—a total trip of 72,522,000 miles. (This is a conservative
estimate. It doesn't include trips across oceans, feeding stops for the
reindeer, etc.) Given the 31-hour time period, Santa's sleigh must maintain an average speed of 650 miles per second, or more then 3,000 times
the speed of sound. To give you an idea how fast that is, the fastest

SOURCE: Reprinted by permission from *Spy,* January 1991.

man-made vehicle ever built, the *Ulysses* space probe, travels at a relatively poky pace of 27.4 miles per second, and conventional, land-bound reindeer travel at a top speed of 15 miles per hour. But let's just assume that Santa's flying reindeer are somehow able to reach hypersonic speeds—thanks, say, to the magical spirit of Christmas giving.

Let's take a closer look at Santa's vehicle. First of all, assuming a cheapo 2 pounds of presents per child (that's like one crummy Lego set), the sleigh must still be able to carry a load of 321,300 tons—plus Santa, an overweight man. On land, a reindeer can't pull more than 300 pounds of freight, and even assuming that flying reindeer could pull ten times that amount, Santa's massive sleigh has to be drawn by 214,200 beasts. They increase the weight of the overall Santa payload to 353,430 tons (not including the weight of the sleigh itself). This is more than four times the weight of the *Queen Elizabeth* ocean liner. Imagine: Santa skimming over rooftops in a gargantuan hypersonic aircraft with even less maneuverability than a Big Wheel.

Here's where things get fun.

Three hundred fifty-three thousand tons of reindeer and presents are going to create an enormous amount of air resistance—especially at 650 miles per second. This air resistance will heat the reindeer in the same way that spaceships are heated up when they reenter the earth's atmosphere. According to our calculations, the lead pair of reindeer will absorb 14.3-quintillion joules of energy per second each. This means they will burst into spectacular, multicolored flames almost instantaneously, exposing the reindeer behind them. As Santa continues on his mission—leaving deafening sonic booms in his wake—charred reindeer will constantly be sloughed off. All 214,200 reindeer will be dead within 4.26 thousandths of a second.

As for Santa, he will be subjected to centrifugal forces 17,500.06 times greater than gravity. A 250-pound Santa will be pinned to the back of his sleigh by 4,375,015 pounds of force (after we deduct his weight). This force will kill Santa instantly, crushing his bones, pulverizing his flesh, turning him into pink goo. In other words, if Santa tries to deliver presents on Christmas Eve to every qualified boy and girl on the face of the earth, he will be liquefied.

If he even exists, he's already dead.

So where *do* the presents come from? Weirdly kindhearted intruders? Stupid robbers? Magic? Your parents, maybe?

We won't insult your intelligence with the answer.

DISCUSSION QUESTIONS

1. What is the purpose of this essay? Is it to discourage the reader from believing in Santa Claus?
2. Look at the use of lines like "rigorous statistical investigation," "an objective inquiry," "a conservative estimate," etc. What do these contribute to the tone of the essay? What is their purpose?

3. Do the scientific numbers and the mathematical analyses seem reliable to you?
4. Do they seem relevant?
5. Does Santa Claus exist? What is the problem when one offers a statistical analysis of love, beauty or religious or traditional beliefs?
6. Is this essay well-written? Why do you think so?

PART TWO

ARGUMENT

FOR ANALYSIS

Do not despise prophesying,
but test everything; hold fast
what is good.
—*St. Paul,* I Thessalonians

An all-electric home?
I think I'll pass!

It doesn't take a Vince Lombardi to figure out that buying an all-electric home is like running your fullback off tackle when it's third and 13. Neither of 'em makes any sense.

Get on the ball. Tackle the high cost of electricity with natural gas.

KnoWhatImean?

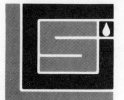

LOUISIANA GAS SERVICE COMPANY

LGS is an independent utility and not affiliated with any other utility.

Courtesy of the Louisiana Gas Service Company and of Carden & Cherry, Inc.

AN IMMODEST PROPOSAL—A LOTTERY
TO PAY OFF THE NATIONAL DEBT

Steven Womack

Geez, is there any good news anymore?

In the last few years, America has gone from being the biggest credi-
tor nation in the world to the biggest deadbeat. We're the only quote-
unquote civilized country in the world that doesn't have universal
health care for all its citizens. Nearly 20% of the children in this country
live below federal poverty guidelines, which were no great shakes to
begin with. The media reported a few weeks ago that we now spend
more on prisons in this country than we do on schools.

Depressing. As I see it, it's going to take two things to get us out of
this mess: leadership and money. The only problem is that our government hasn't got much of either.

Let me suggest an out, a solution, if you will. Our biggest problem
is the staggering national debt. At least that's what the experts tell us.
Nobody wants to pay a cent more in taxes. We don't trust the politicians
to spend it right. We've sold our grandchildren into indentured servi-
tude without even asking their permission. Here's how we get out:

The National Debt-Reduction Lottery Act of 1992. I propose a bill in
Congress that would establish a national lottery to be conducted by the
federal government in every state and territory. The proceeds from this
lottery will, by law, be used solely to retire the national debt. Anyone
attempting to slide money from the NDRL into the federal budget, as is
now done with the Social Security Trust Fund and the Airport fund, will
be exiled to Devil's Island.

When the national debt is completely paid off, which ought to take
about a decade, then the lottery is canceled. Unless, of course, the voters decide they like the lottery enough to keep it going and dedicate it
to some other use—say, education or funding the federal government,
for instance, thereby shutting down the IRS.

Wait, the states scream, you can't have a federal lottery. It will compete with our state lottery. Great, let the feds enact a federal tax on state
lottery proceeds and retire the national debt that way. It'll take a little
longer, but who's counting?

Wait, the fundamentalists scream, gambling is wrong. The government shouldn't condone it. Great, tax the churches. It's about time, anyway. Besides, nearly every state government is condoning gambling already. Maybe it's wrong, but people are doing it everywhere. At least
get some good out of it.

Wait, the promoters scream, there are too many lotteries already.
Who'd play a federal one? Good question. Here's how you make the
NDRL attractive:

SOURCE: Reprinted from *USA TODAY,* July 16, 1991. Reprinted by permission of the author.

- First, set a cap on the lottery prize—say $5 million or $10 million— and make the secondary prizes higher. That way, you don't win a hundred gazillion bucks if you get all six numbers but only $10 if you get four.
- Second, none of this business of paying off a little bit at a time for 20 years. You win 5 million smackers, then baboom, some suit shows up at your front door with television cameras blazing and hands you a check for the whole bazooka. Try not getting excited over that one (this also has the added advantage of incurring no long-term liabilities for the government; the last thing we want to do is cause more debt).
- Third, give everybody a one-time tax exemption on a prize. You hit a grand slam, you keep it all. Of course, anybody who goes on to win more than once ought to be glad to toke the dealer.

It's an outlandish proposal, I know, but stop and think about it for a second. Nobody wants to pay more taxes. The situation is desperate. Think of the lottery as a voluntary tax that gives you the chance to get something back from the government, which is more than most of us can say nowadays. Unless you're counting headaches.

In fact, the only reason I can think of for not passing the National Debt-Reduction Lottery Act of 1992 is that it makes too much sense. And we all know how politicians avoid that.

So there it is. I was glad to provide the leadership. Thank heavens I don't have to provide the other part.

GIVE HOTEL GUESTS
A BIBLE-FREE ROOM

Annie Laurie Gaylor

February 14, 1989

Kenneth F. Hine, Executive Vice President
American Hotel & Motel Association
888 7th Ave.
New York, NY 10106

Dear Mr. Hine:

We urge your Association to inaugurate a simple and much-needed reform. Just as the better establishments now offer smoke-free rooms, our association of freethinkers is requesting "bible-free" rooms.

Currently, a missionary organization with a poor track record of respecting state/church separation uses your member establishments to proselytize a captive audience. We believe it is time that the lodging industry "just say NO" to the Gideons. The Gideons glorify a bible character who is a villain and mass murderer (see enclosed "Gideon Exposed!" bible sticker).

Twenty million Americans are free from religion, and millions more follow other faiths. Many atheists and agnostics are deeply offended that they are paying high fees in order to be proselytized in the privacy of their own bedrooms! Fanatics who must read the bible every day will surely take precautions to travel with their own bibles. The rest of us deserve a break from mindless evangelizing when we are on vacation.

If hoteliers wish to serve customers in possible crisis, it would be far more useful to compile a list of local secular resource numbers: the police, battered woman's shelter, Red Cross, mental health hotline, nearby hospitals, etc. In fact, the bible itself offers not just gruesome bedtime reading (blood is splashed on nearly every page), but potentially violence-inciting and lethal advice. Murderers, child molesters, rapists, sexists, racists and even slaveholders have turned to bible verses to justify crimes. Jesus promotes self-mutilation, the terrifying myth of hell, and the dangerous, primitive belief that sickness results from "demons." The bible also offends by its often pornographic and bloodthirsty language. Why align your association with this image, and insult customers of other faiths, or no faith?

Sincerely,

Annie Laurie Gaylor
FREEDOM FROM RELIGION, Inc.
P.O. Box 750
Madison, WI 53701

When you give blood
you give another birthday,
another anniversary,
another day at the beach,
another night under the stars,
another talk with a friend,
another laugh,
another hug,
another chance.

American Red Cross

Please give blood.

Courtesy of the American Red Cross.

PURIFY YOUR
LANGUAGE!

Douglas G. Peitz

How important to God is the proper use of language?

It is so important that in His coming Kingdom He wants a pure language!

"For then I will restore to the people a pure language, that they all may call on the name of the Lord, to serve Him with one accord," says Zephaniah 3:9, looking ahead to the Millennium.

This language will need to be taught in the world tomorrow, and its rules and principles upheld. As corulers with Christ (Revelation 20:6), part of our job will be to teach and uphold the pure language.

Do you realize that God wants us to prepare now to teach the pure language in the world tomorrow? There are steps we can and should take so we can be ready.

But before we see what those steps are, let's consider some of the qualities of pure language.

QUALITIES OF PURE LANGUAGE

The foundation of pure language is God's Third Commandment: "You shall not take the name of the Lord your God in vain, for the Lord will not hold him guiltless who takes His name in vain" (Exodus 20:7).

This command covers more than most people realize. Not only does it prohibit direct misuse of God's name, but also the indirect misuse through euphemisms and other terms of vulgarity and disrespect that dishonor both God and man, such as racial slurs and obscenities.

As Paul said: "Let no corrupt communication proceed out of your mouth, but what is good for necessary edification, that it may impart grace to the hearers" (Ephesians 4:29).

Also eliminated from the pure language of the world tomorrow will be terms of pagan origin, which often encourage pagan concepts and thoughts. Languages today are filled with these expressions, reflecting the nearly 6,000 years of man's rejection of God and his worship of false gods.

We can also look for words describing evil to drop from the pure language. Words drop out of use because they are no longer needed or because their meaning has been forgotten.

Imagine the words that will drop out of use in the world tomorrow—words such as *war*, *divorce* and *rape*.

This will not be completely accomplished, unfortunately, until after the Great White Throne Judgment period when we are all in God's Family and sin has ceased.

SOURCE: Reprinted from *Good News*, March–April, 1989. Reprinted by permission of the Worldwide Church of God.

LANGUAGE IN THE WORLD TOMORROW

There is yet much more! The pure language will not be contradictory nor ambiguous. Gone will be the many cases of misunderstanding and confusion that arise today from multiple and conflicting usages of words.

Words such as *bad* to describe excellence and *free love* for fornication all have misleading connotations that pervert our understanding of good and evil. This will not be the case in the world tomorrow.

As Isaiah said, "Woe to those who call evil good, and good evil" (Isaiah 5:20). Words will describe accurately and precisely all objects and concepts.

Also, the rules for grammar, spelling and pronunciation will be consistent. God is consistent. He does things decently and in order (I Corinthians 14:40). The pure language of the world tomorrow will reflect God's character.

For example, in the English language today there are at least six different ways to pronounce *ough*, as illustrated by the following words: *through, though, ought, bough, rough,* and *cough.* We can assume such inconsistencies will not exist in the pure language.

The pure language will also be comprehensive. Today all languages limit our range and depth of expression. Even Paul expressed his frustration over sometimes not being able to describe how he felt (Romans 8:26). Because limitations vary from language to language, translation is difficult. The many different translations of the Bible make this obvious.

Language conveys understanding. God has infinite understanding (Psalm 147:5), and He desires to impart understanding to mankind (Proverbs 2:6). He also wants people to communicate clearly and completely to Him and to each other.

Therefore, the pure language will be comprehensive. There will be no more "joy inexpressible" (I Peter 1:8). All thoughts will be expressible.

Finally, the pure language will be perfectly expandable. It will be a living language, and living languages grow. For instance, *The Random House Dictionary of the English Language,* second edition, unabridged, added 50,000 new words just 21 years after its first edition.

But unless a language expands perfectly, it loses its purity. *A Dictionary of Modern English Usage,* second edition, by H. W. Fowler, states: "The [English] language has not been neatly constructed by a master builder who could create each part to do the exact work required of it, neither overlapped nor overlapping; far from that, its parts have had to grow as they could" (page 625).

God's government and way of life will never cease to grow, and God, the master builder, will require the pure language to expand infinitely without losing its purity.

But all of this will be futile unless the rules are upheld. God needs individuals who respect language and who will diligently teach and uphold the pure language. So what should we be doing now as Christians to prepare to uphold and teach the coming pure language? There is much we can do!

STEPS TO TAKE NOW

- *Obey the Third Commandment.* It is essential that we learn to use language now the way God expects. And we must begin by using God's name reverently.

  Some people would never directly use God's name in vain, but many carelessly do so by the use of euphemisms. A euphemism in this respect is any expression used as a substitute for the name of God or Jesus Christ.

  For example, *gee* and *gee-whiz* are used as euphemisms for Jesus, and *golly, gosh* and *goldarnit* are used for God. These and similar terms violate the Third Commandment and must not be used by Christians.

  A Christian should also eschew racial slurs and obscenities. Disrespectful and foul language causes strife and animosity, tearing down society. Christ said, "For out of the abundance of the heart the mouth speaks" (Matthew 12:34). God wants language to be a tool to edify and unify the world.

- *Respect the rules of language.* Although no language is pure today, all have rules that should be respected. We should use proper grammar and pronunciation, and educate ourselves to overcome our shortcomings. We must show God now that we respect language and will use it properly.

- *Let your yes be yes and your no be no.* God wants us to say what we mean and mean what we say (Matthew 5:37). Lying and deceiving are misuses of language that God condemns.

  The Ninth Commandment states, "You shall not bear false witness against your neighbor" (Exodus 20:16).

  Language is a gift from God and a tool. It should not be used for evil.

THE POSITIVE EFFECTS

In Genesis 11 the people were united under one language, and it enabled them to accomplish tremendous things:

"And the Lord said, 'Indeed the people are one and they all have one language, and this is what they begin to do; now nothing that they propose to do will be withheld from them" (verse 6).

Language is powerful! But God realized that human beings influenced by Satan would follow evil purposes, so He confused their language.

"Come, let Us go down and there confuse their language, that they may not understand one another's speech" (verse 7).

God wants language to be used properly.

How different will be the world tomorrow! Satan will be bound, Christ will rule and we will be motivated by God's spirit. God can then unleash the power of the pure language with marvelous results. Magnificent works will be accomplished as talents are combined and used for the good of all.

Foul language will be unknown. God's name will not be taken in vain, but always referred to with the utmost respect. Never again will we wince at a racial epithet or a dirty joke. Language will be used to edify.

And imagine how satisfying it will be to express ourselves fully. As Solomon said, "A word fitly spoken is like apples of gold in settings of silver" (Proverbs 25:11).

It will be tremendously gratifying to be able to express godly thoughts perfectly.

Then, nothing will be withheld from man, for not only will we have a pure language, but we will have pure hearts as well.

Let's prepare now to become stewards and teachers of the pure language!

LOWER THE
CAPITAL GAINS TAX

Richard W. Rahn

The capital gains tax—what you pay on the difference between the price you paid for a corporate stock, farm, small business, family home, and the price you sold it for—is an important tax. Because taxpayers are very sensitive to its rate, it can directly and broadly affect the economy. Indeed, high rates dramatically reduce investment in new ventures, diminish international competitiveness, impede technological innovation and actually reduce federal tax revenues.

In the Tax Reform Act of 1986, Congress raised the top rate for capital gains from 20 percent to 33 percent—a 65 percent increase. That proved to be a mistake. The United States has the highest long-term capital gains tax rate of any major industrialized country. Now, many entrepreneurs and small businesses are unable to raise needed capital. Investors are unwilling to take the large risk of investing in unproved technology or new business if they know that the government will take one-third of the profit.

The capital gains tax also can have a devastating impact on homeowners, small-business owners, farmers or ranchers whose property has been held for a long period. Often inflation will have caused the price to double or triple over a decade or two. Yet, after adjusting for inflation, the homeowner or business owner may have only a modest gain or an actual loss. Taxing purely inflationary gains is both unfair and counterproductive.

Perhaps the most misunderstood aspect of the debate is that our present high rate not only harms economic growth, but also undoubtedly costs the federal government revenue. For instance, during the 1970s, Congress increased the capital gains tax from a maximum of 25 percent to 49 percent. The result? No new tax revenues, stagnation in the economy and the stock market, and a decline in new ventures leading to a loss of competitiveness and jobs.

In 1978, the maximum rate was reduced from 49 percent to 28 percent. Although the rate was almost cut in half, tax revenues from the capital gains tax went up. Why? Quite simply, taxpayers were more willing to sell capital assets at a profit because the tax penalty for doing so was lower. In fact, they sold so many more assets that, even at the lower tax rate, the government came out ahead. In 1981, Congress cut the capital gains tax rate from 28 percent to 20 percent. Again, tax revenues increased.

Research by economists, notably Assistant Secretary of the Treasury Michael Darby and Harvard Professor Lawrence Lindsey, shows that the present 33 percent capital gains tax rate is substantially above the rate

SOURCE: Reprinted from the *Sacramento Bee Final*, February 14, 1989. Reprinted by permission of the author.

that would maximize the federal government's take. In fact, Lindsey's research indicates that 15 percent would be about right.

The predictable crowd of high-tax politicians, economists and media pundits already is claiming that President Bush's proposals to cut the capital gains tax will reduce revenues. But, remember, these are the same people who told you that the 1978 capital gains tax would lose revenue—in fact, the congressional tax staff predicted the rate cut would cost the Treasury $1.8 billion in 1979 and $1.9 billion in 1980. In fact, the government collected an extra $2.6 billion in 1979 and $3.4 billion in 1980.

This is also the same high-tax crowd who said the 1981 tax rate cuts would cut revenues and increase inflation, and that we couldn't possibly have the long and strong economic recovery we have had.

Opponents scream that lowering the rates will benefit the rich—and that's true. What is also true is that lower rates benefit everyone who owns a home, a farm, a small business, corporate stock, or who wants a job or wishes to start a business.

Bush is right when he says that a lower capital gains tax will bring in more revenue and lead to increased competitiveness, more jobs and more economic growth. He understands that to most Americans, fairness does not mean punishing success but creating more opportunity—and a lower capital gains tax would do just that.

Jerusalem is cherished by Jews, Christians and Muslims. And kept open to all by Israel.

Jerusalem, Israel's capital, is one of the most beautiful, inspirational cities in the world.

Fully one-half of the world's population—Jews, Christians and Muslims—regard it as one of the most sacred places on earth. More than a million people visit the city's Holy Places every year.

The ancient city has always been the spiritual and political center of the Jewish people. King David established it as the capital of his kingdom 3,000 years ago, and Jews have lived there ever since. Today, it is the capital of the modern state of Israel.

Jews the world over journey to the Old City's Western Wall, Judaism's holiest place, and Jerusalem has been the subject of Jewish prayers for centuries.

Christians visit Jerusalem to trace the steps Jesus walked to his crucifixion and to see the Church of the Holy Sepulchre, believed to be the site where Christ's body was laid to rest.

Muslims travel to the Dome of the Rock—the third holiest place in the Islamic faith—where the Prophet Mohammed made his ascent to heaven.

But only recently has Jerusalem been open to all who cherish it.

When Jordan controlled the Old City from 1948 to 1967, Jews from around the world were not permitted to enter East Jerusalem, or pray at the Western Wall. Synagogues in the Old City were desecrated. And Christian and Muslim citizens of Israel were denied free access to the Holy Places.

Israel reunited the city in June, 1967, reopened the Holy Places to all religions, and guaranteed freedom of access and worship.

Jerusalem has been profoundly important to Jews, Christians and Muslims for thousands of years. But only since Jerusalem became the united capital of Israel have its Holy Places been open to people of all faiths.

Israel
4,000 years of civilization

America-Israel Friendship League
134 East 39th Street, New York, NY 10016
Tele. (212) 213-8630

Courtesy of the America–Israel Friendship League.

COLLEGE FOOTBALL
DOESN'T NEED A PLAYOFF

Paul Hemphill

Every time the debate flares up about college football rankings, I recall 1957.

Ohio State had led Auburn in The Associated Press poll of writers all year, but with one game to go, Auburn discovered that hundreds of small newspapers and radio stations in the Deep South weren't aware of their right to vote.

"Lay low until we clobber Alabama," they were advised.

The Buckeyes never knew what hit them. An avalanche of votes poured in, and Auburn became the "undisputed" national champ although Woody Hayes did win the less-prestigious United Press poll of coaches.

The AP has since changed its polling system, limiting it to a select group of writers and broadcasters. It's still foolish to think that there could ever be a completely accurate and unbiased poll to determine the best team in the USA, but the alternative—a series of playoff games and the bowls—is downright ludicrous.

College games are greatly swayed by emotion. While these bionic behemoths aren't exactly "student-athletes," they're still teenagers who can be stirred to great highs (or lows) by such factors as fan support, evangelistic coaches, a Dear John letter or a lousy pre-game meal.

So even if we were to have a dream playoff, leading to a single contest to determine a champion, the only issue settled would be that on that given day, one of the two was the better team.

Who in his right mind could say, for instance, that Virginia was superior to Notre Dame, even if Virginia were to win head to head? Virginia is a basketball school, playing the likes of Kansas and Duke, while Notre Dame, loaded with pro draft material, goes up every Saturday against the other football factories.

In spite of the flaws in the polling system, it's the lesser of two imperfect ways to determine a national champion. Better to leave it to the judgment of several hundred writers and broadcasters, however biased their vote might be now and then, than to rely on the results of a single head-to-head match.

Anyone who believes in playoffs must be prepared to say that Stanford, 3–6 and outscored 16–83 in back-to-back games with Oregon and Washington, is superior to Notre Dame because Stanford happened to win when everything came together in one impassioned, 60-minute burst this year.

SOURCE: Reprinted from *USA Today*, November 9, 1990. Reprinted by permission of the author.

REDEEMING THE
VIETNAM WAR

Jud Blakely

Only fifteen years ago, we lost a war. We lost it to an army that had lost to us—to an army we had beaten in the field. But by 1970, the battlefield meant less and less. It was no longer a decisive venue. Even so, the war dragged on for a half-decade more.

Beaten but not broken, North Vietnam kept fighting. It was all they had to do. Americans at home did the rest. We lost to our culture, not their army . . . and we had lost by 1970.

The war was lost to the carnage of the first great Tet offensive—lost at home the same moment we won in the field. Viet Cong and North Vietnamese troops died in droves. It was a crushing, smashing defeat. In military terms, Tet proved to be a catastrophe for them.

But in political terms, Tet was a catastrophe for us. We won the battle yet we lost the war. What we lost was our will at home. We saw more and more gray, less and less black-and-white.

Americans do not fight well or long lacking the broad fire of a crusade. But in Vietnam, our crusade was a fire reduced to embers that slowly turned to ash. We fought on in a dank haze of futility. We killed them, they killed us. Tet was the straw that broke our cultural back. We gave in . . and then we gave up. We just gave up.

Both the purpose and justice of our mission had expired. Stripped of its unifying moral focus, the crusade itself came to expire. We abandoned it. It was over as soon as we began to lose faith in why we were there. The war itself came to an abject end in 1975.

Vietnam has been a personal and a national passage unique in American history. But a passage to what? And from what? The travail is plain. The journey is not. Nor, perhaps, can it ever be. Even so, the questions endure. They tease and torment two generations.

No more than a haunting loose end for some, for others Vietnam has become a wounding obsession. Time in passing has driven it deeper. But time in passing has also revised the glib verdict that the war was "a bright shining lie." It has made more clear the truth of those years—of what was at stake, of why we fought. Time has also made clear much else that divided us then at home. And why.

Our divisions were ferocious. By 1970, the war there had split us into a war here. But the war at home was over more than the war abroad. It was over the aspirations and hostilities in American society—a war of us versus us. Here at home, Pandora's box exploded.

Social issues here had taken on the anger of the times. The country burned with acrimony. We were exhausted and perplexed. The war in Vietnam had sapped our desire for decent disagreement. As a result, our political wars turned into acrid brawls. We flayed each other.

SOURCE: Reprinted in revised form from *Gray Matters*, February 1989. Reprinted courtesy of the author.

In the midst of this melee were the veterans of Vietnam. We were back. I, too, was back, after 13 months as a Marine infantry officer . . . with two wounds and a medal for valor. Unlike some of my comrades, I felt then—as I feel now—no stigma for having gone.

In Washington in 1982, a memorial was raised in behalf of those who served. The project was a lightning rod. It drew in all our fierce ambivalence. When done, this memorial would loom as a solemn ledger of the cost of folly—of those killed by "a bright shining lie."

For years, nothing has so defined the war as has this overwhelming wall. It seems to throb with a life force. This tally in stone is absorbing, disturbing . . . and it does not lack a message. It renders a verdict. The verdict it renders is on the war itself.

Grotesquely serene, the wall is not mute on the value of all that death. It invades us with searing implications—we fought in vain, we died in vain. The wall lets us infer how full of folly was the war. It seeks to win us over to a political view. It seeks to illuminate our grief, then capitalize on it.

This wall reflects the aim of those who built it. They built it as a fable in stone. Their aim was to apprise us of anguish—to offer us the human sum of an unjust war . . . and then to wield our anger in behalf of other political goals. The wall, in short, is propaganda. It seeks to mobilize the emotions of all who feel hurt by Vietnam.

For at least a few of us, the verdict in the wall was vulnerable to time. And time has now passed. For us, the wall was never more than an ugly blemish—a blank, black roll call that implied dark motives, lives wasted, and much disgrace. But time in passing has begun to evoke more and more of the truth. Time has undone the wall's political aim.

We few perceived the wall as a vast scoreboard of sacrifice. We saw it as an arch symbol of failure at odds with what we did and why we went to Vietnam. We saw it as a lie.

We saw Vietnam as a logical tragedy. We saw it as the culmination of our will to deter communism. We did not see it as a wanton, immoral, stupid act of aggression. Nor did we see it as futile.

Though we failed in our effort, we did not fail in terms of who and what we fought. We fought communists in Vietnam, and we fought them to thwart both subversion and invasion. To us, it was right to do so. Was it smart to do so? Only time will tell. But wrong to do so? No.

And time has begun to tell. History since 1975 has overtaken the wall. It has lessened the lie of dark motives, lives wasted, and much disgrace. It has begun to strip the wall of hapless despair.

What time has done is to move the message of the wall from guilt and shame to more of the truth. As it moves, the wall is less and less an affront . . . and the dead are more and more redeemed.

Vietnam was a tragedy. It consumed lives and it crippled lives. But another tragedy was the aim of the left to fix on us a false sense of guilt and shame. This was the context of the Vietnam Memorial. Now time and truth have redeemed the wall.

Reprinted from the *Mobile Press*, March 19, 1990. Reprinted by permission of the author.

FOR A BETTER LIFE,
DON'T EAT ANY BEEF

Dean Ornish

I grew up in Texas chewing on cheeseburgers, chiles and chalupas. Although I like the taste of red meat, I don't eat it anymore. Ever.

Why not? I don't believe in giving up anything I enjoy unless it's to get something even better. I stopped eating meat at age 19 because I felt so much better when I did.

Let's examine just a few of the latest studies:

- My colleagues and I recently found that even severely blocked coronary arteries began to unclog in the majority of heart patients when they stopped eating animal products and made other simple lifestyle changes. Most patients reported dramatic reductions in chest pain after only a few days to weeks after changing their diets.

- Last week, the largest study of diet and colon cancer ever conducted found the more red meat and animal fat women ate, the more likely they were to get colon cancer. Those who ate red meat as a main course every day were *two and a half times* more likely to get cancer than those who ate meat sparingly or not at all. According to the study director, Harvard's Dr. Walter Willett, "The optimum amount of red meat you eat should be zero."

- Earlier this year, a landmark study of 6,500 people by Dr. T. Colin Campbell of Cornell found that the more meat they ate, the more likely they were to die prematurely from coronary heart disease, colon cancer, breast cancer, prostate cancer and lung cancer, among others. "We're basically a vegetarian species. . . . The higher the intake of animal products, the higher the risk of cancer and heart disease," Campbell wrote.

- Many athletes are forgoing the pregame steak for foods high in complex carbohydrates because they find that eating less meat often increases their endurance.

- Some beef is lower in fat than before, but it is still very high in fat. And cholesterol. Studies also indicate that meat protein and perhaps other substances in beef raise the risk of cancer and heart disease.

- Eating meat makes you fat. Most people who consume a low-fat vegetarian or near-vegetarian diet are able to eat a greater amount of food and still lose weight! So there is a sense of abundance rather than deprivation.

When we understand how our diet affects our health and how we feel—for better and for worse—then it becomes easier to make more intelligent choices. These choices are based not out of fear of dying but for the joy of living more fully. Meat. Real food for real death.

SOURCE: Reprinted from *USA Today*, December 18, 1990. Reprinted by permission of the author.

THE RIGHT
TO DIE

Robert Hohler

Dear Friend:

Rudy Linares rushed his infant son, Samuel, into the emergency room of a Chicago hospital. The baby had swallowed a balloon and had stopped breathing.

Despite speedy removal of the blockage and the intensive care he received, Samuel remained in a coma, unable to breathe without the aid of a respirator. Lack of oxygen had caused brain damage, leaving the little baby irreversibly comatose.

The doctors broke the news to Rudy and his family. Samuel had no hope for recovery.

So the baby lay in a hospital room, kept alive by the respirator. Days and weeks passed as the Linares family kept sad watch over the child's body.

Finally, unable to bear the grief any longer, Rudy pleaded with the hospital to disconnect the machinery and permit his son to die a natural death. The hospital refused.

They would not permit Rudy to exercise a crucial right; the right to determine treatment for a loved one.

In effect, they told him: We're in charge here. If you want to change it, find a lawyer and get a court order.

The hospital was wrong. There was plenty of law on Rudy's side.

But Rudy, like so many Americans, didn't know his rights. This young laborer was overwhelmed by his grief and stymied by a hospital bureaucracy.

He only knew that his son was dying and that a machine wouldn't let him go.

After nine months, Rudy took the law into his own hands.

One day he appeared at the hospital armed with a pistol. Holding off the staff, he disconnected his son's respirator, then cradled the child in his arms until he died.

"I did it because I love my son," he said.

Rudy was arrested, jailed and charged with murder.

There was a widespread outpouring of support for Rudy Linares. He was immediately bailed out by friends and neighbors. He and his family received calls and letters of sympathy and encouragement from all over the country.

A few weeks later, a Cook County grand jury heard the case and refused to indict him.

While you and I may not have condoned his actions, we certainly can relate to Rudy's agony and frustration.

Courtesy of the author and the Society for the Right to Die.

You know as well as I do that *any of us at any time could be involved in a similar tragedy.*

The Society for the Right to Die has been fighting these monstrous abuses of medical technology . . . where a family is forced to stand by helplessly as a loved one is connected to a machine that does nothing more than prolong dying.

Here are some of our recent cases involving people who could be maintained artifically for many years:

- Paul Brophy, a 49-year-old fireman who lay permanently unconscious in a hospital bed for 3½ years with no hope of recovery. His wife, a nurse, pursued the long and arduous battle in the courts that finally won his release from futile treatment.
- Daniel Delio, 33, also persistently vegetative (as a result of negligence during routine surgery), whose wife and mother fought and won the right to terminate treatment that extended his dying for more than a year.
- Mary O'Connor, a 77-year-old New York woman, minimally conscious after a series of disabling strokes, and kept alive by tube feeding. Sure they knew what their mother would want, her two daughters appealed to the court to withdraw treatment. The court refused permission, because Mary O'Connor had not made her own wishes clear or put them in writing.
- Nancy Beth Cruzan, a 32-year-old Missouri woman, permanently unconscious for seven years. Doctors say she could continue in a vegetative state for the next 30 years! In a 5–4 decision the U.S. Supreme Court rejected her family's appeal to end the prolongation of her dying.

There are thousands of cases like these in the United States today. And the number grows every year.

Is there anything you can do to protect yourself and your loved ones from situations like this? The answer is **yes.**

In many cases patients are held captive to unwanted treatment **because they have not put their wishes in writing.**

The solution is to make out a document called a Living Will that allows you to describe the kind of treatment you do and do not want.

By filling out a Living Will appropriate for your state, you can protect, in advance, the right to choose your own treatment. For added protection, you can also delegate that choice to someone who knows you well and whose judgment you trust.

The Living Will can speak for you, *even if you cannot speak for yourself.*

You can give this document to your doctor, lawyer, clergyperson and to as many family members and friends as you wish.

Forty states now have statutes recognizing the Living Will as a valid expression of your desires for final care and treatment. Other states have court made law that encourages their use.

You and your family can be spared needless pain, indignity and distress. I urge you to take this simple precaution—make out your Living Will.

To get a form that is legally authorized in your state, just fill out and return the enclosed Living Will order card to the Society for the Right to Die.

Do this for yourself and for your loved ones. Do it now.

SOCIETY FOR THE RIGHT TO DIE
250 West 57th Street
New York, NY 10107

Is it any wonder the prisons are full?

In the mid 1950's, researchers at the University of Pennsylvania began conducting what has become a landmark study.

Its purpose: to determine the effect violent toys have on our children.

What they found was rather disturbing. The researchers stated that violent toys cause children to become more violent.

At Dakin, we've always tried to produce toys that teach children some other things.

Toys that, rather than teach a child how to maim, would teach a child how to love.

That, rather than teach a child how to hurt, would teach a child how to care for something.

Toys that, rather than being designed to be played with in only one way, would challenge the child's imagination to use them in a variety of ways.

You see, as parents ourselves, we at Dakin don't design toys solely on the basis of whether or not they'll make money.

We design them on the basis of whether we'd want our children playing with them.

Gifts you can feel good about.

DAKIN

© 1991 DAKIN, Inc. Available at fine gift and toy shops everywhere.

Courtesy of Dakin, Inc.

THE WHOLE
SCOOP ON COFFEE

We Americans like coffee. But as the estimated 100 million of us sip, on average, some three-and-a-half cups daily, odds are that our morning paper will have some story either confirming or refuting the ill effects of coffee on our health. So, we try to quit, but get dreadful withdrawal headaches (researchers at Johns Hopkins recently reported that even those who drink only one strong cup each day may experience head- aches, fatigue, and other withdrawal symptoms if they stop). But what's the cure for headaches? Coffee (it's practically prescribed for migraines). Before we know it, we're back where we started, sipping a cup of the bad stuff as we read more bad news in the morning paper. Here, we put the whole coffee and caffeine story—which includes tea, cola, chocolate, and certain medications—into perspective.

COFFEE AND HEART DISEASE

The final word *may* finally be in on this one. The latest study, from Harvard last fall, of over 45,000 men between 40 and 75 years old, found not a whit of evidence connecting coffee consumption with stroke or heart disease—even among those men who drank six or more cups a day. Nor was there a connection for tea drinkers, although it's harder to draw a valid conclusion since there were only 664 of them in the group.

While not a *cause* of heart disease, coffee may, in some people, be a marker of those at risk for heart disease for other reasons. A recent study in the *American Journal of Public Health* found that coffee drinkers are also more likely to drink more alcohol, eat more saturated fats and cholesterol, smoke, and be sedentary. In sum, the coffee drinkers were more likely to have a heart-unhealthy lifestyle. Those coffee drinkers who do, however, have a healthful diet and lifestyle seemed no more likely to develop heart disease than non-coffee drinkers. Earlier studies that found a connection between heart disease or elevated cholesterol levels and coffee drinking were too small or flawed because they did not take into account these other contributing risk factors. (The recent Har- vard study largely corrected for these factors.)

One caveat, however, based on a study last year from the Nether- lands: Drinking large amounts of boiled—also known as campfire—cof- fee (made by pouring boiling water directly onto the ground coffee; most common in Europe) does seem to raise cholesterol levels. How- ever, such coffee is rarely drunk in this country, especially at the levels found to increase risk—four to six cups a day.

What if you already have heart disease? Another recent study—of patients taking medication for angina experienced when exercising—ex- amined coffee's effects on their hearts, as measured by endurance on a

SOURCE: Reprinted by permission from the *Johns Hopkins Medical Letter, Health After 50,* March 1991.

treadmill. The researchers found that even three cups of coffee did not affect the intensity of the angina, the heart's function, or the length of time that the subjects could exercise. However, there is some evidence that you should watch your caffeine intake if you have heart arrhythmias. While as yet the evidence is inconclusive, some animal studies have found that caffeine can cause ventricular tachycardia, which poses the risk of sudden cardiac death.

COFFEE AND CANCER

The American Cancer Society has not changed its 1984 statement that coffee does not increase cancer risk. Nonetheless, coffee drinking has been implicated in various studies as a risk factor for certain malignancies, in particular breast, colorectal, bladder, and pancreatic cancer. In all, the evidence is hardly compelling, although the same sort of flip-flop that has plagued research into coffee and heart disease has pervaded the coffee/cancer association. For example, a recent analysis of 24 studies on coffee and pancreatic cancer concluded that you're not putting yourself at risk by drinking coffee. Similarly inconclusive results have been reported on other cancers, including some that suggest caffeine actually protects against colorectal cancer.

COFFEE AND ULCERS

There's no evidence that coffee actually causes ulcers, but you're best off to avoid it if you have one, as it increases secretions of gastric acid and pepsin—just the ticket for aggravating an existing ulcer. In addition, coffee can cause heartburn and has a laxative effect that, in some people, may cause diarrhea.

COFFEE AND OSTEOPOROSIS

Caffeine hastens the excretion of calcium from the body, which could increase the risk for osteoporosis. In fact, one recent finding from the Framingham Study (the ongoing health review begun in 1948 of the residents of a Massachusetts town) is that persons over 50 who drank more than two cups of coffee or four cups of tea a day increased their risk of hip fracture due to osteoporosis by over 50%. However, as with heart disease, it's not clear whether the caffeine itself was linked to the fractures, or if it was merely a marker for other behaviors, such as a sedentary lifestyle or low intake of dietary calcium, that also increase the risk of osteoporosis. Just to be safe, you can add some low-fat milk to your coffee to compensate for the relatively mild calcium loss.

THE BOTTOM LINE

About the worst thing that can be said conclusively about coffee at this time is that it keeps you awake—which, after all, is why most of us drink it. However, caffeine can increase the number of times you wake during the night, and generally disturb sleep—especially as you age. For this reason, many older people have switched to decaf—and about the worst thing that can be said about *it* at this time is that it *doesn't* keep you awake.

DISABLED VETERANS
CAN'T AFFORD GRAVES

Hal Pierce

To the Editor:

I don't think anyone inside the Washington "Beltline" really gives a damn about the federal deficit. They increase their own salaries and hack away at the veterans. One amazing thing they did was stop paying for veteran grave headstones. This means that:

- For a study of Waikiki Beach sand, 1,176 veterans will have to go to unmarked graves.
- For a study of soybean-based ink, another 1,176 will go.
- For a tribute to Lawrence Welk, who still lives, 5,880 veterans will go.
- For a study of bicycling and walking, more than 10,000 veterans will go.

The unmarked graves of 335,294 veterans will pay for congressional and staff salary increases.

This is all O.K., though, because disabled American Veterans were denied the 5.4 percent cost-of-living increase that everybody else got and can't afford the graves anyway.

SOURCE: Letter to the *Mobile Register*, March 12, 1991. Reprinted by permission of the author.

Reprinted from the *Mobile Register*, October 5, 1990. Reprinted by permission of the author.

SLOW DOWN ON FREE
TRADE WITH MEXICO

Lane Kirkland
President, AFL/CIO

While the proposed U.S.–Mexico free-trade agreement would be a dream come true for corporate mercenaries seeking cheap, exploitable labor, it would be a nightmare for workers on both sides of the border.

Proof lies in our experience with the *maquiladora* program, a miniature version of a free-trade agreement that currently enables U.S. firms to set up factories on the Mexican side of the border and export back to the USA with minimal duty charges.

During the 1980s, thousands of Americans lost manufacturing jobs as their employers fled south to escape U.S. safety and environmental regulations and to pay wages ranging from 55 cents to $1 an hour.

And while *maquiladora* workers toil in unsafe conditions and live in cardboard slums amid the waste and pollution of their employers, proponents of the free-trade agreement argue that these jobs are better than no jobs at all.

A few years ago, an article in the pro-*maquiladora* magazine *Twin Plant News* advised U.S. parent companies that they could "keep [their] minimum wage people at the minimum wage" by collecting donated clothing and blankets for their Mexican employees because "many of [their] houses are poorly heated, if heated at all, and warm clothing and blankets feel good on those cold nights."

If these jobs are so good for these Mexican workers, then why do they need handouts to survive?

And to those who tout the market of 88 million that a free-trade agreement will open to U.S. producers—what do they propose we sell to people who earn $25 for a 48-hour week, or to those who have lost their jobs in the USA?

The problems of poverty and economic development in both the USA and Mexico are too serious to be left solely to the interests of private capital. The liberalization of trade is good for workers on both sides of the border only when it is carried out side by side with minimum standards on wages, benefits, safety and the environment.

Lacking this dimension, as the proposed trade agreement now does, workers in our two countries will compete solely on the basis of wages. For U.S. workers, that means lower pay, lost jobs and a declining standard of living. For their Mexican counterparts, it means a future of making products they cannot dream of buying for a market to the north that can no longer pay for them.

SOURCE: Reprinted from *USA Today*, December 10, 1990. Reprinted by permission of the author.

DRUG ABUSERS KILLING SELVES,
SO SOCIETY SHOULD LET THEM

Mike Royko

Slats Grobnik pointed at the bottle of 86-proof skull popper on the back bar and asked: "What would happen if I drank that whole fifth down, just chug-a-lugged it?"

You aren't planning to do it, are you? It would ruin our evening.

"I'm just asking. What would happen?"

You would quickly lapse into unconsciousness, your vital signs would stop blipping and become a steady hum, and your wife would become a weeping widow, until she collected the insurance and moved to a warmer climate.

"In other words, I'd croak."

Something like that.

"I figured. And at my funeral, would you get up and say a few words?"

If asked.

"What would you say?"

With a tear in my eye and a tremor in my voice, I would describe you as a fine friend, a loving father, a doting husband, a hard worker, a solid citizen, and, at the end, a complete idiot.

"Fair enough."

But what is the purpose of this line of questioning?

"Drugs. I think I've read everything about the war on drugs. I've watched all these serious gab shows with the experts on TV. I heard the pitch to legalize and the pitch not to legalize. To spend more money. To go after the peddlers, to go after the users, to put the heat on the foreign producers, poison the drugs.

"I've heard that we got to bring in the military, spend more money to hire more narcs and build more prisons. Or use old Army camps for rehab centers, search high school lockers and frisk our own kids."

Yes, there are almost as many proposed solutions as there are dope-heads. And what is your conclusion?

"Nothin'. I think we ought to do just what we're doing now."

But what we're doing now isn't solving the problem.

"Right. But who says we got to solve the problem?"

Everybody. You've read and listened. Drugs are a menace to our young people. They are eroding our society, attacking our moral fiber. They cause crime, as addicts steal to support their habits and drug gangs shoot it out for control of the markets. It is a terrible crisis.

"I don't believe it."

How can you say that? Aren't you aware of the crack dens in Washington and New York? The addicts littering the alleys of the slums?

"Sure, just like when I was a kid and my old man drove us up Skid

SOURCE: Reprinted by permission of Tribune Media Services. Reprinted from the *Mobile Press*, March 27, 1990.

Row and there were all the winos sitting on the curb drinking muscatel and making their livers big as watermelons. But President Roosevelt didn't say we needed a federal Wino Czar."

So you would just ignore the problem? I can't believe that you are so heartless.

"I got a heart. Call my doc, he'll tell you. But I don't see why it's my job to worry about everybody in this country who wants to sniff and snort, shoot up, smoke up and stick needles in their arms. If they're stupid enough to whack themselves out that way, let 'em."

But many of them are killing themselves. Have you no pity?

"Hey, a friend of mine just came down with cancer. He didn't do anything to get it. Lived clean, ate right. It happens that the docs got it in time and he's OK. Now, I worried about him, but I'm not going to lose any sleep over some goof who shoves a dirty needle in his own arm."

So you would just abandon the war and have society look the other way?

"Nah, I'd keep doing what we're doing now. If the narcs can catch some of the pushers, let 'em do it. It gives the narcs something to do and some of the bums go to prison. So we provide jobs for narcs, prison guards and the TV crews that take pictures of the haul."

But what about the user, the person who is destroying his life and bringing grief to loved ones?

"That's why I asked you about chug-a-lugging that bottle. Don't tell me a dopehead don't know what he's getting into. It's like the lush. One day a lush wakes up with the shakes and sees his wallpaper dancing. He decides that's it. He's going off the stuff. If he does, he makes it."

What if he doesn't?

"Then it's just a matter of time before he croaks. His choice. I'm not pouring the stuff down his throat, he is. It's his liver, not mine, so why do I have to worry about his liver? He don't worry about mine."

So you would just callously turn away from the drug crisis?

"Crisis. Everything's a crisis to newsies. You could put a big black headline on your paper every day that says: 'Thousands Died Yesterday.' And it would be true. Every day thousands of people die."

Of course. But it would be a false alarm, since people are constantly dying of natural causes.

"That's what I mean. Most people aren't lushes. Most people aren't crackheads. Most people aren't putting needles in their arms. Most people are going to die of old age or eating too much cholesterol. Hey, how come the president hasn't appointed a War on Getting Fat Czar?"

You're saying drugs aren't a crisis?

"For most people, nah. For somebody who wants to scramble his brain, yeah. But most people don't want to scramble their brains and they don't. And people who scramble their brains don't worry about the crisis, anyway, because their brains are already scrambled."

And you propose that we let them destroy themselves?

"If they're dumb enough to, yeah. Say, if I pay for that fifth back there, will you chug-a-lug it?"

Of course not. I'm no fool.

"See? We're making progress."

Courtesy of Revlon, Inc.

WHAT RIGHTS

FOR ANIMAL PROTECTION ACTIVISTS?

Heidi Prescott

"We think it's wrong to shoot animals for fun and oppose the fact that the state game agency manipulates wildlife populations to provide more living targets for hunters. Why can't you let these animals live in peace."

Those were some of the last words I uttered before being arrested in Maryland for "hunter harassment" last hunting season.

Not only was I arrested, but convicted on the "hunter harassment" charge and fined $500.

The District Court judge based his conviction of me principally on the testimony of arresting officers who charged I was talking to hunters and rustling leaves with my feet.

Appalled at the idea of being convicted for merely speaking my mind in an appropriate setting, I refused to pay the court-imposed fine. As a result, I write to you from the austere environs of a jail cell in Montgomery County, Md., where I am serving a 15-day sentence—the maximum the judge could have imposed.

Indeed, I am outspoken when it comes to the issue of protecting wildlife. And maybe I'm even a rustler of leaves—incidental though the rustling was.

But I make no apologies for such behavior. In fact, I remain convinced that my actions—especially when conducted at a public wildlife area, as they were—were appropriate and should have been protected by the First Amendment.

I did not physically strike, obstruct, yell at, or insult any of the hunters with whom I communicated, but simply exercised my right to voice my objections to sport hunting and to walk on public lands.

As a longtime wildlife rehabilitator who has seen the misery that hunters inflict on wildlife, I have many means of protesting hunting, such as general education, legislative initiatives, and lawsuits.

But just as a union activist would go to corporate headquarters to protest management policies, it is logical that anti-hunting activists would go to the hunting ground themselves to protest the recreational killing of wildlife.

Protesting at the site—where the hunters are concentrated, identified by their weapons and licenses, and carrying out their activity—serves an irreplaceable function in the efforts of animal activists to abolish sport hunting.

If hunters, whose behavior, ironically, results not only in the harassment, but also in the wounding and killing of wildlife, want absolute solitude and immunity from critical thoughts, they can seek hunting opportunities on private lands.

SOURCE: Reprinted from the *Mobile Register*, August 8, 1990. Reprinted by permission of the author.

But on public lands, hunters should not be afforded special insulation from people who also have a right to use those lands and interact peacefully with wildlife.

I do not deny that my presence might have inconvenienced the hunters and may have incidentally kept wildlife at a safe distance. Neither of those facts, however, seems a sufficient justification to deny my right to speak freely on public land.

Of course, there are limits to free speech. Walking on public lands and talking to hunters, however, is nothing like yelling "Fire!" in a crowded movie theater.

Innocent people are not endangered or put at risk when I talk to hunters on public lands. The fact is, hunting is not a fundamental right, but a privilege granted by the states.

Free speech though is a fundamental right—not something to be unthinkingly squelched when it serves powerful special interests, such as the National Rifle Association and the rest of the hunting lobby.

Ultimately, this issue will be resolved in the nation's highest courts. Already, Connecticut's "hunter harassment" law—the only one thus far challenged—was declared unconstitutional in a U.S. District Court and affirmed as unconstitutional in a U.S. Court of Appeals.

According to the majority of the Court of Appeals for the Second Circuit, "It (the statute) clearly is designed to protect hunters from conduct—verbal or otherwise—by those opposed to hunting. . . . There is no showing that protecting hunters from harassment constitutes a compelling state interest."

Obviously, in issuing their opinion, those judges were aware that trampling First Amendment liberties is a much more serious matter than trampling leaves.

ULCERATIVE COLITIS
IS ASSOCIATED WITH NON-SMOKING

Carol Thompson

About 90% of the victims of ulcerative colitis are non-smokers. In ex-smokers, onset is generally after quitting smoking. Smoking exerts a protective effect against the development of this disease and reduces its severity.

This is important, because the earlier the age at diagnosis, and the more the extent of disease, the greater the risk of developing colorectal cancer. The absolute risk is estimated at 30% to 40%, in 35 years after diagnosis. The actual number of colorectal cancer cases is lower, however, because of the large number of proctocolectomies and rectal amputations the disease compels.

Colorectal cancer risk is about equal in men and women. Women and men, respectively, also have 9.5 to 45.5 times greater risk of liver and gall-bladder cancer. Their overall cancer risk is about 1.8 times that of the general population.

In males, peak incidence is at ages 20–29 and 70–79, and in females, at 30–39 and 70–79. Annual age-adjusted incidence rates in 1973 were 5 to 6 per 100,000, or at least 12,000 to 15,000 new cases per year in 1990. With a greater proportion of non-smokers, it must be more than this. This is a several times greater threat to non-smokers than even the false claims of passive smoking lung cancer deaths that have caused such a stampede.

With a prevalence of 60 to 70 per 100,000, half of all disease onset by age 40, a large proportion of major surgeries, and repeated hospitalizations, this disease associated with non-smoking is surely a significant cause of medical expenses and lost work time.

For many people with ulcerative colitis, smoking could give them many years of disease-free living, or even save their lives. The cause of ulcerative colitis is unknown. Those diagnosed with it could represent just the tip of an iceberg of people at increased risk of colorectal and liver cancer.

The anti-smoking demagogues have concealed these facts from us. How many more are they hiding?

REFERENCES

Ritchie JK, Allan RN, Macartney J, Thompson H, Hawley PR, Cooke WT. Biliary track carcinoma associated with ulcerative colitis. Q J Med 1974; 170:263–79

Garland CF, Lilienfeld AM, Mendeloff AI, Markowitz JA, Terrell KB, Garland FC. Incidence rates of ulcerative colitis and Crohn's disease in fifteen areas of the United States. Gastroenterology 1981;81:1115–24.

SOURCE: Reprinted by permission of the author.

Prior P, Gyde SN, Macartney JC, Thompson H, Waterhouse JAH, Allan RN. Cancer morbidity in ulcerative colitis. Gut 1982; 23:490–7

Harries AD, Baird A, Rhodes J. Non-smoking: a feature of ulcerative colitis (letter). Br Med J 1982; 284:706

De Castella H. Non-smoking: a feature of ulcerative colitis (letter). Br Med J 1982;284:1706

Logan RFA, Edmond M, Somerville KW, Langman MJS. Smoking and ulcerative colitis. Br Med J 1984; 288:751–3

Benoni C, Nilsson A. Smoking habits in patients with inflammatory bowel disease. Scand J Gastroenterol 1984; 19:824–30

Motley RJ, Rhodes J, Ford GA, Wilkinson SP, Chesner IM, Asquith P, Hellier MD, Mayberry JF. Time relationships between cessation of smoking and onset of ulcerative colitis. Digestion 1987; 37:125–7

Ekbom A, Helmick C, Zack M, Adami H-A. Ulcerative colitis and colorectal cancer. N Engl J Med 1990; 323:1228–33

WHEN THEY TELL YOU THAT ABORTION IS A MATTER JUST BETWEEN A WOMAN AND HER DOCTOR

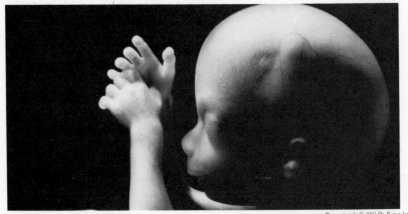

Photo copyright © 1982 Dr. Rainer Jonas

The incredible photograph above by Dr. Rainer Jonas shows what a healthy, active intrauterine child looks like at 19 weeks. Like the bud of a flower, beautiful. But, unfortunately still a candidate for elective abortion.

THEY'RE FORGETTING SOMEONE

Courtesy of Media: Right to Life of Michigan Educational Fund.

MISS AMERICA SWIMSUIT BAN
IS A STUPID IDEA!

Ed Anger

I'm madder than a bird-watcher with busted binoculars over the idiot who heads up the Miss America beauty pageant!

This nincompoop wants to ban the swimsuit competition, for crying out loud!

"I personally find it difficult to rationalize putting a young college woman in a swimsuit and high heel shoes," whined Leonard Horn, the pageant director who just outlawed photo sessions on the beach for these bathing beauties.

Well, excuuuuuuuse me! And not only that, but this mush-for-brains would like Miss America to be picked on how *smart* she is.

Well, there goes the whole damn pageant!

Let's face it, most pretty girls aren't smart and most ugly ones are. That's because plain Janes don't get asked out on dates so they have more time to study. It's that simple.

They don't practice putting on lipstick and makeup because they never go anywhere and it doesn't do any good anyway.

Start putting brains before beauty in the contest and Miss America will have a mug that will crack a mirror—and bowlegs to boot!

And they'll take the pageant off TV because who the hell is going to tune in to watch a bunch of corn-fed wallflowers parade around onstage? For the talent part of the competition, 90 percent of 'em will play the accordion and sing opera!

Great.

I got pig-biting mad when they dumped Miss America master of ceremonies Bert Parks, who always sang, "Here she comes . . . Miss America," on the show. But this has got the metal plate in my head—a little souvenir from the Korean War—hotter than a fire cracker.

Plain old common sense tells you that Miss America is supposed to be pretty. If I want to see ugly, I can invite my daughter-in-law Candy over anytime.

Keep these healthy young things in bathing suits or yours-truly has watched his last Miss America Pageant!

SOURCE: Reprinted by permission from *Weekly World News*, August 14, 1990.

A COMMENT ON "RHETORIC AND IDEOLOGY IN THE WRITING CLASS"

Ellen Quandahi

I was surprised that in his useful essay, "Rhetoric and Ideology in the Writing Class" (*CE*, September 1988), James Berlin fails to consider how rhetorics (his term for pedagogical practices and language about them) represent and thereby transform the theoretical material they draw on. Nor does he consider the extent to which two of the rhetorics he describes, the "cognitive" and the "social-epistemic," have been developed out of two interdisciplinary fields that are pre-occupied with the term *representation*. I'll call these fields the cognitive sciences and interpretive theory.

Broadly speaking, the cognitive sciences consider human cognition in terms of mental representation, asking how things get represented in the mind, whether mental representations are linguistic or non-linguistic, if representation and computation are distinct processes, and so on. Interpretive theorists, on the other hand, study discourses and show how they provide neither fully accurate nor nonideological representation. To the interpreters, linguistic representations are, in a sense, non-representations; language ideologizes rather than stands for, interprets rather than makes present. As far as I know, no one in composition has investigated similarities and differences in the tropes of representation in these two areas. And I think that while the term is inflected quite differently by cognitivists and interpreters, *representation* might serve as a metonymic hinge rather than a point of opposition between their fields. We begin to see such a positioning already in the "social-cognitive" study by Glynda Hull and Mike Ross, in which they ask, "How are [reading and writing strategies] represented in the students' minds, and what personal, social, and historical forces might have influenced these current representations?" (*Written Communication*, April 1989, 152).

Berlin's approach, however, presents the view that cognitive rhetoric, because it does not consider ideology (looking rather at structures of the mind, which correspond to structures of the world, language and audiences), and because it focuses on "the professional activity of experts" in "managerial terms" (481), is suited to appropriation by a university that trains students for corporate capitalism. On the other hand, he believes that social-epistemic rhetoric makes ideology the central issue of the composition classroom. And because it holds that arguments arise from ideology, not from truth, it *"inevitably* supports economic, social, political, and cultural democracy" (489, my emphasis).

Like Berlin, I favor pedagogies informed by interpretive theory and value ideological analysis (as I hope this letter shows), yet the following issues give me pause. To make the argument about cognitive rhetoric, Berlin uses only the work of Flower and Hayes, whom he represents as

SOURCE: Reprinted from *College English*, March 1990. Reprinted by permission of the author.

the leading experimentalists. Flower and Hayes become the representatives of cognitive psychology, and cognitive psychology the representative of the cognitive sciences. This synecdochic argument excludes both those cognitivists who hold that a science ignoring context and culture will lack validity (and I think Linda Flower's recent work would have to be included here), and those who no longer hold correspondence theories of the mind and world. Moreover, it precludes analyses of the language and culture of the cognitive sciences and of the ways in which elements of these have been selected, translated and translocated into the writing classroom by Flower and Hayes. It is disappointing that Berlin's argument is structured in a way that forestalls this sort of rich analysis, because his excellent discussion of ideology early in the essay implies that a pedagogy does not merely transcribe a cognitive (or other) theory of language, but necessarily inflects and interprets the theory in particular ways. That discussion points toward a needed historicist view of the cognitive sciences and their extensions and transformations by writing teachers.

Berlin uses Ira Shor's work as representative of social-epistemic rhetoric. In Shor's classroom, "the liberated consciousness of students is the only educational objective worth considering" (492); therefore the students study ideology, and "are to undergo a conversion from 'manipulated objects into active, critical subjects'" (491). Berlin argues that such a rhetoric is "self-consciously aware of its ideological stand" and "provide[s] itself a defense against preemption" (478). But he does not suggest ways in which the classroom study of ideology may be modified or even subverted by the university in which it is situated, by the aims of composition programs, or by composition teachers—or even students—themselves. He uses extraordinary terms like "libertory classroom," "freedom," "empowering" and "conversion" uncritically (ignoring the fundamentalist implications of his use of the term *conversion*), except to say that this sort of pedagogy is difficult to carry out. It is disturbing that Berlin, who reiterates that what seems valuable and inevitable is imbricated in power relations, sees social-epistemic rhetoric as *inevitably* democratizing or safer from appropriation than any other discourse. Moreover, in his use of Shor, Berlin represents social-epistemic rhetoric as if the study of ideology *per se* is the *necessary* pedagogical move of a teacher using ideological theory. That is, he does not look at how Shor represents ideological theory in the move to pedagogy, or at the ideologizing that in Berlin's own view such a move surely entails.

But if Berlin has been short-sighted in these ways, his essay implies an important insight—that there have been, to date, very few richly developed representations of the cognitive sciences or interpretive theory by compositionists. Thus, while as categories, the terms "social-epistemic" and "cognitive" rhetoric have organizing power, there may be other ways to situate these still-developing fields of study and pedagogical practices.

For example, following Foucault, one could consider the general network of thought that makes it possible, even necessary, for the two apparently opposing fields of cognitive science and interpretive theory to flourish now. One might ask why it is that questions of representation appear with over-determination and urgency in each. If Foucault is right, one might expect that the cognitive sciences operate within a space of knowledge—a system of thought, a set of conditions for what counts as knowledge—together with interpretive theory; thus the cognitive sciences may have as much to do with interpretive theory as with the rationalist-Cartesian thought where they seem to be rooted. For example, each of these fields, the cognitive sciences and interpretive theory, intersects with Foucault's "human sciences" (see *The Order of Things*, final chapter), investigating non-conscious forms and processes and favoring metaphors of network, system and function; each shows how needs, conflicts, and desires take form in representation and how these are organized by unthought systems and rules; each tries to look at the real conditions of consciousness, uncovering the elusive powers that shape it. And each, dealing with signification and language, the things that animate the ghost in the machine or orchestrate the human subject, has a troubled relationship to "science." We need to look carefully at the ways in which interpretive theory and the cognitive sciences are used to establish students as the subjects of stories about learning.

Courtesy of the advertiser (Phone Vision, Inc., San Rafael, CA) and the advertising agency (R.M. Barrows, Inc., Burlingame, CA).

CONCERNING ABORTION:

AN ATTEMPT AT A RATIONAL VIEW

Charles Hartshorne

My onetime colleague T. V. Smith once wrote a book called *Beyond Conscience,* in which he waxed eloquent in showing "the harm that good men do." To live according to one's conscience may be a fine thing, but what if A's conscience leads A to try to compel B and C to live, not according to B's or C's conscience, but according to A's? That is what many opponents of abortion are trying to do. To propose a constitutional amendment to this effect is one of the most outrageous attempts to tyrannize over others that I can recall in my long lifetime as an American citizen. Proponents of the antiabortion amendment make their case, if possible, even worse when they defend themselves with the contention "It isn't my conscience only—it is a commandment of religion." For now one particular form of religion (certainly not the only form) is being used in an attempt to tyrannize over other forms of religious or philosophical belief. The separation of church and state evidently means little to such people.

WHAT SENSE "HUMAN"?

Ours is a country that has many diverse religious groups, and many people who cannot find truth in any organized religious body. It is a country that has great difficulty in effectively opposing forms of killing that *everyone* admits to be wrong. Those who would saddle the legal system with matters about which consciences sincerely and strongly differ show a disregard of the country's primary needs. (The same is to be said about crusades to make things difficult for homosexuals.) There can be little freedom if we lose sight of the vital distinction between moral questions and legal ones. The law compels and coerces, with the implicit threat of violence; morals seek to persuade. It is a poor society that forgets this difference.

What is the *moral* question regarding abortion? We are told that the fetus is alive and that therefore killing it is wrong. Since mosquitoes, bacteria, apes and whales are also alive, the argument is less than clear. Even plants are alive. I am not impressed by the rebuttal "But plants, mosquitoes, bacteria and whales are not human, and the fetus is." For the issue now becomes, *in what sense* is the fetus human? No one denies that its origin is human, as is its *possible* destiny. But the same is true of every unfertilized egg in the body of a nun. Is it wrong that some such eggs are not made or allowed to become human individuals?

Granted that a fetus is human in origin and possible destiny, in what further sense is it human? The entire problem lies here. If there are pro-life activists who have thrown much light on this question, I do not know their names.

One theologian who writes on the subject—Paul Ramsey—thinks

SOURCE: Reprinted by permission of the *Christian Century,* January 21, 1981.

that a human egg cell becomes a human individual with a moral claim to survive if it has been fertilized. Yet this egg cell has none of the qualities that we have in mind when we proclaim our superior worth to the chimpanzees or dolphins. It cannot speak, reason, or judge between right and wrong. It cannot have personal relations, without which a person is not functionally a person at all, until months—and not, except minimally, until years—have passed. And even then, it will not be a person in the normal sense until some who are already fully persons have taken pains to help it become a human being in the full value sense, functioning as such. The antiabortionist is commanding some person or persons to undertake this effort. For without it, the fetus will *never* be human in the relevant sense. It will be human only in origin, but otherwise a subhuman animal.

The fertilized egg is an individual egg, but not an individual human being. For such a being is, in its body, a multicellular organism, a *metazoan*—to use the scientific Greek—and the egg is a single cell. The first thing the egg cell does is to begin dividing into many cells. For some weeks the fetus is not a single individual at all, but a colony of cells. During its first weeks there seems to be no ground for regarding the fetus as comparable to an individual animal. Only in possible or probable destiny is it an individual. Otherwise it is an organized society of single-celled individuals.

A possible individual person is one thing; an actual person is another. If this difference is not important, what is? There is in the long run no room in the solar system, or even in the known universe, for all human eggs—even all fertilized eggs, as things now stand—to become human persons. Indeed, it is mathematically demonstrable that the present rate of population growth must be lowered somehow. It is not a moral imperative that all possibilities of human persons become actual persons.

Of course, some may say that the fertilized egg already has a human soul, but on what evidence? The evidence of soul in the relevant sense is the capacity to reason, judge right and wrong, and the like.

GENETIC AND OTHER INFLUENCES

One may also say that since the fertilized egg has a combination of genes (the units of physical inheritance) from both parents, in this sense it is already a human individual. There are two objections, either one in my opinion conclusive but only one of which is taken into account by Ramsey. The one he does mention is that identical twins have the same gene combination. The theologian does not see this as decisive, but I do.

The other objection is that it amounts to a very crude form of materialism to identify individuality with the gene-combination. Genes are the chemical bearers of inherited traits. This chemical basis of inheritance presumably influences everything about the development of the individual—*influences*, but does not fully determine. To say that the entire life of the person is determined by heredity is a theory of unfreedom that my religious conviction can only regard as monstrous. And there are biophysicists and neurophysiologists who agree with me.

From the gene-determined chemistry to a human person is a long, long step. As soon as the nervous system forming in the embryo begins to function as a whole—and not before—the cell colony begins to turn into a genuinely individual animal. One may reasonably suppose that this change is accompanied by some extremely primitive individual animal feelings. They cannot be recognizably human feelings, much less human thoughts, and cannot compare with the feelings of a porpoise or chimpanzee in level of consciousness. That much seems as certain as anything about the fetus except its origin and possible destiny. The nervous system of a very premature baby has been compared by an expert to that of a pig. And we know, if we know anything about this matter, that it is the nervous system that counts where individuality is concerned.

Identical twins are different individuals, each unique in consciousness. Though having the same genetic makeup, they will have been differently situated in the womb and hence will have received different stimuli. For that reason, if for no other, they will have developed differently, especially in their brains and nervous systems.

But there are additional reasons for the difference in development. One is the role of chance, which takes many forms. We are passing through a great cultural change in which the idea, long dominant in science, that chance is "only a word for our ignorance of causes" is being replaced by the view that the real laws of nature are probabilistic and allow for aspects of genuine chance.

Another reason is that it is reasonable to admit a reverse influence of the developing life of feelings in the fetus on the nervous system, as well as of the system upon the feelings. And since I, along with some famous philosophers and scientists, believe in freedom (not solely of mature human beings but—in some slight degree—of all individuals in nature, down to the atoms and farther), I hold that even in the fetus the incipient individual is unconsciously making what on higher levels we call "decisions." These decisions influence the developing nervous system. Thus to a certain extent we *make our own bodies* by our feelings and thoughts. An English poet with Platonic ideas expressed this concept as follows:

The body from the soul its form doth take,
For soul is form and doth the body make.

The word "soul" is, for me, incidental. The point is that feelings, thoughts, experiences react on the body and partly mold its development.

THE RIGHTS OF PERSONS

Paul Ramsey argues (as does William Buckley in a letter to me) that if a fetus is not fully human, then neither is an infant. Of course an infant is not fully human. No one thinks it can, while an infant, be taught to speak, reason, or judge right and wrong. But it is much closer to that stage than is a three-month fetus. It is beginning to have primitive social relations not open to a fetus; and since there is no sharp line anywhere between an infant and a child able to speak a few words, or between the latter and a child able to speak very many words, we have to regard the infant as significantly different from a three-month or four-month fetus. Nevertheless, I have little sympathy with the idea that infanticide is just another form of murder. Persons who are already functionally persons in the full sense have more important rights even than infants. Infanticide can be wrong without being fully comparable to the killing of persons in the full sense.

Does this distinction apply to the killing of a hopelessly senile person (or one in a permanent coma)? For me it does. I hope that no one will think that if, God forbid, I ever reach that stage, it must be for my sake that I should be treated with the respect due to normal human beings. Rather, it is for the sake of others that such respect may be imperative. Symbolically, one who has been a person may have to be treated as a person. There are difficulties and hazards in not so treating such individuals.

Religious people (I would so describe myself) may argue that once a fetus starts to develop, it is for God, not human beings, to decide whether the fetus survives and how long it lives. This argument assumes, against all evidence, that human life-spans are independent of human decisions. Our medical hygiene has radically altered the original "balance of nature." Hence the population explosion. Our technology makes pregnancy more and more a matter of human decision; more and more our choices are influencing the weal and woe of the animals on this earth. It is an awesome responsibility, but one that we cannot avoid. And, after all, the Book of Genesis essentially predicted our dominion over terrestrial life. In addition, no one is proposing to make abortion compulsory for those morally opposed to it. I add that everyone who smokes is taking a hand in deciding how long he or she will live. Also everyone who, by failing to exercise reasonably, allows his or her heart to lose its vigor. Our destinies are not simply "acts of God."

I may be told that if I value my life I must be glad that I was not aborted in the fetus stage. Yes, I am glad, but this expression does not constitute a claim to having already had a "right," against which no other right could prevail, to the life I have enjoyed. I feel no indignation or horror at contemplating the idea that the world might have had to do without me. The world could have managed, and as for what I would have missed, there would have been no such "I" to miss it.

POTENTIAL, NOT ACTUAL

With almost everything they say, the fanatics against abortion show that they will not, or cannot, face the known facts of this matter. The inability of a fetus to say "I" is not merely a lack of skill; there is nothing there to which the pronoun could properly refer. A fetus is not a person but a *potential* person. The "life" to which "pro-life" refers is nonpersonal, by any criterion that makes sense to some of us. It is subpersonal animal life only. The mother, however, *is* a person.

I resent strongly the way many males tend to dictate to females their behavior, even though many females encourage them in this. Of course, the male parent of a fetus also has certain rights, but it remains true that the female parent is the one most directly and vitally concerned.

I shall not forget talking about this whole matter to a wonderful woman, the widow of a philosopher known for his idealism. She was doing social work with young women and had come to the conclusion that abortion is, in some cases, the lesser evil. She told me that her late husband had said, when she broached the subject to him, "But you can't do that." "My darling," she replied, "we *are* doing it." I see no reason to rate the consciences of the pro-lifers higher than this woman's conscience. She knew what the problem was for certain mothers. In a society that flaunts sex (its pleasures more than its serious hazards, problems and spiritual values) in all the media, makes it difficult for the young to avoid unwanted pregnancy, and does little to help them with the most difficult of all problems of self-discipline, we tell young persons that they are murderers if they resort to abortion. And so we should not be surprised that Margaret Mead, that clearsighted observer of our society (and of other societies), should say, "Abortion is a nasty thing, but our society deserves it." Alas, it is too true.

I share something of the disgust of hard-core opponents of abortion that contraceptives, combined with the availability of abortion, may deprive sexual intercourse of spiritual meaning. For me the sacramental view of marriage has always had appeal, and my life has been lived accordingly. Abortion is indeed a nasty thing, but unfortunately there are in our society many even nastier things, like the fact that some children are growing up unwanted. This for my conscience is a great deal nastier, and truly horrible. An overcrowded world is also nasty, and could in a few decades become truly catastrophic.

The argument against abortion (used, I am sorry to say, by Pearl Buck) that the fetus may be a potential genius has to be balanced against the much more probable chance of its being a mediocrity, or a destructive enemy of society. Every egg cell is a possible genius and also a possible monster in human form. Where do we stop in calculating such possibilities?

If some who object to abortion work to diminish the number of unwanted, inappropriate pregnancies, or to make bearing a child for adoption by persons able to be its loving foster parents more attractive than it now is, and do this with a minimum of coercion, all honor to them. In view of the population problem, the first of these remedies should have high priority.

Above all, the coercive power of our legal system, already stretched thin, must be used with caution and chiefly against evils about which there is something like universal consensus. That persons have rights is a universal belief in our society, but that a fetus is already an actual person—about that there is and there can be no consensus. Coercion in such matters is tyranny. Alas for our dangerously fragmented and alienated society if we persist in such tyranny.

SHOULD
PRIESTS MARRY?

Martin Ridgeway

I'm told there are hundreds and thousands of priests in this country who want to have wives. Either they've applied for laicization or they're contemplating it or they hope that the Vatican will change the rules and let them marry.

I can see a lonely priest fantasizing about a warm comfortable home and a wife who says, "Is it OK if we have shrimp again tonight?" or "Snuggle up; I'm cold."

I'm sorry, Father, but it doesn't work like that. As you walk through your quiet rooms, you might want to reflect on the language of marriage—the true sounds of a "good" marriage.

"Don't use those. Those are the good scissors."

"You said you'd be home by five."

"Not tonight. I have a headache (or cramps or a cold or depression or toothache or indigestion or swelling or thyroid tiredness . . .)."

"Don't say 'fixin' to.'"

"Do you really need another drink?"

"I'm having a Tupperware party tomorrow night."

"Take this back to the store for me; tell them I lost the sales-slip."

"Come on, everyone, it's time to watch *Family Feud*."

"Anyone can put up a swing-set."

"We'd better leave early. I'm worried about the kids (or the car or the baby-sitter or the furnace or nuclear waste . . .)."

"If you'd put things in their place, they wouldn't be lost."

"Not in front of the children."

"At least try to talk to my mother."

"How could you forget? Tommy's piano recital is tonight."

"Jimmy says his little-league team needs a coach."

"You didn't get me anything nice last Christmas (or Valentine's Day or birthday or Easter or Thanksgiving or anniversary or Mother's Day . . .)."

"Be in by 11:30. You know I can't sleep when you're out."

"The Wilsons feed their cat in the morning." [A line doesn't have to make sense to express a serious complaint.]

"That dog of yours has ruined the carpet."

"Do you have to see *every* Super-Bowl game?"

SOURCE: Reprinted by permission of *The National Catholic Reporter*, April 10, 1981.

Think about it, Father.

In Mark's gospel, the Sadducees ask Jesus about a woman who has married seven times. They ask whose wife she is in the next life. Jesus answers that in the hereafter there is no marriage.

That might be why they call it Heaven.

AND ON THE EIGHTH DAY, WE BULLDOZED IT.

Elusive jaguars, rarest orchids, colorful birds-of-paradise.

Rainforests are haven to half of all the plant and animal species on earth. But how much time do they have left?

Fifty thousand rainforest acres are lost each day worldwide. At that rate, the last traces of original, irreplaceable paradise will vanish in a single human lifespan.

To preserve the splendid variety of life we must save the endangered rainforests.

Please support our efforts to conserve a miracle of creation. Tomorrow won't wait.

Save the rainforests and safeguard the survival of half of the species on earth, including our own. Here's my donation of ☐ $25 ☐ $50 ☐ $75 ☐ $100 ☐ _____ .

NAME _____
ADDRESS _____
CITY _____ STATE ____ ZIP_____

RAINFOREST ACTION NETWORK

300 BROADWAY, SAN FRANCISCO, CA 94133

AND ON THE EIGHTH DAY, WE BULLDOZED IT.

Worldwide, fifty thousand acres of rainforest will be destroyed today. Paradise lost at horrendous cost of half the species left on earth. To ensure their survival, we must act now. Learn how by writing us.

RAINFOREST ACTION NETWORK

300 BROADWAY, SAN FRANCISCO, CA 94133

AND ON THE EIGHTH DAY, WE BULLDOZED IT.

The oldest rainforests date back to the time of the dinosaurs, 100 million years ago. Today they offer the last refuge for half of all the plant and animal species on earth.

But how much time do rainforests have left?

Each day, fifty thousand acres of rainforests are bulldozed, burned, degraded, destroyed. At this rate, the last traces of paradise will be gone in a single human lifespan.

A miracle of creation wiped out, at horrendous cost to our environment.

What can you do to save the last rainforests on earth?

You can support activists in more than a dozen nations fighting to conserve the splendid variety of living things which depend on these endangered environments.

Jaguars, orchids, boas, birds . . . not to mention 200 million people.

To get involved, simply mail the coupon below. Tomorrow won't wait.

Tell me more about the rainforests and what I can do to save them.

NAME _____
ADDRESS _____
CITY _____ STATE ____ ZIP_____

RAINFOREST ACTION NETWORK

300 BROADWAY, SAN FRANCISCO, CA 94133

Courtesy of the Rainforest Action Network.

MANDATORY BUSING
PROTECTS BLACKS' RIGHTS

DeWayne Wickham

Most people who complain about busing schoolchildren aren't concerned about the ride.

Every day, hundreds of thousands of children are bused to school. Largely white, they are picked up in suburban neighborhoods or along rural roads and carted off to class with the doting approval of their parents.

Today, lawyers go before the Supreme Court to argue against an Oklahoma City school busing plan—designed to desegregate the school district. Their objections will make no mention of a desire to return to the "separate but equal" system that existed before the court ruled school segregation unconstitutional. But that will be the effect if the high court rules in their favor.

Before the court's 1954 ruling in the *Brown v. Board of Education* case, school segregation was mandated by law. Today, it's caused mostly by segregated housing patterns. The result is the same. The white flight that followed court-ordered desegregation has recreated the separate and "unequal" system that existed before 1954.

Predominately black public schools are underfunded. They get fewer resources and less experienced teachers than schools with largely white student bodies.

Across this country, urban school districts have less money to fund education than their suburban counterparts. Most states don't do enough to balance out these inequities.

School busing plans are the leverage judges need to push local and state officials to share educational resources equally among all students, regardless of race.

Opponents of the Oklahoma City busing program argue segregation resulting from housing patterns is less insidious than that which resulted from law. They are wrong.

Ironically, most of the children bused under the Oklahoma City plan are black, not white. Still it is the white-controlled school board, not black parents, who want to end court-ordered busing there.

If busing opponents can convince the court the cause of school segregation is more important than its results, the *Brown* decision will effectively be overturned.

Abandoning busing as a means of ending segregation does more than deny trial judges an effective remedy. It also means this Supreme Court rejects the admonition of Earl Warren, the chief justice who presided over the court that handed down the *Brown* decision.

"Separate educational facilities," he warned us, "are inherently unequal."

SOURCE: Reprinted from *USA Today*, October 2, 1990. Reprinted by permission of the author.

SOCIETY SHOULD
NOT DECIDE LIFE'S END

D.L. Cuddy

One can sympathize with the Cruzan family's distress concerning their daughter Nancy's medical condition for the past decade.

But a Missouri court's Dec. 14 decision that her food and water could be withheld, causing her to starve and dehydrate within two weeks, has ominous implications.

James Bopp Jr., president of the National Legal Center for the Medically Disabled, said, "There was absolutely not one shred of evidence that she had made an informed-consent refusal (of food and water while in a coma) in the past. This shows the lengths to which those who believe that the best thing for people with disabilities is to be dead will go to implement that view."

The Missouri court said recent testimony by three of Nancy's friends that they'd heard her indicate she wouldn't want to live "like a vegetable" satisfied the U.S. Supreme Court's requirement of "clear and convincing" evidence that she'd want food and water withheld. Yet, one must wonder why these friends hadn't come forward in court before.

Now there will surely be a push for legalization of suicide, because if people other than Nancy Cruzan, who was in no pain, can decide she should die, the argument will be that those with painful terminal illnesses should be able to end their lives. After all, a Michigan court on Dec. 13 dismissed a murder charge against the doctor there whose machine helped an Oregon woman commit suicide.

And the U.S. Supreme Court's own "clear and convincing" standard for withholding sustenance is an acceptance of suicide, too. What then is to stop someone, for the purpose of a financial inheritance or body organ transplant, from committing murder and saying, "My friend couldn't stand the pain, so I helped him/her commit suicide"?

The Missouri court's decision is equally disturbing because people across the USA may be discussing this case and casually remark that they wouldn't like to live in a coma. Then, if they're in a coma sometime in the future, and despite the fact that they (like Nancy Cruzan) may have chosen not to have a living will regarding denial of food and water, some friends could say they heard them make the above remark and proceed to starve them to death.

No one should be denied food and water, and suicide shouldn't be legalized.

SOURCE: Reprinted from *USA Today*, December 19, 1990. Reprinted by permission of the author.

" Views From A Heartland Campus "

"In John Doe We Trust" Is Not A Good Motto.

A generation ago, a former president of Harvard remarked, "The least that can be expected from a university graduate is that he or she pronounce the name of God without embarrassment."

That minimum requirement is no longer being met today.

Modern education, dominated by a cold naturalism and a shallow humanism, is often hostile to any expression of faith.

Courses in science and literature often dismiss or caricature religion. Psychology texts often treat religious motivations for behavior as neuroses and God as a psychic aberration. Throughout the academic disciplines, objective standards of moral values have given way to a normless diversity and a pervasive attitude that it is better to accept all values, all beliefs, than to choose among them. The danger is, Chesterton observed, not that man will believe in nothing, but that he will believe in anything.

But our concept of the dignity of the individual, our laws, our very freedom — these are all products of Judeo-Christian, Western values that have been central to our history and the American experience for over two hundred years. To ignore their importance on the campuses of our universities is to deny our human qualities and simply make us intelligent barbarians.

Nature alone simply can't account for the miracle of life or for the heights that are reached by man's spirit, his dreams and his inward longing for truth. Nor can an anonymous God-in-general or a John Doe God or scientism alone satisfy.

In denying God and all moral authority, we can ultimately deliver ourselves into the coercive powers of the state.

Immanuel Kant once wrote: "Two things impress me with increasing awe — the starry heavens without and the moral law within." Education should embrace both the universe without and the soul within us.

At Hillsdale College we stress the liberal arts, but we also believe that a truly educated person should have a spiritual dimension to his or her academic experience. We are not afraid to discuss the place of God in our heritage and in our lives.

We hope our students leave our campus with values to guide them that will help shape not only individual lives but communities and countries as well.

I would like to tell you more about Hillsdale College and the philosophy of its leadership. Write me, George Roche, for more information about the educational principles of Hillsdale College and why it refuses federal funds and federal control, though we provide a substantial number of our students with private financial assistance. We would like to explain our reasons for encouraging a national discussion of the need to revive the spirit of the authentic American revolution. Write Hillsdale College, Dept. NM-6, Hillsdale, Michigan 49242. Or call us, toll free, at 1-800-535-0860.

Dr. George Roche
President, Hillsdale College

HILLSDALE COLLEGE

Courtesy of Hillsdale College.

AT STANFORD, A SETBACK
TO WESTERN CIVILIZATION

Charles Krauthammer

Washington—Western civilization has suffered a setback at Stanford University. Civilization will recover. Whether Stanford will is another question.

At issue is the core curriculum in Western civilization instituted in the early 1980s at Stanford and elsewhere. At Stanford, it consisted of 15 required and 18 "strongly recommended" political and philosophical classics.

It was one of the most popular courses at Stanford, but two years ago a campaign was launched by minority and feminist groups, which denounced it as a racist, sexist compendium of "European-Western and male bias."

Last month the faculty capitulated. It did not quite abolish, but it emasculated the program. Fifteen required works became six. Eighteen "strongly recommended" are recommended no more.

The slack will be taken up with works that emphasize "cultural diversity and the processes of cultural interaction." A less oblique instruction to the faculty is to include a substantial number of "works by women, minorities, and persons of color."

Even the term "Western civilization"—"anachronistic and inappropriate," explains history professor Judith Brown—will have to go. The new name for the program is "Culture, Ideas and Values."

There is everything to be said for having students learn about non-Western cultures, but not as a substitute for one's Western heritage.

In pursuit of intercultural understanding, the Stanford faculty could find neither the nerve nor the will nor the arguments to insist that Homer, Dante and Darwin be read. Or to "strongly recommend" Locke and Mill, to say nothing of Jefferson, Madison, Hamilton and Jay.

In fact, it had trouble defending the very idea of Western civilization, which is what the protest was about.

The protesters oppose the core curriculum on the grounds that white male authors are overrepresented and the groups to which these critics owe their allegiance—women, blacks, Native Americans, Hispanics, etc.—are missing.

Bill King, a student leader of the protest, not only accused Stanford of "crushing the psyche of those others to whom Locke, Hume and Plato are not speaking" but of suppressing facts such as that "the Iroquois Indians in America had a representative democracy that served as a model for the American System."

It is unfortunate that the Iroquois left no written language. It is a crime that blacks were excluded from intellectual life (and much else, of course) during centuries of slavery. It is a great injustice that women were denied opportunity and education until very recently.

SOURCE: Reprinted by permission of the Washington Post Writers Group. Reprinted from the *Seattle Times*, April 24, 1988.

But these are historical facts. And they explain why the corpus of great works, of which these excluded people were obviously capable, were either lost or never created. It does no good to pretend otherwise and to invent or exaggerate historical influences (such as the Iroquois on the Federalist Papers) as a gesture of historical restitution.

Affirmative action for people is problematic but, on the whole, a good thing: It gives those who were denied opportunity an extra chance to compete. Affirmative action for great books is an embarrassment.

The critics further charge that the core curriculum not only denies American ethnics their due. It denies the "global culture" its due. In today's global village, the idea of a Western culture is seen as narrow, biased and ethnocentric.

(The aversion to ethnocentricity does not, however, prevent the critics from demanding great works that come from the right ethnic, racial and gender groups.)

There is nothing wrong with believing in a world culture and wanting students to gain familiarity with it. But before approaching the larger world, it is essential to have a sense of self, to know who you are and where your ideas come from.

One has to know one's own culture first. Without understanding it, how can one be intelligently critical of it?

It makes no sense to recommend a dab of East Asian history, a few semester hours of African art, and a bit of American Indian architecture for 17-year-olds, the majority of whom don't know when the Civil War was, what the Magna Charta was, or who wrote "The Canterbury Tales."

The first obligation of a university is to help a student fulfill the injunction: Know thyself. Or is that too Western an idea?

A pastiche of "global culture" for a population utterly ungrounded in its own culture produces the most haphazard jumble of knowledge. It guarantees intellectual disorientation and perpetuates in college the cultural illiteracy produced by high school.

To say that a Western core exists and that it is valuable is not to say that it is immutable. For the foreseeable centuries, the Bible and Plato will not become less relevant to the West.

One should, however, always be prepared to add to the core as history requires—but on the basis of the genius and the influence of a book, not on the basis of the race or sex of the author.

The declared project of the anti-Western-culture forces is to eliminate not just the course or the books but the concept. Last year 500 demonstrators (led by—who else?—Jesse Jackson) celebrated Stanford's acquiescence to a new ideologically correct history course with the chant, "Hey hey, ho ho, Western culture's got to go!"

At Stanford, they won. If they win elsewhere, we will be firmly embarked on another round of cultural deconstruction.

STOP FOREIGNERS FROM
BUYING OUT AMERICA

June M. Collier

Thank you, ladies and gentlemen. I want to start off my speech today by assuring you that I am not against trade among the nations of the world. Trade and commerce are good for the United States as well as for all other nations. I have deep feelings for all nations, and I'm ready for us to defend freedom wherever in the world it may be threatened.

But our country must be strong and prepared in order to do that—not only for the sake of other nations, but for our own as well. Our national economy is sick. Unfortunately, by the time our elected leaders realize how sick it is, it may be too late.

Today, Americans are more productive than ever. Our manufacturing quality is up. Even our foreign competition admits that. But we still can't compete, and there's a very good reason why we can't—and why the situation will get even worse. Our workers cannot turn out products of equal quality as cheaply as workers offshore who make 21 cents to a dollar-and-a-half an hour. That's the long and the short of it.

Workers in other countries have access to the same machinery and technology as we do. There's no advantage there to either side. A worker in Alabama can work at about the same speed as a worker in Taiwan. There's no advantage there to either side. The real advantage that a Mexican company or a Phillipine company has is labor cost. In order to get the same output per dollar of labor cost, an American worker has to build products at least five times faster than workers in other countries. And we wonder about the quality difference!

That problem is not going to go away by itself. Worse than that, it is leading to another problem that is far more dangerous to us and our children than the trade deficit could ever be.

Ask yourself this: If foreigners are accumulating our dollars by selling us products, and if they aren't buying our products in return, what can they possibly do with all those dollars? They are using those dollars to buy America, piece by piece.

Again, this is not just conjecture; it is based on solid fact. It is a fact that foreign investment in the U.S. has tripled in just the past ten years and has accelerated even faster in 1988 and 1989. And let me stop right here to tell you that when I say "investment" I really mean "buying." I could give you the figures—or what figures the government has, but even our government admits that the figures are just estimates, and they're all too low. For example, there is a reported 200 billion dollar difference between what the Commerce Department says has been acquired here over the past five years and what has been reported in the home countries of the buyers. Except in very few cases, foreign interests don't have to report on what they're doing here. And even when

SOURCE: Speech to the American Business Women's Association, Montgomery, AL, February 11, 1991. Reprinted by permission of the author.

reporting is required, there are enough loopholes in the law to drive a Volvo through.

I'm from Missouri. I like to use simple words for things. I said it before, but it's so important that I'll tell you again: Honest and plain-speaking people would never say that foreigners are "investing" in America. They'd say that foreigners are "buying" America. And when you buy something, you control it.

My concerns about America are very concrete and very immediate. Our resources are being drained off. The independence of our country is being threatened. The future of our children is in jeopardy. All of that is real, and it's now. Right now—as far as we know—only about ten percent of the private wealth of America is in foreign hands.

Please, will somebody tell me what we have in the law to keep that from becoming fifty percent or ninety percent? Is there anybody in this room who can tell me what the countries who are making huge profits by exporting to us will do with that money other than to use it to buy us? Where is there even one law that will slow down this process?

Where is there even one law that will keep foreign companies from employing over half our work force by the turn of the century? That's what the trends show today. That's our future.

Ladies and gentlemen, if that future comes to pass—and it will unless we act to stop it—our destiny will be out of control. With that sort of economic control, political control is sure to follow. For an example, I would call your attention to the fact that foreign-controlled political action committees spent more than 100 million dollars during the last Congressional election cycle.

For more specific examples, look at what happened to California's unitary tax structure after intense lobbying by the chairman of Sony. Look at what happened to the so-called "serious" sanctions we imposed against Toshiba for giving away our critical strategic lead in submarine technology to the Soviets. Those sanctions virtually disappeared after Toshiba spent 60 million dollars in Washington in less than one year.

And where did they get the money? That money, which was used to buy favor for Japan over America in our halls of Congress, came directly from the pockets of U.S. consumers. And it was obtained as a direct result of giving foreign companies unfettered access to those pockets. Enough about politics. Let's talk technology.

Do you realize that most of the top companies winning U.S. patents over the past several years are owned by foreign interests? Did you know that the Japanese today hold over 32 thousand U.S. patents? We do have laws against transferring sensitive technology to foreign countries. So those interests have not bought that technology; they have bought the companies that have developed it, and they get the technology along with the company. There's no law against that.

Here's an example for you: The CIA recently discovered a plot by which the Soviet Union was trying to buy four banks in Silicon Valley. That purchase would have given the Russians tremendous leverage over the customers of those banks. I'll leave the rest to your imagination. The point is that it took the CIA to uncover the plot. The Treasury Department couldn't; neither could the Commerce Department.

Here's another example: Japan is being given the latest we have in the way of aerospace technology along with their purchase of 60% of the FSX fighter deal. Do we know that Mitsubishi will guard that technology any better than Toshiba did?

To me, the government is charged with only a very few responsibilities, such as guarding the shores and carrying the mail. I'm not sure how well our government is doing at either one, but I do know that guarding the shores means more than just keeping us safe from bombs and bullets. People seem to think the Soviet Union is the enemy we need to watch for because they have bombs and bullets.

Mark this well: the real enemy is the same one that we faced on a different battlefield over 45 years ago. Russia could not take over and control as much American property if they won a nuclear war as Japan has already bought on the open market. Now, what's the difference? An economic takeover is far more dangerous to us in the long run than an armed invasion. All the more so because we seem to welcome it. You see, other nations have found out—very painfully—that we tend to get really mad when people try to take us over by force. But what they've recently learned is that it's cheaper to buy us than to bomb us.

Even if you can possibly discount all that, look to the future of your own children. When American companies have been bought out or frozen out by foreign companies here, what career hopes will they have? How high they rise with an American company depends on how smart they are and how hard they work. How high they rise with a foreign-owned company depends on what language their parents speak. Tuck this thought away: No American child will ever direct the corporate policy of Honda or Hyundai, except as a token.

I can tell you that the trends are all in that direction. Nobody has been able to dispute that. Nobody can deny the increase in foreign control over our most basic industries. And here's something else they can't deny: *there is absolutely nothing we are doing to reverse it.*

SMOKING SHOULD NOT BE A PART OF GROWING UP

One of the most trying aspects of being a parent is encouraging your child to make the right choices—not just to follow along. In today's complex society, growing up involves more pressures and choices than ever before. Studies show that young people do things because their friends do. Smoking is one of those things.

We don't want young people to smoke.

That's why we are offering a booklet aimed at helping parents meet the challenge of providing their children with the tools to resist peer pressure. The booklet, "Tobacco: Helping Youth Say No," is the third in a series designed to keep parents and children communicating about important issues like smoking.

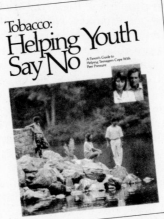

To continue its longstanding commitment that smoking is not for young people, the tobacco industry also has strengthened its marketing code and is supporting state legislation to make it tougher for young people to buy cigarettes. We are also working with retailers for strict compliance with state laws prohibiting sales of cigarettes to minors. Look for ITS THE LAW displayed wherever cigarettes are sold.

And, for your free copy of "Tobacco: Helping Youth Say No," return the coupon today.

THE TOBACCO INSTITUTE

P.O. Box 41130, Washington, DC 20018

The Tobacco Institute
P.O. Box 41130
Washington, DC 20018

**PLEASE SEND ME MY FREE COPY OF
"TOBACCO: HELPING YOUTH SAY NO."**
Please Print
NAME

ADDRESS

CITY

STATE   ZIP
01

Courtesy of the Tobacco Institute.

SEMI-AUTOMATIC FIREARMS:
THE CITIZEN'S CHOICE

National Rifle Association

Semi-automatic firearms are used extensively by millions of citizens throughout America—bird hunters, water-fowlers, competitive shooters, and collectors.

Semi-automatic rifles, shotguns, and pistols are nothing new, employing basic designs that date from the turn-of-the-century. Their distinctive feature is that after firing a single shot by one pull of the trigger, a mechanism reloads another cartridge for firing. The mechanism is simply equivalent to, and sometimes *slower* than, some other commonly used methods of providing additional shots. For instance, some pump shotguns can be fired more rapidly than semi-automatics.

Current legislative proposals to ban the sale, ownership and possession of semi-automatic firearms are uninformed and misdirected at best, and represent clear dangers to all law-abiding American gun owners.

The national media and organized "gun control" groups have advanced from demanding prohibitions on certain handguns and ammunition, to calls for banning semi-automatic firearms. The pattern is obvious, and the strategy has long been clear—isolate certain types of firearms, label them as inherently "evil" or "crime prone," then try to segregate and drive a wedge between firearms owners.

All firearms owners should beware. Those who would willingly sacrifice handguns as a compromise, and who may now be willing to sacrifice semi-automatic firearms, will eventually find themselves having to defend their shotguns or any other type of firearm they choose to own.

Can you imagine the government ordering citizens to give up their word processors for goose quills and ink wells? or sophisticated stereos for gramophones? or televisions and video cassettes for radios? Of course not.

For most Americans, it is impossible to imagine being forced to give up modern, effective, and often "better" products for throwbacks to the past.

The development and improvement in firearms are similar to all of the technological progress that Americans have experienced in a wide-range of products applicable to any facet of American life. In fact, like semi-automatic firearms, many advances occurred as a direct result of modifications in goods from the military to domestic use: the development of canned and concentrated foods, commercial jet flight, medical breakthroughs, and mass transportation. Individual tastes cause each change or trend to be accepted or rejected. The marketplace rules.

When it comes to firearms, however, forces dominated by an anti-firearms phobia seek by legislative fiat to once again play "divide and conquer." By crafty use of pseudo-issues and negative media labeling, they aim to halt the lawful use and ownership of military style firearms.

Courtesy of the National Rifle Association.

Anti-gun groups—like the National Coalition to Ban Handguns and Handgun Control, Inc.—have branded an entire class of firearms "assassination machines," "modern combat weapons," "assault guns," and "exotic weaponry" to stigmatize these lawfully owned rifles, shotguns, and handguns.

In effect, the gun prohibitionists have set their sights on making the semi-automatic firearm the heir-apparent to the "Saturday Night Special." To garner support for a ban on so-called "assault" rifles, pistols, and shotguns, the gun prohibitionists prey on fear. They seek to create inordinate fears based on what auto-loaders look like or their alleged "awesome lethality." As with the "Saturday Night Special," the myths perpetrated by these groups do not stand up to clear, factual examination.

Deliberately obscured in the propaganda barrage are the inherent appeals, the historic significance, and the legitimate uses of semi-automatic firearms in today's society.

WHY NOT A
FOOTBALL DEGREE?

William F. Shughart, II

Clemson University's football program was placed on probation last spring for the second time in six years, and the coach who guided the team to a national championship in 1981 quit or was forced to resign. Last season's Heisman Trophy winner played at the University of Houston, a school banned from TV and postseason bowl appearances by the National Collegiate Athletic Association; Southern Methodist University fields a team barely resurrected last fall from the "death penalty" it received three years ago; and scandals have rocked the basketball programs at Kansas, Kentucky, Memphis State and North Carolina State.

Each of these events, which are only the latest in a series of NCAA rules violations, has generated the usual amount of hand-wringing about the apparent loss of amateurism in college sports. Nostalgia for supposedly simpler times when love of the game and not money was the driving force in college sports has led to all sorts of reform proposals. The NCAA's decision to require its member institutions to make public athletes' graduation rates is perhaps the least controversial example. Proposition 48's mandate that freshman athletes must meet more stringent test score and grade point requirements to participate in intercollegiate sports has been criticized as a naked attempt to discriminate against disadvantaged (and mostly minority) high-school graduates who see athletics as a way out of poverty.

HALF-MEASURES

But whether or not one supports any particular reform proposal, there seems to be a general consensus that something must be done. If so, why stop at half-measures? I hereby offer three suggestions for solving the crisis in college athletics.

1. *Create four-year degree programs in football and basketball.* Many colleges and universities grant bachelors' degrees in vocational subjects. Art, drama and music are a few examples, but there are others. Undergraduates who major in these areas are typically required to spend only about one of their four years in basic English, math, history and science courses; the remainder of their time is spent in the studio, the theater or the practice hall honing the creative talents they will later sell as professionals.

Although a college education is no more necessary for success in the art world than it is in the world of sports, no similar option is available for students whose talents lie on the athletic field or in the gym. Majoring in physical education is a possibility, of course, but while PE is hardly a rigorous, demanding discipline, undergraduates pursuing a degree in that major normally must spend many more hours in the class-

SOURCE: Reprinted from *The Wall Street Journal*, December 26, 1990. Reprinted by permission of the author.

room than their counterparts who are preparing for careers on the stage. While the music major is receiving academic credit for practice sessions and recitals, the PE major is studying and taking exams in kinesiology, exercise physiology and nutrition. Why should academic credit be given for practicing the violin, but not for practicing a three-point shot?

2. *Extend the time limit on athletic scholarships by two years.* In addition to practicing and playing during the regular football or basketball season, college athletes must continue to work to improve their skills and keep in shape during the off-season. For football players, these off-season activities include several weeks of organized spring practice as well as year-round exercise programs in the weight room and on the running track. Basketball players participate in summer leagues and practice with their teams during the fall. In effect, college athletes are required to work at their sport for as much as 10 months a year.

These time-consuming extracurricular activities make it extremely difficult for college athletes to devote more than minimal effort to the studies required for maintaining their academic eligibility. They miss lectures and exams when their teams travel and the extra tutoring they receive at athletic department expense often fails to make up the difference.

If the NCAA and its member schools are truly concerned about the academic side of the college athletic experience, let them put money where their collective mouth is. The period of an athlete's eligibility to participate in intercollegiate sports would remain four years, but the two additional years of scholarship support could be exercised at any time during the athlete's lifetime. Athletes who use up their college eligibility and do not choose a career in professional sports would be guaranteed financial backing to remain in school and finish their undergraduate degrees. Athletes who have the talent to turn pro could complete their degrees when their playing days are over.

3. *Allow the competitive marketplace to determine the compensation of college athletes.* Football and basketball players at the top NCAA institutions provide millions of dollars in benefits for their respective institutions. Successful college athletic programs draw more fans to the football stadium and to the basketball arena. They generate revenues for the school from regular season television appearances and from invitations to participate in postseason play. There is evidence that schools receive increased financial support from public and private sources—both for their athletic and academic programs—if their teams win national ranking. There is even evidence that the quality of students who apply for admission to institutions of higher learning may improve following a successful football or basketball season.

Despite the considerable contributions made to the wealth and welfare of his or her institution, however, the compensation payable to a college athlete is limited by the NCAA to a scholarship that includes tuition, books, room and board, and a nominal expense allowance. Any payment above and beyond this amount subjects the offending athletic program to NCAA sanctions. In-kind payments to players and recruits in the form of free tickets to athletic contests, T-shirts, transportation and accommodations are also limited. These restrictions apply to alumni and fans as well as to the institutions themselves. The NCAA also limits the amount of money athletes may earn outside of school by curtailing the use of summer jobs as a means by which coaches and team supporters can offer higher wages to athletes.

The illegal financial inducements reported to be widespread in collegiate football and basketball represent conclusive evidence that many college athletes are now underpaid. The relevant question is whether the current system of compensation ought to remain in place. Allowing it to do so will preserve the illusion of amateurism in college sports and permit coaches, athletic departments and college administrators to continue to benefit financially at the expense of the players. On the other hand, shifting to a market-based system of compensation would transfer some of the wealth created by big-time college athletic programs to the individuals whose talents are key ingredients in the success of those programs.

It would also cause a sea change in the distribution of power among the top NCAA institutions. Under current NCAA rules, some of the major college athletic programs, such as those of Alabama, Notre Dame and Penn State in football, and North Carolina and Indiana in basketball, have developed such strong winning traditions over the years that they can maintain their dominant positions without cheating.

These schools are able to attract superior high school athletes season after season at the mandated NCAA wage with the offer of a package of nonmonetary benefits (well-equipped training facilities, quality coaching staffs, talented teammates, national exposure and so on) that increases the present value of an amateur athlete's future professional income relative to the value added by historically weaker athletic programs. Given this factor, along with NCAA rules that mandate uniform compensation across member schools, these top institutions have a built-in competitive advantage in recruiting the best and brightest athletes.

ILLEGAL INDUCEMENTS

It follows that under the current system, the weaker programs are virtually compelled to offer illegal financial inducements to players and recruits if they wish to compete successfully with the traditional powers. It also follows that shifting to a market-based system of compensation would remove some of the built-in advantages now enjoyed by the top athletic programs. It is surely this effect, along with the reduction in the incomes of coaches and the "fat" in athletic departments to be expected once a competitive marketplace is permitted to work, that is the cause of the objection to paying student–athletes, not the rhetoric about the repugnance of professionalism.

It is a fight over the distribution of the college sports revenue pie that lies at the bottom of the debate about reforming NCAA rules. And despite the high moral principles and concern for players usually expressed by the debaters on all sides of the issue, the interests of the athlete are in fact often the last to be considered.

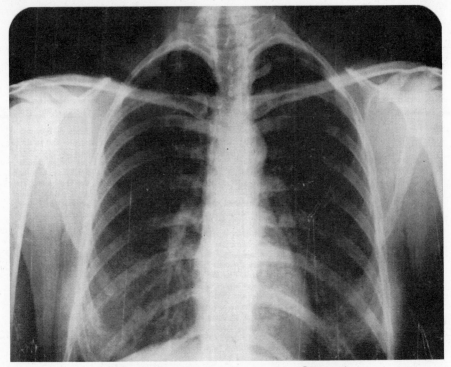

If a doctor can't find
asbestos damage here, a lawyer will.

These days, asbestos litigation is fast becoming a giant grab bag. And nobody's grabbing more than America's personal injury lawyers. These opportunists are rounding up workers all across the country, herding them into vans equipped with x-ray and breathing machinery, and examining them for traces of asbestos-related disease.

The lawyers who invented this screening technique brought suits in 12 states on behalf of 8,000 tire workers. Yet in a May 1990 opinion, a Kansas City district judge called their litigation project "a professional farce...The process makes a mockery of the practices of law and medicine."

As Forbes pointed out in a February 18th cover story, it's not just lawyers that are at fault, but the vagueness of the law itself. Consider the case of a mechanic who had occasional contact with tractor parts containing not-so-dangerous chrysotile asbestos. When he died from cancer, lawyers saw to it that his wife received a large settlement from the companies that made those parts. But in all likelihood, his

death was caused by deadly amphibole asbestos, which he was exposed to when he worked at a naval shipyard during World War II.

Right now, the U.S. has 115,000 pending asbestos cases. Forbes has learned that between 65% and 80% of the claimants involved in them have symptomless maladies unrelated to asbestos. Then why is it that asbestos claims have already forced 15 companies into bankruptcy? And why is it that litigation could end up costing companies, and their insurers, as much as $100 billion?

When it's all too easy to attack today's businesses, count on Forbes to tell things as they really are. With gutsy, insightful reporting. The kind of reporting that other publications either can't go after, or won't go after. At least not until it first appears in Forbes.

Advertisers are well aware of our distinctive editorial. That's why Forbes is the only business magazine up in ad pages for 1990. What's more, it's the only biweekly magazine that's ever ranked second in total ad pages.

If you want your ads to make a stronger impact, run them in Forbes. The magazine that does justice to every story.

No guts. No story.

Forbes Magazine·60 Fifth Ave. N.Y. NY 10011

Courtesy of *Forbes*.

DON'T STEP ON THE RIGHTS OF THE DESTITUTE

John A. Powell

All across the country, sympathy and tolerance for the homeless and their plight seem to be in a tailspin.

In Washington, for example, the police have announced plans to use an almost-forgotten law to begin arresting beggars.

In Martinsburg, W. Va., the city council votes today on a proposal to require panhandlers to pay an annual $50 licensing fee.

No one begs for the fun of it; it is a degrading process and quickly strips human beings of their dignity. Society's declining tolerance toward the homeless—and increasing desire for quick-fix solutions—demonstrates a lack of knowledge about the causes of homelessness and the rights to which we all have equal claim.

Government has many policies and programs—from capital gains taxes to rent subsidies—meant to enhance housing opportunities. But, increasingly, those programs benefit only certain segments of the population—mainly those in the upper-income economic brackets.

These inequities in the government's housing policies and programs raise questions about basic principles of fairness and equality. Nowhere are these inequities more evident than in the government's failure to help the homeless.

Without a place to live, these Americans cannot exercise other basic rights. Without a home, they suffer a denial of rights basic to the fabric of our country, such as the right to vote, the right to privacy, the right to family integrity and, ultimately, the right to liberty itself.

Finally, it is also painfully clear that homelessness in the USA is inextricably tied to questions of race and discrimination. A greater percentage of African-Americans and Latinos are poor. They therefore have no choice but to live in substandard housing that often becomes uninhabitable, forcing additional people onto the streets. Also, members of minority groups face severe discrimination in finding and keeping affordable housing. Not surprisingly, many minority-group members are homeless.

No one sets out to be homeless. Instead of arresting the homeless and charging them ridiculous fees to eke out the barest of livings, we must focus our attention on attacking the root causes of homelessness, on making government housing and assistance programs more equitable and on providing better educational and employment opportunities for all our citizens.

SOURCE: Reprinted from *USA Today*, November 15, 1990. Reprinted by permission of the author.

COMMUNITY

TOXIC REPORT

Greenpeace

Your participation in this community survey on hazardous wastes is urgently requested. The questions are easy to answer. Estimated time of response is two to three minutes. Please complete and return to Greenpeace within ten days.

1. Each year, more than 300 million tons of hazardous waste are produced in the U.S. alone. Do you believe your state, local, and federal authorities are doing all they can to protect you and your community from these wastes?

        ☐ Yes   ☐ No   ☐ No opinion

2. Rather than reducing production of toxic wastes, chemical and industrial giants propose "new" and "better" ways of disposing of them. What would be your response to locating the following waste disposal facilities in or near your community:

    A. Toxic waste
       incinerator   ☐ Opposed   ☐ Unopposed

    B. Toxic storage
       facility   ☐ Opposed   ☐ Unopposed

    C. Toxic
       landfill   ☐ Opposed   ☐ Unopposed

    D. Injection
       well   ☐ Opposed   ☐ Unopposed

3. Do you feel safe with the quality of drinking water in your community?

        ☐ Yes   ☐ No   ☐ No opinion

4. The use of pesticides, herbicides and other chemicals by U.S. agribusiness is a major source of toxic pollution in our water, soil, and food supplies. Would you favor more vigorous regulation of agricultural chemicals?

        ☐ Yes   ☐ No   ☐ No opinion

5. Toxic chemicals are suspected to be causing the deaths of dolphins, beluga whales and other animals. Do you think Greenpeace should invest its resources in investigating the impact of toxic pollution on wildlife habitats?

        ☐ Yes   ☐ No   ☐ No opinion

Courtesy of Greenpeace.

6. Rather than waste disposal or toxic waste management, Greenpeace believes that the best solution to the problem of hazardous wastes is to stop it before it starts, to reduce the quantity and toxicity of these wastes by improving industrial processes—*source reduction*. Do you agree that source reduction would be an effective way of reducing pollution?

☐ Agree   ☐ Disagree   ☐ No opinion

7. Recent surveys show that many Americans consider toxic wastes to be a serious threat to their health, but feel incapable of doing anything about it. How would you characterize your attitude toward toxic wastes?

☐ Serious problem, and
   want to do something about it

☐ Serious problem, but
   feel I can't do anything about it

☐ Not a serious problem

8. Would you be willing to spend just a few cents a day to help Greenpeace expose and confront the major toxic polluters—and to establish source reduction as a policy of major industrial nations as soon as possible.

☐ Yes   ☐ No

If your answer is "yes," Greenpeace invites you to join our historic effort to reduce and eventually eliminate toxic wastes from our communities. Simply check the appropriate box below, and return this form with your contribution today.

A lot of campus rapes start here.

Whenever there's drinking or drugs, things can get out of hand.
So it's no surprise that many campus rapes involve alcohol.

But you should know that under any circumstances, sex without
the other person's consent is considered rape. A felony, punishable
by prison. And drinking is no excuse.

That's why, when you party, it's good to know what your limits are.
You see, a little sobering thought now can save you from a big
problem later.

© 1990 Rape Treatment Center, Santa Monica Hospital.

Courtesy of the Rape Treatment Center, Santa Monica Hospital.

SIZISM—ONE OF THE LAST "SAFE" PREJUDICES

Sally E. Smith

As obscene as it sounds, a generation or two ago, Black people were considered to be inherently ugly, stupid, unsanitary, lazy, and enslaved by creature comforts. Today, fat people are assumed to be inherently ugly, stupid, unsanitary, lazy, and enslaved by creature comforts. Such stereotypes are reinforced by both the media and the public. Even in "politically correct" circles, where one would never hear derogatory remarks about people of color, gays and lesbians, or people with disabilities, one continues to hear disparaging remarks about fat people.

Stereotypes, and the resulting prejudice, develop from a belief that a group of people share common characteristics. This belief is almost always grounded in myth. The central myth surrounding the prejudice against fat people is that, if fat people really wanted to, they could lose weight. It doesn't seem to matter that research indicates that fat people are fat because of heredity and metabolic factors; that 95–98% of all diets fail within three to five years; that much of the $33 billion that the diet industry earns annually comes at the expense of the health and well being of fat people; that more people will die from weight loss surgery than died in the Vietnam War; that yo-yo dieting makes a person fatter; that most fat people have no more choice in their size than a person does in the color of their skin. Our society, which accepts that in the bell curve of the human species, some people will be shorter or taller than average, and some people will be thinner than average, cannot accept that some people will be fatter than average.

This climate of non-acceptance creates a "blame the victim" mentality, wherein myths and stereotypes are used to justify treating fat people as second-class citizens. This has a devastating effect on the quality of life for fat people. Fat people are discriminated against in employment, in that they are denied employment, denied promotions and raises, denied benefits, and sometimes fired, all because of their weight. Fat people are discriminated against in education, in that they are not accepted into graduate programs, and are harassed and expelled because of their weight. Fat people cannot adopt children, solely because of their weight. Fat people are denied access to adequate medical care, in that they are denied treatment, misdiagnosed, harassed, and treated as though every medical condition, from a sore throat to a broken bone, is a weight-related condition. Fat people are denied access to public accommodations, such as public transportation, airline travel, theatres, and restaurants because seating is not available for them.

Because fat people are fair game for ridicule and public humiliation, they face substantial social discrimination. Epithets are screamed at fat people; ice cream cones are snatched out of the hands of fat people "for

SOURCE: Reprinted from *The California Activist,* July 1990. Reprinted by permission of the author.

their own good"; fat people are run off of public beaches and out of health spas, because they do not look "acceptable."

This discrimination takes an enormous toll on a fat person's self-esteem, particularly when the person is a child. Unlike children in many other oppressed groups, fat children get little support from parents, teachers, or peers; instead of receiving support from her parents or teachers when other children make sizist remarks, a fat child will often be told, "If only you lost weight, you wouldn't have this problem."

Research has documented that women are most often the victims of size discrimination. Perhaps this is because men have traditionally garnered credibility through the power and wealth they accumulate, and women have garnered credibility through how closely they conform to society's ideals of beauty. Size discrimination is therefore linked to sexism. Because women of certain ethnic groups tend to be fatter than white women, size discrimination is linked to racism. Because women get fatter as they get older (a physiological phenomena), size discrimination is linked to ageism. Because lower income women tend to be fatter than higher income women, size discrimination is linked to classism. There should be no doubt that size discrimination is a feminist issue.

In most places, discrimination against fat people is perfectly legal. Currently, there is only one state, Michigan, which has a statute prohibiting size discrimination. And there are only a few cities which have ordinances prohibiting discrimination based on personal appearance. When a fat person decides to fight size discrimination, she most often has to litigate using disability rights laws. But the truth is, while some fat people are disabled, most fat people aren't disabled, leading some courts to create a Catch-22 for fat people. There was a case in Pennsylvania, for example, where the court said that even though the employer didn't want to hire the person because of their physical problems, those problems were not a handicap, and therefore the fat person was not protected by the handicap law. Can you have it both ways? "We're not hiring you because you're physically inadequate, but you're not protected because you are physically adequate."

Fat people desperately need statutory protection, both to raise their quality of life, and to ensure an avenue of redress should they be discriminated against. The words "height and weight" should be added as a protected category, so that an employer cannot arbitrarily dismiss a candidate or an employee because of her size. Schools and universities should not receive state or federal funding if they discriminate against fat people. High school curriculum dealing with civil rights movements should include the size acceptance movement. Training for teachers should include material to raise sensitivity about size issues, and school health care professionals should have accurate information about fat and health, and the self-esteem issues of fat children. There should be a mandate that every public building, from jury boxes in courtrooms to desks in schools, be accessible to fat people.

Neither the California Legislature nor Congress has taken an interest in size discrimination issues. A Congressional subcommittee is holding a series of informational hearings on regulating the diet industry. Legislation coming out of these hearings may give fat people some consumer

sumer protection, but will do nothing for problems of size discrimination.

Because this is a feminist issue, NOW should take a public stance against size discrimination. An anti-size discrimination resolution, first passed by California NOW at our 1988 Conference, will be considered at the 1990 National NOW Conference in San Francisco.

MINORITIES SHOULD HAVE
AN EDGE IN TEST SCORING

Richard T. Seymour

If tests were perfect, and if test scores were always fair and accurate measures of a person's ability to perform, it would be reasonable to ban adjustments to test scores.

Unfortunately, tests are often culturally biased and the scores people obtain on them are often of limited use in predicting their ability to perform. When the test scores themselves are unfair, banning adjustments to test scores will interfere with merit selection, not protect it.

Suppose that you are an employer hiring several inexperienced typists. You use a typing test, and find that every increase in test score corresponds to greater ability to type. If these are all the facts, it would clearly be unfair for you to add points to the test scores of blacks just because they obtained lower scores on the typing test.

Suppose, however, that there were other facts clouding this simple picture: some of the lower-scoring black applicants impressed you in their interviews. You found that their inner-city schools still used manual typewriters in typing classes, and they were not used to the electric typewriters used for the tests. The white applicants had all used electric typewriters in their typing classes.

Now what do you do? You know that the scores obtained by black applicants cannot directly be compared with the scores obtained by white applicants. You check with a friend at another firm, and she confirms that black hires routinely out-perform white hires who had scored up to 10 points higher on the same typing test.

If you are still interested in hiring based on merit, you have to regard a typing score of 75 for a white applicant as being the equivalent of a typing score of 65 for a black applicant in order to make hiring decisions truly based on ability to perform the job.

This kind of situation occurs frequently. In 1989, a federal court barred New York State from awarding Regents' scholarships based solely on the scores obtained on the Scholastic Aptitude Test, a test developed to predict first-year college grades.

Women receive lower scores than men on the SAT, so men received most of the scholarships. However, women's first-year grades are higher than men's even when controlling for course of study. The SAT substantially under-predicted women's ability to perform well. Without a score adjusted, its use would be unfair.

The Labor Department's Specific Aptitude Test Batteries are used by State Employment Service in deciding which applicants to refer to employers with job vacancies.

The government has published studies performed on current employees. The results are staggering: the test-passing rate for whites who

SOURCE: Reprinted by permission of the Scripps Howard News Service. Reprinted from the *Mobile Register*, April 10, 1991.

turned out to be poor workers was close to the test-passing rate for blacks who turned out to be good workers in more than half the studies; in nine of the 47 studies, white workers who turned out poorly passed the test at higher rates than blacks who turned out well.

Whites do a lot better on the tests than they do on the job, and blacks do a lot better on the job than they do on the test.

The "intelligence" tests administered by the Army during World War I are a chilling example of what can occur when differences in test scores are treated as if they have intrinsic meaning—38 percent of Irish draftees, and 68 percent of black draftees were regarded on the basis of these tests as having a mental age of 8 or younger.

The lower scores received by blacks and by recent immigrants from Ireland and southern and eastern Europe were used to support theories of racial superiority, and were relied upon in efforts to limit the immigration of southern and eastern Europeans.

Clearly, there was something seriously wrong with the tests, and not necessarily anything wrong with the test-takers. With this example in mind we should not again make the mistake of treating test scores as automatically meaningful in themselves.

We know that minorities score lower on most tests than whites, that women score lower than men, and that southerners of any race score lower than northerners of the same race.

Before we engrave test scores in stone, we must first ensure that the test scores themselves are fair measure: that they really are related to ability to perform, that the differences in performance they predict are meaningful, and that their predictions are equally accurate for all race, gender, and regional groups affected by the tests.

Courtesy of People for the American Way.

LEFT-HANDERS (THOSE SICKOS) GOT NO REASON TO LIVE!

Roger L. Guffey

If you ask me, the U.S. Supreme Court ruling concerning certain sexual acts between consenting adults in the privacy of their own homes heralds a much welcome return to the right rather than an invasion of privacy and individual rights. To further this admirable goal of moving to the right, I want to encourage the Court now to go after one of the most despicable and un-American groups that threaten our great country today: left-handed people.

Ha, ha, you say. Most people do not realize how truly malevolent these subversive little perverts are. Look up the word "sinister" in the dictionary, and you find two meanings: evil or left-handed. Still not convinced, eh? Historically, the U.S. government has fought leftists worldwide, so let's do it in this country before we take on those in Nicaragua. In this century, every other English speaking nation makes its citizens drive on the left (i.e., wrong) side of the road. If that doesn't prove how un-American left-handers are, I don't know what does.

Besides, left-handers are not normal. They are so unnatural that I can pick them out of a crowd a mile away. Our society has no use for their sick, twisted kind. Just think of all the things we have designed exclusively for the right-handers: scissors, shirt pockets, phone dials, wrist watches, toilet flush handles, books, etc. Have you ever seen a car with the ignition switch on the left side of the steering column? No, and you won't, because that's not the way God told Henry Ford to make them. You can even turn right against a red light, but if you try to make a left-hand turn against the light, you will find yourself going against society because it is not natural.

Oh, sure, the bleeding hearts will say that we need compassion for these sickos because they were born that way. Hogwash! It's a choice they make. If every mother would give her children a swift rap in the chops at the first sign of this filthy, disgusting left-handed behavior, this degenerate psychosis would vanish. Now, I am all for respecting everybody's rights to be different as long as I agree with what they are doing, but you have to draw the line somewhere. There won't be any left-handers in heaven, you can count on that.

The solution is not just social ostracism. We should all band together and pray fervently that God will strike these little perverts dead. Once this society returns to the moral character and justice that made this country great and prosecutes these deviant miscreants and genetic mistakes to the fullest extent of the law, everything will be all right. Act now before we all go out and buy left-handed bicycles. Take heart. God is on our side.

SOURCE: Reprinted from the *Lexington Herald-Leader*, July 10, 1987.

THE GANG THAT COULDN'T SHOOT
STRAIGHT STILL AIMS TO DECONSTRUCT US

Jud Blakely

A rose is a rose is a rose. No. In fact, a rose is *not* a rose is *not* a rose. That's right. Yes, it's not. And no, it is. Or so say the oracles of the theory of Deconstruction. These days, though, they're a beaten claque in mean retreat. Soon a rose may be a rose again. Good. So what?

Deconstruction arrived in the U.S. in 1970. It emerged at Yale in the person of Paul de Man, a Belgian intellectual. He had come to the States in 1948. Before Yale, he studied or taught at Harvard, Johns Hopkins, and Cornell. With de Man came too a revolutionary era in "lit-crit."

TYING TIN CANS TO THE TALE OF AMERICA

Paul de Man died in 1983 of cancer. During his tenure at Yale, de Man turned literary criticism inside-out. He brought to it a virulent new form of radical skepticism. This was Deconstruction. It has had far-flung negative side-effects.

The impact of Paul de Man is not academic. It is obliquely profound. And it is national. It long ago slipped its literary leash to infect such fields as law, history, and art. No field is immune to the reach of Deconstruction. As a theory, it's a godsend for the "marginalized"—for those who feel put down, fed up, left out. It gives them a potent intellectual weapon. Or has. It let them tie a lot of tin cans to the tale of America.

THE SWASTIKA THAT CAME IN FROM THE COLD

In 1987, the integrity of Paul de Man went up in smoke. He'd been a Nazi stooge. He'd been an intellectual sell-out. During 1940–42, the guru of Deconstructive rigor had written a steady stream of pro-Nazi articles. In 1987, they came to light.

The revelation broke like a clap of thunder. It echoed and echoed, and echoed. A Nazi collaborator? If there was a worse crime, no one could name it. This was an unspeakable trespass. For a liberal scholar like de Man, such craven acts defied belief. They were hopelessly vile.

All told, de Man wrote 170 pieces extolling the virtues of Hitler's New Order in Belgium. He toiled for *Le Soir,* a collaborationist newspaper. Not exactly a slip of the tongue.

Having died four years earlier, the guru failed to defend himself. But his followers circled the wagons. They strove to exculpate him. Or at least to interpret what he'd done in less horrific terms. They tried at first to whitewash de Man. That didn't work. So they graywashed him.

In the eyes of Deconstructionists, Paul de Man was not guilty. Nor

SOURCE: Reprinted in revised form from *Gray Matters,* July 1991. Reprinted by permission of the author.

was he a fascist. He was, in fact, quite the opposite—an infinitely complex *anti*-Nazi! His writings? They were in code.

Yeah! That's the ticket! Code! De Man wrote in, uh, *code!* He didn't say what he'd said. No! What he said was what he *didn't* say. It was as clear as an unrung bell. He only seemed to say what a Nazi suckling would say. But no! It was a code. Decoded, de Man said the opposite.

For hard core Deconstructionists, that was the party line. Outrageous? Sure. But it was not just an *ad hoc* defense of Paul de Man. It was Deconstructive theory at work. As gospel.

GEORGE ORWELL, CALL YOUR OFFICE

As gospel, Deconstructive theory has leaped off the pages of *1984.* It tries to subvert. It tries to yank words and deeds out of old patterns and ram them into new ones. Fine. Except the new ones erase the old, and mock them. Criticism? No. It's cynicism. With a smirk and a sneer.

So it is with Deconstruction. The theory is a smirking, sneering act that exalts the *self,* the *here,* the *now.* It draws us into a dire funk of nothing at the edge of nothing. We end up with black on black. Or with gray on gray—as in the case of Paul de Man. We end up befogged.

Where we end up with Deconstruction is at a choice we dare not make. What is real, what is not? As gospel, Deconstruction seeks to numb us—to leave us unfree to choose. Or to act.

THE GOSPEL ACCORDING TO PAUL

Unfree to choose. Or *free not to choose.* Such is the gospel of Deconstruction as preached by Paul de Man. *Either/And.* With his past, there is much to be said for a theory that deters the possibility of choice. Deconstruction does that. It presents a quandary. It makes us shrug.

As preached by Paul de Man, Deconstruction is a defiant abuse of moral clarity. It works to seduce us at the point of moral choice—to con us with an abstruse lie. The lie is that life is a "text." It isn't words, it isn't deeds. Life is what we describe. It's *language*—no more, no less.

Marx defined life as economic. Freud defined it as psychological. To Paul de Man, life was a "linguistic predicament," an ironic flux. It had to be read—lived—in terms of a coy novel.

KILLING KING AUTHOR

In Deconstructive theory, the authors have all been killed. They no longer exist. They are the victims of de Man, his mentors, his colleagues, and their minions. Readers are the new kings. King Author is dead! Long live the king!

The reader rules a kingdom of text—which is words and deeds neutered into *signs.* They are the family jewels of Deconstructive theory. But signs are mere coinage-in-waiting. Their value is nil. They wait King Reader, who them dubs them with value—the imprint of himself.

In short, Wm. Shakespeare isn't who he was. He's who I-the-Reader say he is. And I say he's dead, gone, and/or never was. Therefore, he is irrelevant—as person, as author. I decree it.

That is the Deconstructionist death sentence. Authors are not relevant. They are, at best, no more than accidents of language. It's not what they said that counts—for they said nothing. It is what the *words* say that counts. But words are *signs,* not words. It's signs that count.

"SIGNS 'R' US"

To Paul de Man, the signs of life were life. He wrote that, "Instead of containing or reflecting experience, language constitutes it." In other words, language is life. Language happens, not experience. Hmmm. So..."Signs 'R' Us."

But signs 'R' not us. We are flesh and blood. We do confront right and wrong. Life is no text. Nor can its sole essence be language. Essence lies in what and how we choose, and in how we bear the result. No text, life is also no trick. Yet Paul de Man preached it was both.

The trick is self-contradiction—of all signs at all times. Of life. Thus, any choice is as moral as one that refutes it. Or indicts it. Those not chosen are no more or less real. Or unreal.

Paul de Man taught the marginalized how to pitch. He taught them how to throw spitballs, curves, and knucklers. He taught them a nifty new way to pitch the misdeeds of America to America. The aim? To deconstruct us—to read us as a text. Then find us sinful or remiss.

Hey! This really isn't a joke! Anyway, the bad guys are bad due to Phallogocentrism. They're all stoked up on that *phallus/logos/egotistical I* stuff. This warps them into linear thugs.

Linear thugs are fond of logic. They find logic a good tool for diagnosing most matters. They tried it, they like it. Alas, logic is all too linear. Being linear is a Deconstructionist no-no. As are hierarchies. Or the notion that we live and die in a world of moral choice.

YANKEE DOODLE ISN'T DANDY

In literature first, voices on the margin rose to decry Western works. But Paul de Man did not fire up their anti-Western drive. He just added the cunning theory of Deconstruction. It soon spread from its 1970 beachhead at Yale.

There was no puzzle to its appeal. It appealed *as* a puzzle. In Deconstructive theory, nothing was what it was. Nothing was not a text. And all texts were words that were signs—none of which was certain. Example: dog means dog, unless dog means cat. Or something else.

Honest! This is no joke! It's Deconstruction. It's a form of intellectual catnip. Or dognip.

At any rate, Paul de Man was a boon to those on the outside looking in. He made them a gift of Deconstruction. With it, they had a new way to twist America's tale—to declare that Yankee Doodle isn't dandy. Via Deconstructive theory, the story of America was boldly revised. Now it became a conspiratorial epic. It was rewritten. Now it was an encyclopedic rap sheet.

America was a Phallogocentric bully. We were center-loving, margin-hating goons. We had an insatiable yen for racist, sexist oppression. We were Uncle Sham—the West at its worst.

THE GANG THAT COULDN'T SHOOT STRAIGHT

Deconstruction is one part of America's shame game. Since 1970, it's been a deft intellectual tool of great use to America-bashers. They use it to debunk us—to "expose" all we were, all we are, as a morbid, bloody mega-scam. Our past is a fraud. The West is a fraud. It's all bad.

White middle-class non-gay males are at the controls. All others are victims. They include those who are black, red, brown, female, poor, gay, handicapped, and so on. This indictment is hardly fresh. Even so, Deconstructive theory layered it with a fresh intellectual gloss.

This impressive gloss has now paled where it first shone so brightly—in the world of lit-crit in higher education. But it's long since moved on. These days it has a worrisome hold in the less arcane fields of art, history, law, architecture, and political science. That's the short list.

Are lies the same as the truth? Paul de Man's Deconstructionists say no. Except when they say yes. Or maybe. Are they just a gang that couldn't shoot straight? No? Maybe? Yes.

Courtesy of the Adolph Coors Company.

STOP BANNING THINGS
AT THE DROP OF A RAT

Elizabeth M. Whelan

In 1959, the nation experienced its first food-related cancer scare: An official said that a chemical used on cranberries caused cancer in rodents. Panic ensued. Cranberry products were destroyed.

In 1989, a movie star and an environmental group announced Alar on apples caused cancer. Panic ensued. Apple products were destroyed across the land.

And in between these two events, artificial sweeteners, hair dyes, bacon, muffin mix and more were targeted because they had "cancer-causing agents."

The common link: the animal test and the assumption that any chemical which at megadoses causes cancer in rodents must be assumed to cause cancer in humans, even at minuscule levels of exposure.

This has no basis in science. There is not a shred of evidence that the barely measurable levels of these much-maligned chemicals cause *any* cancer in humans.

And continuation of policies which require chemicals to be banned "at the drop of the rat" threaten both our quality of life and our health. If we continue to ban everything which causes cancer in rodents, we will reduce our food supply (by banning pesticides), raise taxes (to pay for chasing down trace chemicals), and otherwise burden our economy and diminish our standard of living without preventing *any* cancer cases—while diverting attention from real causes of human cancer.

The solution to "mouse terrorism" and the "carcinogen of the week" phenomenon is not to abandon animal tests. Instead, we must:

- Acknowledge that exposing animals to near-fatal doses of chemicals itself causes tissue changes that predispose to cancer. If the alleged effect occurs only in the highest dose, the results should be considered suspect.

- Before automatically issuing the label "carcinogen," ask relevant questions: Does this cause cancer in more than one species or sex? In multiple experiments? The Alar scare, for example, was triggered on the basis of one study on mice alone.

- Avoid an exorcist approach to purging our environment of every trace of the chemical in question. Instead, prudent and safe tolerance levels of exposure should be set as we do with known *human* carcinogens (radiation, sunlight exposure) and with known natural carcinogens.

Animal studies are critical in biomedical research—but so is common sense in interpreting the implications and applications for humans.

SOURCE: Reprinted from *USA Today*, October 19, 1990. Reprinted by permission of the author.

SUBLIMINAL ADVERTISING:
HOSTILITY AMONG THE ICE CUBES

John Leo

Seagram's gin ads have been spoofing the idea that subliminal messages are tucked away in advertising. "Can you find the hidden pleasure in refreshing Seagram's gin?" says one. Not so hidden among the bubbles and ice of a gin drink is a couple dancing or perhaps a woman floating along in an inner tube. A helpful arrow points to the image, along with the copy line, "If you think this is just a bubble, look again."

No one knows why, but we appear to be in the midst of a boom of ads mocking subliminals. The spoofers include Toyota, Schweppes, Miller Lite, Absolut and Round Table Pizza, which features a slice of pepperoni that turns into a human face and shouts "Buy this pizza!" The Seagram's campaign looks like a satirical poke at the author Wilson Bryan Key, who has been arguing for years that images of skulls are hidden in ice cubes and the letters "S-E-X" deviously embedded in Ritz crackers. Years ago, when I was working at *Time* magazine, Key phoned to argue that whole bunches of the letters S, E and X had been hidden in a *Time* cover photo on Vietnam. I had to tell him this was impossible: Since decision making at *Time* is modeled on that of the Austro-Hungarian civil service, the authorizations required to approve the placement of each forbidden letter would have instantly converted the magazine into a monthly.

Key's zealotry has deflated what might have been a serious debate about motivational research and advertising. Forget crackers and ice cubes. If you define subliminal ads as those that appeal on an unconscious level as well as a conscious one, then subliminals surely exist. The best current example is Newport's long-running and immensely successful "Alive With Pleasure!" campaign. The photos always show outdoorsy yuppies horsing around. But amid all this jollity, there is a strong undercurrent of sexual hostility, usually directed at women. Many depict women who seem to be off-balance and menaced, or at least the target of berserk male energy. Women are about to be clanged by a pair of cymbals, carried off on a pole, pulled along in a horse collar, or slam-dunked in the face by a basketball-wielding male. I once collected more than a hundred of these ads, about 80 percent of which, I think, are coded scenes of sexual aggression, though everyone is shown wildly laughing to indicate the opposite. We flip past these ads every day without the theme puncturing our consciousness, but if they are laid out together, the point is hard to miss. When I showed a batch to Betty Friedan, she immediately called them "absolutely perverse."

No other recent campaign seems as dubious as Newport's, but there are many examples of similar ambiguity. Nike's "Just do it" slogan and Burger King's "Sometimes you've gotta break the rules" are evocative, open-ended statements, likely to be read quite differently by the com-

SOURCE: Reprinted by permission of *U.S. News & World Report*, July 15, 1991.

fortable middle class and the struggling poor. To the well-off, Nike's advice is to get in shape and Burger King's is to allow yourself a fatty hamburger once in a while. But in harsher neighborhoods, both campaigns seem to identify their products with lawbreaking and freedom from impulse control. The Hispanic agency employed by Burger King got the point right away, declining to translate "Breaking the rules" into Spanish because it implied approval for violating laws or Hispanic traditions. (Merrill Lynch's "Your World Should Know No Boundaries" campaign was a totally up-scale variation on the same antisocial theme, playing with the idea of an infinite self, free of bothersome restraint and obligation.)

As might be expected, alcohol and tobacco ads seem to resort to subliminal themes most frequently. Most of these are nonverbal and can't easily be analyzed in a column, so let's take one of the more verbal ones. In the Bacardi Black "The Taste of the Night" campaign ("Some people fear the night because it liberates the other senses"), the overt message is sexual (partially clad woman standing by), but the stronger covert one circles around the theme of night and liquor as liberators of the real you (and your darker side) from the bonds of civilized society. A second ad in this series makes the theme explicit, in fact too explicit: "Some people embrace the night because the rules of the day do not apply." Possible translation: They can hold you responsible during the day, but not at night, when you're drunk. This dreamy appeal to booze-induced wildness is echoed in the Bacardi white rum ads ("Wild for Bacardi," women in leopard bathing suits). Bacardi's symbol, by the way, is a bat.

Use of feral animals as a come-on for drinking is an old story. The malt liquors, marketed primarily to poor members of minority groups, use cobra, bull, dragon, tiger, stallion and pit bull. The idea is to sell wildness and power to the powerless (high alcohol content is part of the same strategy). So long as this theme is covert, nobody seems to object, but the G. Heileman Brewing Co. has just found out what happens when the fig leaf is dropped. By naming a strong malt liquor Power-Master, Heileman provoked minority protests, and the Bureau of Alcohol, Tobacco and Firearms withdrew approval for the brand name. In a reasonable world, Newport would have been jumped on years before PowerMaster, but then Newport is subtle and Heileman isn't.

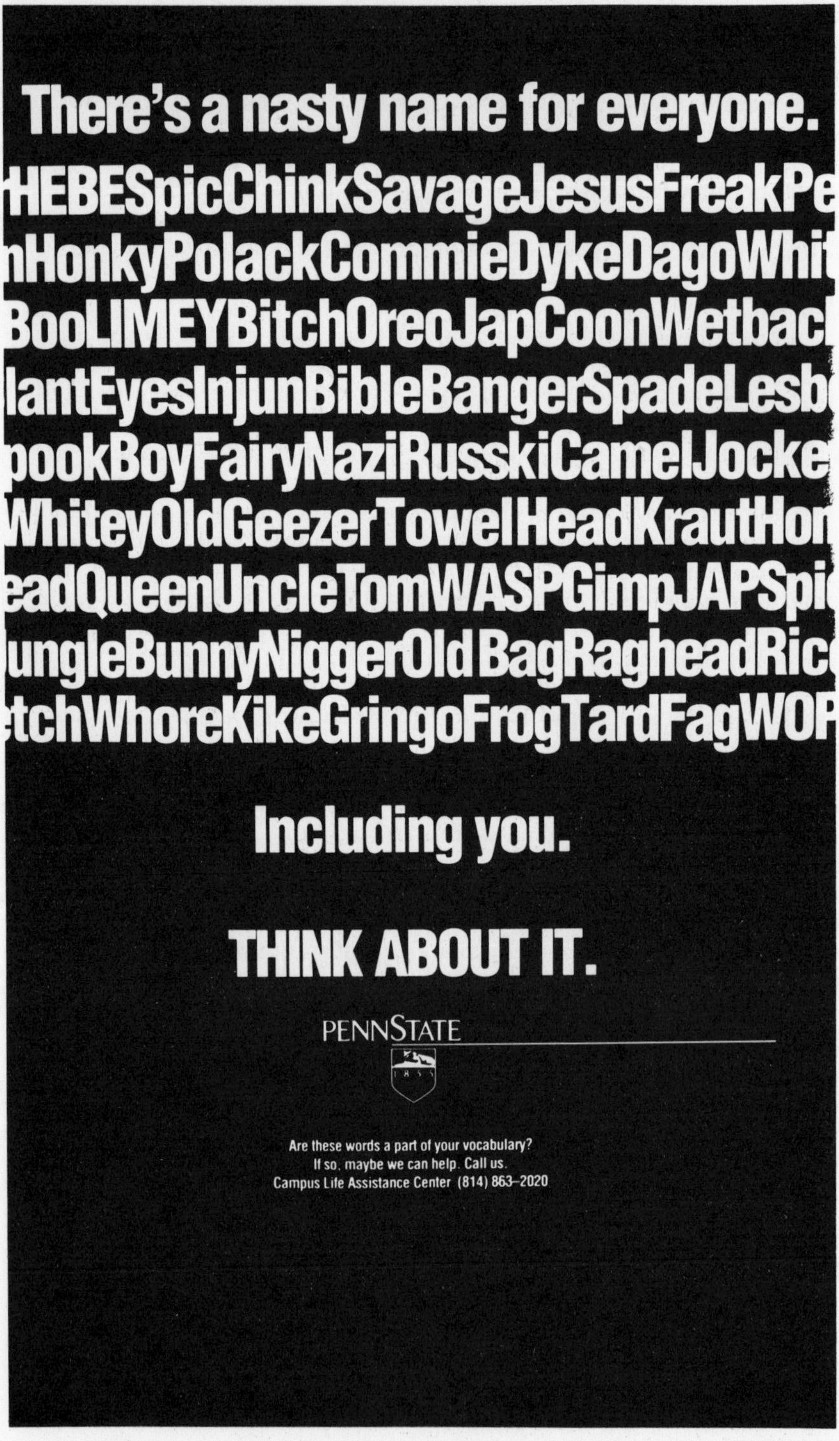

Courtesy of Pennsylvania State University.

ASKING GOD TO
CHEAT IN SPORTS

Dexter Martin

Should people pray for their team to win? Isn't that asking God to cheat? The rules of a game permit only a certain number of players. If God were to help one side more than the other, wouldn't he be breaking the rules? Wouldn't he be dishonest and illegal?

And wouldn't he be unfair? God's power is said to be infinite; and if that is true, he's irresistible. (I'm using masculine pronouns for convenience, instead of clumsily repeating "he or she or it.") A team with God behind it or in it would be unbeatable, wouldn't it?

And if God were to favor one team more than another, he wouldn't be acting like a father. If we're all his children, shouldn't he treat us equally? Would a decent father like to see some of his children defeat his other ones and make them feel miserable? Would he be proud to be the cause of this?

If you beg God to give your team a victory, aren't you unconsciously hoping he'll be unjust and unpaternal? If you thank him afterwards, shouldn't you also say, "I'm grateful to you, God, for granting us an unfair advantage by your invisible presence and influence"? And shouldn't you add, "I'm happy you didn't behave like a father"? In sports, you want God to be unethical, don't you?

You don't? Then stop praying before, during, and after games.

Coaches leading teams in the Lord's Prayer in locker rooms; spectators imploring God visibly and audibly; the wife of a notorious basketball coach frantically repeating her rosary behind him and rushing off to church afterwards to thank God, Jesus, Mary, and a favorite saint; baseball players crossing themselves before they bat (or strike out); a Protestant pitcher falling to his knees on the mound to thank God for letting him win the final game of the World Series; pro football players who kneel in the end zone after their touchdowns and thank the Lord; Notre Dame appealing to Jesus by installing a mural of him in the football stadium, holding up his arms like a referee signalling "Touchdown!"—such people unwittingly want an immoral God, a divinity who would be guilty of unsportsmanlike conduct if he were a human being.

Some editors may be afraid of this article because some Christians will disagree with me. But only a very few will, I'm sure, because I've tested these opinions on students at several universities when I was an English professor. (I've retired.) I told them, "I'm not attacking your denominations or preaching atheism. I'm merely suggesting that you should draw a distinction between childish religion and adult religion." As a beautiful nun said in class, "There's a difference between superstition and religion. Praying for a team is just superstition. I agree with you."

And she said it in a paper. Let me quote her:

> *Catholics used to call Notre Dame God's Team because it was usually ranked first in the nation. I called it that myself when I was much younger. But then Gerry*

Faust became coach and the team slumped for four years, even though he was extremely pious. His record was only 30-26-1. He was fired. Now that Lou Holtz has made Our Lady Number One again, I suppose some Catholics are thinking of it as God's Team again. But the phrase seems very childish to me now. Religion isn't the secret of Notre Dame's success. Coaching is, and that includes recruiting.

(Later, she told me, "If I weren't a nun, I'd be a sports reporter.")

In pro football, the Dallas Cowboys were number one so often that some fans called *them* God's Team. I knew one who was serious and so there were probably more. But then America's Team (as it was also known) sank into a slump even worse than Notre Dame's. Coach Landry had to be fired, although he had become more religious than ever.

There's no evidence that any team has ever been God's. If there were one, it would be easily recognizable because it would never lose. How could Almighty God be clobbered?

Shouldn't we assume that God realizes he shouldn't interfere in games, that he'd be cheating if he guided footballs and baseballs and basketballs, that he'd be unsporting if he provided an athlete with an extra spurt? Spiritual steroids are as dishonest as medicinal ones.

If you were running the universe, would you cheat for your favorite athletes? Of course not. Why would God?

DON'T RETIRE TENURED
PROFESSORS AT 70

Mary W. Gray

To believe that professors who reach the age 70 suddenly become incapable of carrying on successful research and teaching is no less misguided than to believe that women cannot do mathematics or that African-Americans cannot manage baseball teams.

With the elimination of mandatory retirement for the vast majority of employees, the nation has learned that many over-70 doctors, lawyers, secretaries and carpenters are far more valuable than many of their younger colleagues.

If Congress accepts the recommendation of the National Academy of Sciences/National Research Council Commission on Mandatory Retirement, beginning in 1994 tenured faculty will also enjoy the full protection of the Age Discrimination in Employment Act.

Tenured faculty, along with such workers as airline pilots and firefighters, originally were exempted from the abolition of mandatory retirement because university administrators convinced some members of Congress that higher education deserved special treatment. They argued that research and teaching ability declines with age (not necessarily true) and that older employees cost more (generally true, but not confined to tenured faculty).

Tenure, they asserted, protects incompetent faculty, and the nation's campuses would be burdened by doddering, expensive older professors.

In the first place, tenure protects academic freedom, not incompetency; although some faculty and administrators fail to use them, dismissed-for-cause procedures exist and can be effective.

Second, there are incompetent professors of age 40 as well as of age 70. Civil rights laws require that we judge individuals on their own merits, not make arbitrary judgments based on age, race or gender.

Finally, others who have tenure have been protected by the abolition of mandatory retirement—public school teachers, for example—and others have never been subject to mandatory retirement—members of Congress and most judges.

Although each of us probably has a member of Congress or judge whom we would like to retire, lack of mandatory retirement seems not to have wrecked the institutions.

Those arguing for the retention of mandatory retirement maintain that colleges and universities are "different"; the same argument has been made for exempting higher education from all anti-discrimination laws.

I agree that government should not interfere with academic freedom, but academic freedom does not include a license to discriminate, I also have little sympathy with the argument that the precarious financial

SOURCE: Reprinted from the *Mobile Register*, September 11, 1991. Reprinted by permission of the author.

situation of colleges and universities will be worsened by the abolition of mandatory retirement. It would be better to seek savings by curbing expensive sports programs and reining in the administrative bloat that has occurred in higher education over the past 20 years.

It is true that we need to provide opportunities for younger faculty, particularly women and minorities. However, the same people arguing in favor of mandatory retirement have failed to make much progress over the last 20 years while mandatory retirement has been in effect. For example, although approximately 20 percent of the Ph.D.'s in mathematics go to women, only 1 of the 86 junior faculty members in the nation's top 10 mathematics departments is a woman. In fact, most of those arguing for the retention of mandatory retirement are college and university administrators who seek in whatever way they can to exert more control over tenured faculty in the name of "flexibility."

The NRC commission recommended that mandatory retirement be eliminated for two reasons. First, it found little evidence to justify the arbitrary assumption that older faculty are less productive. Second, it found that in those states where mandatory retirement has already been abolished, few faculty stay beyond age 70 so that the concerns over financing and closing off opportunities for younger scholars seem unjustified.

Currently the average age of retirement for faculty is under 65, far less than the mandatory 70. However, the commission did find that a few research universities where the teaching loads are very light, the salaries high, and the working conditions generally very pleasant, a large proportion of faculty might choose to stay on beyond age 70.

Nonetheless, it did not feel that the civil rights of hundreds of thousands of Americans should be violated by continuing their employers' ability arbitrarily to retire them just because a handful of problems might arise at a few elite institutions.

*This may be
the very best idea
you've ever had.*

*Bells and whistles,
the works.*

*The one you
could ride all the way
to the corner office.*

*When it's important,
it belongs on
Hammermill paper.*

An idea acquires a little more
impact when you put it on Hammermill paper.
A little more immediacy. Why Hammermill?
It could be the sharp, down-to-business
readability of our copier papers. The leading-
edge look of our desktop publishing papers.
Or the commanding quality of our
bond papers. Hammermill makes just
about every kind of business paper around.
And every one has that air of importance
that helps make sure what you have to say
gets the attention it deserves.

**Where America
conducts its business.**

INTERNATIONAL⊕PAPER

Courtesy of Hammermill Papers.

RIGHT OF THE LAW-ABIDING
CITIZEN TO PROTECT WHAT IS HIS

Bill Hodges

While visiting relatives recently in your lovely city, I read an article in the *Press Register* that I found very disturbing. A man, Mark Mc-Clammy, who had taken steps to try to protect his home from repeatedly being burglarized, was found guilty of negligent homicide because a booby trap he had set for burglars killed one of them. What happened to the right of the law-abiding citizen to protect what is his? Was the reason he was negligent because he wasn't present and holding the gun when it fired?

I don't think any jury would have found him guilty if he had shot the burglar himself as he was breaking into his home. Are we to stand by and just watch our valuables being taken by thieves? The police do an excellent job, but they can't be everywhere at the same time.

The man who was killed, Lee Roy Woodard, had an extensive criminal record dating back to 1970. It's bad enough that a piece of human debris like this was allowed to continue preying on others, but to send a man like McClammy, (who, by the way, reportedly has no criminal record) to jail for trying to protect his home, his property and his and his family's lives, would be the ultimate travesty. Instead of sending him to jail, we should be sending him an award for doing something to benefit the community.

No longer will Lee Roy Woodard cause suffering and anguish to any others. No one forced him to burglarize McClammy's residence. He knew the risks involved in such an evil deed.

Each member of the jury that voted to convict McClammy and every member of the prosecuting team should be thoroughly ashamed of themselves for the decision reached. This is something they will have to live with the rest of their lives. I only hope that the judge who will issue the sentence, Judge Ferrill McRae, will lessen the wrong done to Mc-Clammy by issuing the most lenient sentence the law will allow. At least Judge McRae has the opportunity to dampen this unjust blow to Mc-Clammy and his family.

SOURCE: Letter to the *Mobile Register*, August 15, 1990. Reprinted by permission of the author.

129,001

IN MEMORIAM In memory of all the lives lost to AIDS. All 129,001 of them. ◆ Every American man, woman and child who has contracted the HIV virus and died since 1981. Remembered by the men, women and children who loved them, and whom they loved. ◆ Their mothers and fathers, sisters and brothers. Their wives and husbands and lovers, colleagues and friends. ◆ Remembered as particular, unique human beings, not as statistics. Each one with a name, a face, a heart, and a mind. Each one with a favorite song, songs which will forever evoke a look and a touch for the millions of us left behind. ◆ We who cannot help but mourn. ◆ We who remember them in joy and fondness for how they lived. ◆ And in deepest sorrow and hottest anger for how they died. ◆ Their bravery unacknowledged, their pain ignored, their needs neglected and mocked by those without the basic human decency to choose love over hatred, compassion over fear. ◆ One out of every hundred adults in the United States has acquired HIV, the virus that causes AIDS. ◆ We will lose every one of them far too soon unless we do what's right, and good, and possible. ◆ And we will lose millions more in years to come unless we begin to talk honestly to each other and to our children, spread awareness instead of panic, and insist that the people we call our leaders embrace their true responsibilities. ◆ America's men, women, and children with AIDS. ◆ They are our friends. They are our family. They are the missing from among us. Today, remember them all.

AIDS. THE ONLY CURE IS TO CARE.

In the time it has taken to read this, one more American has needlessly died of AIDS. For the facts about HIV transmission, testing, and treatment, please write the nation's oldest and largest AIDS organization, providing advocacy, education, and care for men, women, and children with AIDS: Gay Men's Health Crisis, 129 West 20th Street, New York, New York 10011.

NEUTRALSPEAK IS TOO HIGH
A PRICE TO PAY FOR SENSITIVITY

Donald K. Emmerson

What price sensitivity?

That is the question inadvertently posed by two pieces of paper that recently crossed my desk.

The first is a page from the Summer 1991 newsletter of the Modern Language Association, to which I belong, announcing a new project to oppose "anti-feminist harassment in the academy." According to the MLA, the intellectual harassment of feminists is related to sexual harassment, though different from it. Examples include the "easy dismissal of feminist writers"; "the automatic deprecation of feminist work as 'narrow,' 'partisan' and 'lacking in rigor'"; and "malicious humor directed against feminists."

Harassment is nasty business. As the Modern Language Association should know, "to harass" originally meant to cause someone to be attacked by dogs. My dictionary gives two meanings: physical assault and repeated pestering. By linking it with sexual harassment, the MLA makes anti-feminist harassment sound almost like arguing with intent to rape.

Easy dismissal, automatic deprecation, malicious humor . . . are these things harassment? Is it not possible that the logical or factual weakness of an argument, made by a feminist, a chauvinist, or anyone else, could make it easy to dismiss? To avoid being charged with anti-feminist harassment, when we hear a feminist make such an argument, are we to sacrifice candor for sensitivity by camouflaging what we mean, dressing up in some feigned difficulty the ease of our dismissal?

As for automatic deprecation and malicious humor, who is to define these adjectives? No argument, feminist or otherwise, should be deprecated "automatically" if that means the deprecator hasn't bothered to read it or listen to it. But who is to say where quick criticism stops and automatic deprecation begins? If the object of a joke does not laugh, does that make the jokester malicious? The best advice for anyone wishing to avoid the accusation of harassing feminists might be to avoid humor altogether. Is that a small price well worth paying to ensure no one gets angry? Or is the value of discourse thereby lowered to the level of the thinnest skinned?

The second piece of paper is a list of guidelines for speakers written by the Wisconsin Union Directorate. WUD sent it to help me prepare for a slide lecture I've agreed to give for them this week. The guidelines request my "sensitivity" and ask me to "avoid sexist and/or biased language" and "be aware of language which may offend others or show unintentional bias, such as gaudy versus ornamental; shack versus building; etc."

I too wish to avoid sexist language; I consider myself a feminist. But

SOURCE: *Wisconsin State Journal*, 2 October 1991, p. 11A

whose definition of "sexist" should guide me? Fortunately, I will be speaking, not writing, so although I may have to say the word "women," I won't have to risk upsetting someone by writing it with an "e" rather than a "y." (The "y" in "womyn" decontaminates "women" from the taint of "men.") "I will not try to utter the word "mankind," which might be offensive to some.

But Wisconsin Union Directorate asks me to eliminate even unintentional bias from my language. How am I going to do that? Language is rich and subjective, it carries emotive impact; its connotations move us. And whose bias is to be avoided here? The bias of the "racist homophobes" so automatically deprecated by some, or the bias of the "politically correct" so easily (though less hurtfully) dismissed by others? Doesn't it depend on whose ox is being gored?

Should I reduce my risk while showing the slides by saying as little as possible? But then I would violate another WUD guideline that asks me to explain such slides. Maybe I should remove from my carousel in advance any slides of things that look like shacks, just so I won't make a mistake and forget not to call them buildings. As for the shots of certain multicultured structures in Malaysia that I was going to include, if I do dare to show them, I must remember to call these buildings ornamental, even though when I look at them the word "gaudy" comes—I confess!—more readily to mind. But even if I purge my vocabulary in these specified cases, how can I know what other traps and transgressions WUD may have planted inside "etc.", the minefield of a word with which that guideline ends?

I do not mean to disparage the all too real issues of prejudice to which the MLA and the WUD are trying in their own ways to respond. Not at all. But surely we can oppose harassment and insensitivity without exaggerating the hostility of those who honestly, vigorously disagree with us, and without disguising our opinions in euphemistic neutralspeak. Scholarship and diplomacy are not and should not be the same profession. In the mission statement of the University of Wisconsin, let's not segue from "fearless sifting and winnowing" into walking on tiptoes, or self-censorship.

For sensitivity, that's too high a price to pay.

Reprinted by permission of John Trever, *Albuquerque Journal*.

PART THREE

EIGHT RULES FOR
GOOD WRITING

What matters is that we get done
what we have to do and get said what
we have to say.
—*Donald J. Lloyd*

The following pages will show you how to write clear, straightforward prose. This is the language you would use in explaining a situation or arguing an issue. It expresses itself in a direct, informal style.

There are other styles of writing. For an inaugural address or an academic essay, you will want a more formal, balanced presentation. For an emotional appeal or an angry condemnation, you may want a more colloquial style. But such occasions are rare. The informal style recommended here will serve you in almost all writing situations. You can use it to propose marriage, explain entropy, or plead not guilty.

The eight rules that follow should make you a better writer. They offer material you should know, and they omit areas you don't need to worry about. The intent is practical—not to tell you about "good writing," but to show you how to do it.

These rules will be sufficient for most people on most writing occasions. The weak student who cannot recognize a sentence and doesn't know that a period goes at the end of it will need additional help; so will the refined writer who seeks a singular style. Nevertheless, the rules can help most people become correct and effective writers.

RULE 1

Find a Subject You Can Work With

Choosing a subject is one of the hardest parts of writing, and perhaps the most important. In many writing situations, of course, you don't have to choose a topic. You want to write the power company protesting the latest rate hike. You have to send a thank-you letter to your aunt. Your boss asks you to prepare a marketing report. In these cases the subject is there, and you have to tell a particular audience about it.

Still, there are occasions when you select a topic for an essay or speech, and there are times when you might be given a general subject ("The American Dream" or "Tomorrow's Promise") but can approach it in a number of ways. You need to recognize the problems in making a choice.

To produce a good essay, you need a topic that will interest your audience, that lends itself to detail, and that can be covered in a prescribed number of words. (The point here will be clearer if you recall the last dull sermon you heard.)

If you were assigned to write a 500-word theme for a general audience (think of the people you see around you in class or at a movie), how good would these topics be?

1. "Death Awaits All Men"   Unless you are going to write of something unusual—an exploding sun, the bloody prophecies of Revelation, or the mathematics of entropy—this will be a boring subject. When you write of "all men," you tend to say what everyone knows.

2. "My Brother, the Practical Joker"   This topic concerns an individual rather than all men. The experience, however, is pretty close to that of all men. Most people have met practical jokers. Unless your brother's jokes are particularly brilliant or outrageous, you would do better with a different subject.

3. "I Am Sure I Have Pierced Ears"   This subject does not lend itself to detail. What can you write after the first sentence? Why should anyone be interested?

Remember that everything you write—every essay, every paragraph, every sentence—has to answer the question "Who cares?"

4. *"The Sun Also Rises*—Hemingway's Masterpiece"   This topic is interesting and rich with detail, but it is more suitable to a 300-page book than a 500-word theme. If you wish to write on a novel, you must restrict yourself to one feature of it. Here you could limit yourself to one character

("Robert Cohn—the Outsider") or to one fairly defined theme ("Fishing in Spain—a Symbolic Quest"). Remember that, almost invariably, you will choose a subject that's too broad rather than one that's too narrow.

5. "Hank Aaron Was a Better Hitter Than Babe Ruth" This could be a good choice. The subject would interest many readers. It provides a lot of detail—comparison of number of times at bat, number of hits, quality of opposing pitchers, the kinds of baseballs used, sizes of stadiums, and so on. If you keep the focus on batting and avoid discussions of fielding, base running, and personality, the theme can be finished in 500 words.

Another element that makes this a good subject is that it presents a minority opinion. This always adds interest. "Cleanliness Is Important" is a vague truism, but "Cleanliness Is Dangerous" could make a fascinating theme.

6. "How to Clean a Bassoon" This subject lends itself to detail; it can be covered in 500 words; and it is beyond the experience of "all men." But it would have little appeal for most readers.

Of course, if you're a knowledgeable and creative writer (like Tom Wolfe), you can make any subject interesting. And you can imagine particular readers (like your mother) who would respond to any topic you choose. But these exceptions don't change the situation for you. You need a subject that will keep the interest of a fairly general audience.

Probably, you should write on the subjects you know most about and are most interested in. What do you think about? What do you and your friends talk about on Friday night? This is what you'll write best about.

EXERCISES

Which of these subjects would be more likely to produce an interesting 500-word theme? Why?

1. The Virtue of Thrift
2. Space Travel Will Have a Drastic Effect on Contemporary Art
3. A Sure Way to Pick Winners at the Dog Track
4. The Importance of a College Education
5. Tennis Balls
6. My Brother Collects Green Stamps
7. Dogs Are Better Than Cats
8. Drag Racing Cars Perform Mathematically Impossible Feats
9. Robert Redford
10. Aspirin, Bufferin, Anacin—Somebody's Lying
11. The World Is Ending: Prophecy, Weaponry, and Ecology
12. My Baby Is a Joy!

RULE 2

Get Your Facts

An interesting theme has to be specific. No one can write a compelling essay on entropy or Hank Aaron or space-age architecture or much else without seeking out a body of factual information. Writing involves research.

Unless you are writing from personal experience, you will probably want to build your theme around people you can quote and facts you can bring forward. You obtain such material from a number of sources.

VISIT THE LIBRARY

Large stores of information can be unearthed by using the card catalog and the *Reader's Guide*. The card catalog, which is probably computerized, lists author, title, and subject for every book in the library. The *Reader's Guide*, under subject headings, lists magazine articles printed over the years. (You can find the magazines in the periodicals section or on microfilm.)

This list illustrates some of the titles available to you and the kinds of information they contain.

Acronyms and Initialisms Dictionary
   (What is the N.A.U.I.?)
American Movies Reference Book
   (Who won the Academy Award as Best Supporting Actor in 1966?)
Bartlett's Familiar Quotations
   (Who said, "A reformer is a guy who rides through the sewer in a glass-bottomed boat"?)
Baseball Encyclopedia
   (Who was the only major league pitcher to pitch two consecutive no-hit games?)
Benet's *Reader's Encyclopedia*
   (Who is the hero of Henry James' *The American?*)
Black's Law Dictionary
   (What is the Miranda rule?)
Book Review Digest
   (When David Garnett's *Shot in the Dark* was published in 1959, how did critics react to it?)

College Handbook
(What is the ratio of male to female students at Loras College?)

Crime in the United States (The FBI Report)
(How many aggravated assaults were reported in Madison, Wisconsin, in 1985?)

Current Biography
(Name the two daughters of jazzman Chuck Mangione.)

Cyclopedia of Literary Characters
(Name the Three Musketeers.)

Dictionary of American History
(Who founded the NAACP? When?)

Dictionary of American Slang
(What is a "hodad"?)

Dictionary of Classical Mythology
(Who is Aemonides?)

Dictionary of Foreign Terms
(What does *ignis fatuus* mean?)

Encyclopedia of the Opera
(Why couldn't Hoffman wed his beloved Olympia?)

Facts on File
(Why was New York Police Chief John Egan sent to prison in 1974?)

Famous First Facts
(Who received the first kidney transplant?)

Funk's *Word Origins and Their Romantic Stories*
(What is the source of the word *tantalize*?)

Gallup Poll
(In 1977, what percentage of Americans believed that homosexuality is a condition some people are born with?)

Gray's Anatomy
(If you strain the muscles of your thenar eminence, where do you hurt?)

Guinness Book of World Records
(How long was the world's longest hot dog?)

International Who's Who
(Who is Gaetano Cortesi?)

Interpreter's Bible
(What did Jesus mean when he said it is easier for a camel to go through the eye of a needle than for a rich man to enter the kingdom of God?)

McGraw-Hill Encyclopedia of Science and Technology
(What are the characteristics of synthetic graphite?)

Menke's *Encyclopedia of Sport*
(What golfer and what score won the U.S. Open in 1989?)

Mirkin's *When Did It Happen?*
(Name two famous composers born on May 7.)

The Murderers' Who's Who
(How did an earlobe figure in the "death" of murderer Charles Henry Schwartz?)

Oxford Companion to Music
(What is the Impressionist School of music?)
Oxford English Dictionary
(When was the word *fair* first used to mean "average"?)
Prager Encyclopedia of Art
(What is the real name of the painting usually called *Whistler's Mother?*)
Rock Encyclopedia
(Who was the lead singer in the original Jeff Beck Group?)
Statistical Abstract of the United States
(How many American women used poison to commit suicide in 1986?)
Telephone Directory (any large city)
(If you want tickets to a Chicago White Sox game, where should you write? What 800 number can you call?)
The Way Things Work
(Why doesn't the ink leak out of your ballpoint pen?)
Webster's Biographical Dictionary
(What is Mary McCauley's better-known name? Why is she famous?)
Webster's Dictionary of Proper Names
(When and what was the Chicken War?)
Webster's Geographical Dictionary
(In what county and state is Black River Falls?)
Who's Who in American Women
(What is Linda Ronstadt's birthday?)
World Almanac
(Name the junior senator from Oregon. What is the capacity of the Notre Dame stadium?)
World Encyclopedia of the Comics
(What was Blondie's maiden name?)

Also, make particular use of the *New York Times Index.* This gives you references to names mentioned in that information-packed newspaper. Many libraries have microfilm collections of the *Times* dating back to the 1890s. Learn to thread the microfilm projector, and you can have a fine time reading how Red Grange scored four touchdowns in ten minutes or how Neil Armstrong walked on the moon.

You will need all these sources to provide facts for your essays. And don't be afraid to ask for help in the library. Most librarians are nice people.

USE YOUR TELEPHONE

Libraries employ reference people who spend a good part of every day answering questions over the phone. If you need to know Babe Ruth's batting average in 1928, you can either find the answer in a baseball almanac or phone your local reference librarian, who will look up the information and call you back. (The Public Library in Mobile, Alabama, boasts it answered 227,000 questions in 1990.)

You can phone others too. If you need to know whether there is an apostrophe in "Diners Club," call an elegant restaurant and ask the cashier. If you have a brief legal question ("What would it cost to change my name?"), phone a lawyer. If you need to know the current price for wastepaper, call a junkyard. For specific information, don't be afraid to call a priest or banker or news reporter or sheriff or insurance agent. Most of these people are willing to help you, and many will be happy to.

When necessary, don't hesitate to call long-distance. Suppose you have to write to "Leslie Johnson" and don't know if the person is male or female. Suppose you're applying for a job and don't know the personnel manager's name. In such cases, call long-distance and get the information you need. These calls are relatively cheap.

It helps to have a WATS line or to know someone who has access to a WATS line. Think about this when you're making new friends.

WRITE FOR FACTS YOU NEED

Many sources are available to you. U.S. government agencies will send you documents on a range of subjects. Organizations with a cause will send you stacks of literature. (The American Cancer Society and the Tobacco Institute have dozens of pamphlets on smoking and health.) You can base your writing on materials from Common Cause, the National Rifle Association, the Confraternity of Christian Doctrine, Greenpeace, the National Organization for Women, People for the American Way, and any number of Right to Life organizations. (When the National Rifle Association was asked to send material that might appear in this book, they responded with a packet that weighed 3½ pounds.)

Two sources deserve special mention. If you want the script of a particular news program, say, *60 Minutes*, write and the network will send you a copy. For anything related to new laws, politics, or government programs, write your senator or representative in Washington. You will *always* get an answer from them.

If you make the effort, you will find plenty of information to give meaning and interest to your argument.

Warning: Get your facts right. Factual errors in your writing are just like spelling and punctuation errors. They make you look ignorant or careless. In persuasive writing, they are fatal.

EXERCISES

Use your library and other sources to locate this information.

1. What was the front-page headline in the *New York Times* on the day you were born?

2. What is the source of these lines?
   a. "Watchman, what of the night?"
   b. "When in doubt, punt."
3. What causes blue babies?
4. Name the individuals who won more than one Academy Award, Cy Young Award, and Heisman Trophy.
5. What day of the week was June 16, 1904? Why is that day important in English literature?
6. What was the famous crime involving Winnie Ruth Judd?
7. What does *in gremio legis* mean?
8. How many women did Don Giovanni seduce?
9. Name six performers who appeared in the movie *George Washington Slept Here*.
10. What is meant by "filial regression," "blood-packing," "googolplex," and "lycanthropy"?
11. Identify as many of these as you can:
    Sir Andrew Aguecheek
    Asiatic Annie
    Allan Paul Bakke
    Melvin Belli
    Suzette Charles
    Denton Cooley
    Pete and Frank Gusenberg
    Nile Kinnick
    Nathan F. Leopold, Jr.
    Greg Louganis
    Captain Midnight
    Donald T. Regan
    Django Reinhardt
    Christopher Robin
    Son of Sam
    Daley Thompson
    Tommy Tittlemouse
    Uriah the Hittite
    Johnny Vander Meer
    Sigourney Weaver
    John A. Zaccaro
    Pinchas Zukerman

ALTERNATE EXERCISES

Use your library and other sources to locate this information.

1. What were two of the leading sports stories in the *New York Times* on the day you were born?

2. What is the source of these lines?
    a. "Hold the fort, I am coming."
    b. "I begin to smell a rat."
3. Name the victims of Jack the Ripper.
4. Give ten words that rhyme with "aggle."
5. In *Cavalleria Rusticana*, who kills Turiddu and why?
6. Give the complete major league batting record of Ernest William Rudolph.
7. Will State Farm pay off on a suicide?
8. Give the source of the words *buxom*, *cravat*, *sabotage*, and *vermouth*.
9. What movie stars played *The Duke of West Point* and *The Duchess of Idaho*?
10. Distinguish between *Chapter Two*, Leo II, *Walden Two*, and helium II.
11. Identify as many of these as you can:
    Kathy Boudin
    William H. Bonney
    Reginald Bunthorne
    Hilda Doolittle
    Morgan Fairchild
    Doctor Fell
    Louis Farrakhan
    Uri Geller
    Bruno Hauptmann
    James Huberty
    Meadowlark Lemon
    Ed "Strangler" Lewis
    Marian McPartland
    Mercutio
    Professor Moriarty
    Linus Pauling
    Sneaky Pete
    Raina Petkoff
    Baron Scarpia
    Frank Sinkwich
    Uncas
    Frank Urban Zoeller

RULE 3

Limit Your Topic to Manageable Size

Most writing is subject to space and time limitations. You are preparing a magazine advertisement or a campaign document (one page). You are writing an editorial or a letter to the editor (under 1000 words). You are preparing a sermon or an after-dinner speech (20 minutes or less). Rarely will you have an opportunity that will permit, or an audience that will tolerate, a discussion of all aspects of an issue.

Therefore, you must limit your topic. Do not, for example, write about "Dieting." Even "Crash Dieting" is too broad a subject. But you can argue that "Crash Dieting Is Dangerous." Similarly, do not speculate about "America's Unjust Drug Laws"; write "Alabama's Marijuana Laws Violate the Fifth Amendment."

Narrowing a topic is particularly important when you write argument. A vague and rambling essay is never persuasive.

Don't write an "about" theme—that is, a general theme about fishing, about communism, about heart disease, or about marriage. These aren't helped by bland titles like "The Joys of Fishing" or "The Truth about Communism." Such unfocused subjects lend themselves to vague generalizations. They produce themes that lack unity and speeches that put an audience to sleep.

Your essay is probably unfocused if it discusses unnamed or hypothetical people, such as "students," "Cora Crazy," "Tom J.," or "a doctor in Florida." When you find yourself writing "some people" or "in life," you can be sure you're in trouble.

You probably shouldn't write about your most serious and profound feelings. You can have a wonderful love and commitment to your father, your spouse, your baby, or your dog. You can have a warm and genuine belief in God or in democracy. But when you write such things on paper, they turn into clichés. The way you love your baby is the way other people love their babies. It's something everyone already knows about. So it's dull.

A good way to focus your topic is to put a space or time limitation on it. Don't write, "My sister is a slob"; say "My sister is a slob. Let me tell you what her junk drawer looks like." Don't write, "My father-in-law is crazy"; say "My father-in-law is crazy. Let me tell you what happened Wednesday night."

A carefully focused theme demands specific detail. You will need these details to keep your reader awake.

EXERCISES

Limit each of these topics; that is, isolate parts that you can discuss in a 500-word theme.

1. Improving American Education
2. LSD—A Blessing or a Curse?
3. The Assassination of John Lennon
4. Women in Politics
5. Jim and Tammy Bakker
6. God in Everyday Life
7. Traffic Signs
8. Travel Is Educational
9. Current Slang
10. Extrasensory Perception
11. Situation Ethics
12. Animals Can Talk
13. Cocaine

RULE 4

Organize Your Material

Most essays—and indeed most reports and business letters—are made up of an *introduction, a body,* and a *conclusion.* The introduction says, "I am going to write about X." The body discusses X in some organized way. And the conclusion says, "That's what I have to say about X." Good writers keep this pattern from being too obvious, but this is the pattern they use.

THE INTRODUCTION

The purpose of the introduction is to catch the reader's attention, to declare your subject, and sometimes to outline the direction of your essay.

The best way to get the reader's interest is to announce your subject and get on with it. You can, of course, try a witty opening ("If my brother had two more IQ points, he would be a tree") or a dramatic one ("I know who killed Jimmy Hoffa"); these might work for you. If you are not confident about such lines, however, it is best to rely on a straightforward opening.

Just say it. Write, "America can't afford nuclear power" or "*Dallas* had all the characteristics of a morality play." Then get on with proving your point.

Although you may not seek a dramatic opening line, you should try to avoid sentences that turn off your readers. If you begin your essay by saying, "Time is the auction block of the world" or "Young people to-day . . .," it won't make much difference what you write afterward. Nobody will be reading it.

The line in your opening paragraph that announces the main idea or purpose of your theme is called the *thesis statement.* You may include another sentence with it, giving a general outline the essay will follow.

Most topics can be divided into parts. Your essay praising Joe Di-Maggio might discuss his fielding, base running, and hitting. Your argument against abortion might describe the growth of the fetus month by month. Your analysis of a physical or social problem (lung cancer, skyjacking, etc.) might first describe the effect, then indicate some probable causes.

See how these introductions announce the outline of the essay:

There can be no doubt that extrasensory perception exists. How else can one explain the results of the Spranches-Malone experiment at UCLA in 1975?
[The theme will discuss the experiment.]

Legal abortion is necessary. Otherwise we will be back with vast numbers of women getting amateur surgery in bloody abortion mills.
[The theme will discuss earlier years: (1) vast numbers of women and (2) bloody surgery.]

Remember, the first paragraph has to give your audience a reason to read on. And you have to do it quickly. An opening paragraph should rarely be longer than three lines of type.

THE BODY

The introduction and conclusion are little more than a frame surrounding what you have to say. The paragraphs of the body *are* your essay.

Each paragraph presents a unit of your message. This does not mean that each division of your topic, as announced in the introduction, must be covered in one paragraph. In the ESP theme just introduced, your discussion of the UCLA experiment might take two, three, or six paragraphs.

Just as the introduction has a thesis statement announcing what the whole theme is about, so most paragraphs have *topic sentences* telling what they will cover. Usually this is the first sentence. Because they show exactly what the rest of the paragraph will discuss, these are effective topic sentences:

These gun laws haven't reduced the crime in Cleveland.

Why did the price of electricity go up in July?

Secretary Baker was equally unsuccessful with the Arabs.

Your paragraph should not bring in material beyond the scope of the topic sentence. In the paragraph about gun laws in Cleveland, for example, you should not discuss other crime-fighting measures in Cleveland; you shouldn't mention crime in Detroit.

Topic sentences are effective in linking paragraphs. In the examples given, the references to *"these* gun laws" and to Secretary Baker's being *"equally* unsuccessful" show a relation to material in previous paragraphs. Words like *therefore, however, such, second,* and *similarly* have the same effect.

Within each paragraph, try to give the sentences the same grammatical subject. (In the paragraph on Secretary Baker, the subject of most of the sentences should be "he" or "Baker" or "the Secretary.") If you vary the kinds of sentences, as in this example, the practice won't seem monotonous.

A variation popular with *exposé writers* is to make an extravagant claim and then point to conclusive evidence—which happens to be unavailable. *They* argue that superbeings from outer space built Stonehenge and that President Warren G. Harding was murdered by his wife; then *they* regret that evidence is lost in the past. *They* talk confidently about Bigfoot, Atlantis, and the Loch Ness Monster—and then lament that proof remains out of reach. *They* insist that UFOs are extraterrestrial spaceships and that a massive conspiracy led to the attempted assassinations of President Reagan and Pope John Paul II—then *they* protest that government officials and law enforcement agencies are withholding crucial evidence.

Remember that the grammatical subject is not necessarily the first word of a sentence. It may follow an introductory phrase ("After the dance, *he* . . .") or clause ("When Kathy remembered the accident, *she* . . .").

In some paragraphs, keeping the same subject will prevent you from saying what you want. Or it can make your writing seem stilted and artificial. In such cases, don't do it.

Here's an important point. *Avoid long paragraphs.* Part of writing well is making someone want to read your work, and people are turned off when they face long, block, single-spaced paragraphs. (Think how you feel beginning a chapter in your sociology textbook.) Make use of short paragraphs, headings, blank space between sections, indented material, bullets, lists, and similar devices to make your ideas easy to read. *Write with white space.* (Notice how material is laid out on these pages.)

When in doubt about whether to begin a new paragraph, always begin the paragraph.

THE CONCLUSION

The last paragraph of your essay echoes the introduction. It summarizes and generalizes about the subject discussed.

Unless your paper is long or particularly complicated, you don't need to restate the structural outline. ("In this theme, I have discussed first the language of Mark's gospel, then its historical qualities, and finally its theology.") Instead, just give a sentence or two expressing the main point. Here are some acceptable concluding paragraphs:

Mark's gospel is more like a sermon than a biography. It is a work of profound faith and impressive artistry.

No one favors abortion. But we have to admit that, in many cases, it is the only humane alternative.

The Spranches-Malone experiment proves conclusively that ESP exists. Now we have to figure out what we can do with it.

Keep your conclusions short.

EXERCISE

Discuss the strengths and weaknesses of this essay. Consider the thesis statement, the topic sentences, transitions between paragraphs, keeping the same subject within a paragraph, unity of a paragraph, and so on.

POETRY

All my life I have hated poetry. I hated it in high school, in grade school, and in the sophomore poetry course I've just completed here at South Alabama. Why we serious students have to study jingled nonsense, I will never know.

I live in Reedsburg, a community of farmers, merchants, and practical people. Nevertheless, the Reedsburg Grade School subjected me to all sorts of frivolous and impractical poetry. From the first grade on, my class endured semester after semester of cute rhyme. We read teddy-bear poems from *Winnie the Pooh*. We read Mother Goose rhymes about Simple Simon, and Robert Louis Stevenson poems about a "friendly cow all red and white." We read jingles telling us to drink our milk. I always wonder why the poets didn't just *say* things instead of chanting and jingling then. It was silly.

I had some poetry in Reedsburg High School too. However, I escaped much of it by signing up for speech classes. In speech, I studied more sensible subjects. I learned to think on my feet. I learned to make a talk interesting by referring to the audience and adding humor. Most important, I learned to say things directly, without all the cute ornament of poetry.

The sophomore poetry class I've just finished at South Alabama has only made me dislike poems more. Mr. Remington, my instructor, was incompetent. The way he read them, all poems sounded just alike. When he wasn't mumbling about Shelley, we were taking impossible tests on Keats and nightingales. Either it was assumed we knew everything about epics or he was talking down to the class as though we had never heard of metaphor. The day before the final exam, he didn't even show up for class. The whole quarter was a waste of time.

In fact, all the poetry discussions I've had from grade school up to now have been a waste of time. I just don't like poetry.

EXERCISES

How effective are these first paragraphs? After seeing this introduction, would you read the rest of the message? Why or why not?

1. Here is the information you asked for about the No. 2 chimney. It looks like we may have trouble with it.
2. I want to tell you about the three C's of a good marriage: commitment, communication, and common sense.

3. It's been proven: Diet drinks cause cancer.
4. This is to record the conversation we had yesterday about responsibility for the new computer programs.
5. Young people today must learn a new set of priorities. The future of our nation depends on it.
6. There are a lot of keen church-going people in Mobile, Alabama, but they can't tell you the religious truths I can. My Baptist friends can't; the priests at my church can't. Even the high-powered Jesuits at Spring Hill College can't. They don't read the tabloids.
7. The programs and actions growing out of libertine thought and its ideologies have put society in bondage to the indifferent with disturbing results. It strikes me in this manner.
8. Michael Jordan did it again last night!

RULE 5

Make Your Writing Interesting

Remember that no one *has* to read your writing. And if people have to hear your speech, they don't have to pay attention. The burden is on you to make your subject interesting.

This is not a huge task. If you have a topic you think is important, and if you present it with clarity and specific detail, your audience will pay attention.

Generally, you maintain interest by avoiding certain practices that deaden language.

TRUISMS

Do not say what everyone knows. Don't be like actress Brooke Shields, who told a congressional subcommittee, "Smoking can kill you. And if you've been killed, you've lost a very important part of your life."

Your readers will not be thrilled to hear that third-degree burns are painful or that the president of the United States bears great responsibilities. Don't write, "Every great man has moments of profound sorrow, but Thomas Eaton's life was genuinely tragic." Write, "Thomas Eaton's life was tragic."

CLICHÉS

Some phrases have lost meaning through overuse. Your writing will lose emphasis and interest if you use tired phrases like these:

acid test
and . . . was no exception
at this point in time
at your earliest convenience
beginner's luck
bite the bullet
bottom line
constructive criticism
could care less
the cutting edge
down to the wire

few and far between
first and foremost
in a very real sense
an in-depth study
is invaluable
last but not least
let's face it
meaningful relationship
needs no introduction
nitty-gritty
pure and simple
on the other hand
share this idea with you
shot in the arm
slowly but surely
sneaking suspicion
snow job
state-of-the-art
status quo
touch base with
uncanny ability
user-friendly
white elephant
viable alternative

Watch out for emerging clichés—words that were once new and colorful but are now becoming overused. There's a danger in writing about an "awesome" blonde, a "Type-A" personality, or a "Catch-22" situation. The language is losing force even as we speak.

A good rule: If you suspect a particular phrase is a cliché, it is. Don't use it.

Remember that avoiding a cliché can produce a rich substitution. A CBS sports announcer once described a Green Bay quarterback as (not "cool as a cucumber" but) "cool as the other side of the pillow."

Some readers will find clichés insulting. If you write "In conclusion, do not hesitate to contact me at your earliest convenience," you're saying you don't care enough to really talk to them; you're just giving them a set of words. It's like telling someone "You're wonderful. I love you. This is a recording."

GENERALIZED LANGUAGE

The point cannot be overemphasized: *To be interesting, you must be specific.* Let's call this "the Ginger Principle." (You'll see why in a minute.)

Write of real things. Use proper names, words that begin with capital letters. (Don't say "lunch"; say "a Big Mac.") Use real numbers. (Don't say "a lot"; say "725.") Give specific places, dates, and quotations. You can, for example, refer to the same person in a number of ways:

an athlete
a ball player
a baseball player
an infielder
a shortstop
a Cardinal shortstop
Ozzie Smith

Always choose the most specific word that serves the purposes of your essay. Good writing uses proper names.

Generally, your ideas will be more interesting if you can avoid the words *good, bad,* and forms of *to be.*

Substituted words are always more meaningful. Instead of "good," write "even-tempered," "inexpensive," "compassionate," or "crisp." Instead of "bad," write "moldy," "pretentious," "degenerate," or "unfair."

Similarly, try to avoid forms of the verb *to be*—that is, the words *is, are, was, were, am* and *been.* Much of the time, you will have to use these words, of course, but substitutions are usually more effective. For example, "Sue Walker *was* injured" becomes "Sue Walker smashed two bones in her right foot." And "The weather *was* horrible" becomes "Eight inches of snow fell on Buffalo yesterday." (Some scholars have designated the English language without *to be* forms as "E-prime.")

To see the degree of interest that specific detail can give a sentence, compare Irving Berlin's lyric "I'll be loving you always" with George Kaufman's suggested emendation, I'll be loving you Thursday."

The best way to win interest is to force a lot of real names and numbers into your prose. Don't write, "His cousin drove me to a nearby woods, and we sat drinking beer and listening to music until very late." Write, "Ginger drove me over to Johnson's Woods, and we sat in her red Toronado till four in the morning. We drank a six-pack of Coors and listened to her Frank Zappa tapes." Look at the "Ginger" in those sentences. This kind of writing doesn't just tell you of an event, it shows it to you.

Another good rule; *Don't write about nobody.* Look at this infirm passage: "The American public is tired of football. People are bored by all the hype. Every time you turn on your TV set, you see another ad for the Super Bowl." Here, the words "public," "people," and "you" refer to nobody in particular. They express a dull generalization. Write of real people—Henry Kissinger, Carry Nation, or yourself. Say, "Every time *I* turn on my TV set, *I* see another ad for the Super Bowl."

This doesn't mean you can't generalize. It means that when you want to talk about the generation gap, you begin "I can't talk to my mother."

INFLATED LANGUAGE

Except in rare cases, you will want your writing to be clear. To do this, keep your language as simple and direct as possible. When addressing a general audience, try to avoid these forms:

Foreign words—*bête noir, ne plus ultra, coup d'état*
Learned words—*penultimate, symbiotic, alumna*
Poetic words—*repine, oft, betimes*
Technical words—*input, societal, kappa numbers*
Odd singular and plural forms—*datum, stadia, syllabi*
Literary allusions—*Lot's wife, protean, the sword of Damocles*
Current in-words—*parameter, viable, ambience*

Such words are more acceptable if you are writing for an educated or specialized audience. But a really fine writer wouldn't use them there either.

Reading William F. Buckley's column in your morning newspaper can be a useful exercise. You, like almost everyone else, will stop reading early on, probably at his first reference to "biblical irredentism." Columnist James J. Kilpatrick gave us a useful rule. He wrote, "Whenever we feel the impulse to use a marvelously exotic word, let us lie down until the impulse goes away."

Write with everyday words, words you would say. Don't use "in view of the above" or "for the above reasons"; write "consequently" or "for these reasons." Try not to use "the addressee," "the executrix," "the former," or "the latter"; write "Sylvia Mitchell" (or "she" or "her"). Never refer to yourself as "the writer" (or "we"); say "I."

The next time you hear a dull lecture or sermon, don't tune it out. Ask yourself why it is dull. Probably you're hearing a collection of truisms, clichés, and vague or inflated phrases. You can learn from such examples.

EXERCISES

Rewrite these sentences. Make them more likely to sustain the interest of a general audience.

1. This insult was the last straw. I decided to leave Marcia, and I spent the next few hours preparing for the trip.
2. The Book of Jonah illustrates the ludicrous intractability of a particular mind-set.
3. Scott Daniel was a fine basketball player. I believe he was the best to play in the league in the last 20 years. He was really fine.
4. Vis-à-vis our tête-à-tête, I must say the rendezvous filled me with ennui.

5. It is true that some rhetorics have denied their imbrication in ideology, doing so in the name of a disinterested scientism.
6. Driving the L.A. freeway is like crossing the river Styx.
7. In the following weeks at school, I worked frantically. Every day I became busier and busier.
8. As we entered the restaurant, Nick stated that the chicken there was good but the service was bad.
9. Anyone can suffer with a rotten tooth or a sprained thumb, but the man with kidney stones endures a superexcruciating kind of pain.
10. In the final analysis, there are few rugged individualists in this day and age who are really down to earth in expressing nothing but the truth about the seamy side of life. Perhaps in the near future . . .
11. We will never know everything about the atom, but some of the recent discoveries have been fascinating.
12. Graduate school can be a procrustean bed.
13. Sorting on the part of mendicants should be interdicted.

RULE 6

Make Your Writing Emphatic

Sometimes unnecessary words or particular word-forms detract from the point you want to make. These recommendations should help you emphasize the important ideas in your writing.

AVOID WORDINESS

Unnecessary words may bore or antagonize your reader. Say what you have to say as briefly as possible. Too often writers use a series of words where one word will do.

> *am of the opinion that* = believe
> *due to the fact that* = because
> *the man with the dark complexion* = the dark man
> *people who are concerned only with themselves* = selfish people
> *I disagree with the conclusion offered by Professor Lally* = I disagree with Professor Lally

Certain pat phrases have extra words built into them. You don't need to write "end result," "component parts," "advance planning," "large sized," or similar forms. Omit the extra word.

Some introductory forms can usually be dispensed with:

Needless to say . . .
Let me say that . . .
It is important to recognize the fact that . . .

And commonly one or more words appear where none is necessary.

Molly *really* is a *very* beautiful girl.
Personally, I agree with him.
I asked whether *or not* the twins looked alike.
I dislike his personality *and his temperament.*
There were several people at the party *who* saw the fight.

Eighty percent of the time, you can omit words ending in "ly." Ninety percent of the time, you can delete "very." You'll never need to put three adjectives before a noun, and you should try to avoid using two.

Don't worry about wordiness when you're putting together the first draft of your essay; just get down what you have to say. It's in rewriting that you can change "And I think it is necessary to add that Tom wasn't there" to the more forceful phrase "Tom wasn't there."

WRITE IN THE ACTIVE VOICE

In sentences written in the active voice, the grammatical subject is the acting agent. ("*The Brezinsky Commission* has attacked public apathy.") In sentences written in the passive voice, the subject receives the action of the verb. ("*Public apathy* has been attacked by the Brezinsky Commission.")

You can use the passive voice in sentences where the acting agent is obvious or irrelevant ("The president was reelected") or where you want to deliver bad news and avoid personal involvement ("The decision is to buy our supplies from a different source" or "Your contract will not be renewed next year").

A world-class use of the passive voice occurred during the Iran-Contra hearings. When a committee member asked what happened to some implicating documents, Colonel Oliver North answered, "I think they were shredded."

Generally the passive voice is a bad thing. It doesn't sound natural and seems wordy and evasive. Where you may want particular emphasis, it can produce a mushy effect: "Home runs were hit by both pitchers during the game."

Often, using the active voice means beginning your sentence (or beginning the main clause of your sentence) with acting agents: *we, she, Jim Phillips,* or *the Brezinsky Commission.* This gives force and directness to your prose. Try to avoid forms that keep you from doing this. Here are some examples:

> My intention is . . .
> It was soon evident that . . .
> There were . . .
> . . . was seen
> . . . could be heard
> The assumption was that . . .

If you are writing a personal essay, begin most sentences (or main clauses) with *I.*

Think of the passive voice as you do a visit to the dentist. It's necessary sometimes, but you want to avoid it when you can.

EXPRESS YOUR MAIN IDEA IN THE SUBJECT–VERB OF YOUR SENTENCE

Make the subject–verb unit of your sentence express your main thought. Put less important information in modifying phrases and clauses.

Don't write your main thought as a modifying phrase ("Harold Lord slipped in the outfield, *thus breaking his arm*") or as a *that* clause ("I learned *that Aunt Rita has been arrested for arson"*). Give your point subject–verb emphasis: "Harold Lord slipped in the outfield and broke his arm"; "Aunt Rita was arrested for arson."

DO NOT WASTE THE ENDS OF YOUR SENTENCES

Because the end of a sentence is the last thing a reader sees, it is a position of emphasis. Don't use it to express minor thoughts or casual information. Don't write, "Both candidates will speak here in July, if we can believe the reports." This is effective only if you want to stress the doubtfulness of the reports. Don't write, "Pray for the repose of the soul of John Bowler, who died last week in Cleveland." Your reader will wonder what he was doing in Cleveland. Notice how emphasis trails away in a sentence like this:

> The B-1 bomber, a brainchild of the U.S. Air Force and Rockwell International, is trying a comeback as one of America's leading defense weapons after President Carter, in June 1977, put a stop to the plans to complete the project.

For particular emphasis, write your thought in subject–verb form (see previous section) and give the unit an end-of-the-sentence position. Don't write, "The union reluctantly approved the contract." Write, "The union approved the contract, but they didn't want to do it."

Because the beginning of a sentence also conveys a degree of emphasis, you should not waste that position either. Try to put words like "however," "therefore," and "nevertheless" in the middle of sentences. ("The mail carrier, however, didn't come till five o'clock.") Don't do this if it makes your sentence sound awkward.

KEEP YOUR SENTENCES RELATIVELY SHORT

To avoid a monotonous style, you should build your essay with sentences of different kinds and lengths. But using short or relatively short sentences will help you avoid difficulty.

When sentences go beyond 15 or 20 words, punctuation—which can be a problem—becomes complicated; meaning gets diffuse; their pronouns are separated from the words they refer to; and the reader or listener finds it difficult to see the continuity and may lose interest. Short sentences are better.

When you finish a sentence of reasonable length, fight the temptation to extend it by adding a unit beginning "which" or "when" or "because" or "according to" or some other "-ing" form. Put the additional material in a new sentence.

If you're typing, try to end your sentence within two lines of type. Only rarely should it go beyond three lines.

KEEP YOUR DOCUMENT AS SHORT AS POSSIBLE

Don't waste your audience's time.

Remember the purposes of your writing are to be read and to win a particular effect from your readers. Probably you won't do either if your document is too long.

If you turn in a 40-page report at work, your boss will be frustrated. If you write a 6-page sales letter people will throw it away. When Ann Landers receives letters of 10 pages or more, she concludes, "These people need professional help."

You can write long term-papers for your school classes, however. Here, there is no purpose other than to show how much you know. And no one has to read them.

Your writing will be longer or shorter as the subject and occasion require. But keep it as short as possible. You can learn from the emphatic message that appeared on bulletin boards at a southern university. It said, "Free Kittens. Call 342-7098."

"It says he's out to lunch."

Reprinted from the *National Enquirer*, August 16, 1988. Reprinted courtesy of Orlando Busino.

EXERCISES

What changes would make the meaning of these sentences more emphatic?

1. I was born in the city of Chicago, Illinois.
2. Trapped in a drab life with a dull husband, Hedda Gabler shoots herself, partly because she is threatened by Judge Brack.
3. The eagle suddenly loosed its grip, allowing me to escape.
4. Though I had more than several reasons to dislike and distrust Libby MacDuffee before the accident, I found still more when she tried to take me to court to pay for the hospital costs and when she claimed I had had three martinis at the Red Oak Bar an hour (or at the most two hours) before the wreck.
5. Reviewing the past history, we found that the team was weak on basic fundamentals and that the average age of the players was 17 years old.
6. Nevertheless, I must refuse your kind offer.
7. His hope was that he could conquer Paris by June.
8. Although Jeannine feared flying, she took the 9:02 flight from Milwaukee, being already two days late for the convention.
9. This book concerns itself with language intended to deceive.
10. It is greatly feared by the crowd that an honest decision would not come from the referee.
11. I'm very sorry to hear you recently and tragically crashed your new red Cutlass convertible.
12. Guilt is a fact of life, an emotion that everyone has to deal with constantly, which is no surprise when you consider that guilt is the subject of more fiction and nonfiction than any other emotion.
13. With the great potential for savings existing, the implementation stage of the project should immediately be proceeded with.

RULE 7

Avoid Language That
Draws Attention to Itself

You want your audience to follow your ideas, to follow the argument you're developing. Don't break their attention by using odd words or phrases that catch their eye. Try to avoid these distracting forms.

SEXIST LANGUAGE

If you want to persuade your audience, you can't use words that offend them. And today, many people—of both sexes—are turned off by terms they consider offensive to women. They don't like masculine forms of words used in references that can apply to either men or women. Here are some examples:

> chair*man*
> spokes*man*
> *man*kind
> *man*power
> all *men* are created equal
> everyone did *his* best
> a doctor earns *his* money
> separate the *men* from the *boys*
> take it like a *man*

Don't use this kind of language.

Find synonyms. Instead of "chairman," "spokesman," and "man-power," write "chair," "advocate," and "work force." Instead of "man-kind" and "all men," write "humanity" or "all people." When you come to "a doctor earns his money," go plural—"doctors earn their money." Rewriting "separate the men from the boys" and "take it like a man" can call for some creativity. Try "separate the winners from the losers" and "shape up."

Avoid "his or her" whenever you can; it always sounds artificial.

Unless there's a reason for it, don't bring in gender. The best way to denote a woman doctor is to say "a doctor." (This is also the best way to refer to an African-American doctor, a homosexual doctor, or a doctor who uses a wheelchair.)

REPETITION

Repeating a word for emphasis can be effective ("government of the *people*, by the *people*, and for the *people*"), but often it distracts attention. Avoid repetition of sentence forms ("I went to see the accident. Fifteen people were there. Each told a different story."); of particular words ("Going to school is not going to be easy. If the going gets tough . . ."); and even of sounds ("The black boxer was bloody, beaten, and battered.").

Don't write three adjectives in a row. ("Suzanne is a lovely, energetic, red-haired girl.") This becomes a habit.

Time magazine once wrote of a New York police officer with problems. It said, "The people he works for have cases to break, headlines to make, careers at stake." *Time* can write that way occasionally, but you shouldn't.

DANGLING AND MISPLACED MODIFIERS

Make it clear what words your adjectives and adverbs are modifying. You do this by putting modifiers close to the words they refer to. Avoid examples like these:

When nine years old, my grandmother took me to the circus.

He was reported drowned *by the Coast Guard.*

Dr. Ruth talked about sex *with newspaper editors.*

By knowing what you want to say, your essay will progress more easily.

Notice that these sentences are clear enough; in context, your reader would know what they mean. But such awkward and even humorous lines draw attention to themselves and away from your meaning.

ELABORATE FIGURES OF SPEECH

A mixed metaphor often produces irrelevant laughter. ("You're the salt of the earth and the light of the world, but you've thrown in the towel.") Even a meaningful figure of speech can be distracting. You could write, "Reagan steered the ship of state over treacherous seas; he was a star-crossed president." Such a sentence, however, stops your readers. Instead of following the rest of your ideas, they pause to interpret the metaphor.

You will, of course, want to use figures of speech in your prose. But don't let them obscure your meaning by being too dramatic:

Auto sales got a big *shot in the arm* in March from the *price slashes.*

Or pointless:

Lee Bailey wore a suit *the color of a thousand-dollar bill.*

Or redundant:

At the wedding, the champagne *flowed like wine.*

Or strange:

When God fights your battles, He *does it in spades.*

Remember that if you keep a metaphor simple, it can create an effective argument. Consider the force of the ad "Happiness is a Met Life security blanket."

FAULTY PARALLELISM

You should express coordinate ideas in similar form. You do this mainly to avoid awkward and distracting sentences. Clearly, "I was *alone, uncertain,* and *possessed of a considerable degree of fear*" is less emphatic than "I was *alone, uncertain,* and *afraid.*" Consider these examples:

The teachers were burdened with *large classes, poor textbooks,* and *the necessity to cope with an incompetent principal.*
I love *seeing my daughter* and *to hear her voice.*
For a settlement, I will accept *a new stove* or *having my old stove repaired.*

Some sentences cannot be made parallel. You cannot change "Ted was tall, charming, and wore a blue hat" to "Ted was tall, charming, and blue-hatted." In such cases, write the first units so your reader doesn't expect the final one to be parallel. Write, "Ted was tall and charming; he always wore a blue hat."

Many of these problems occur when you write units in a series. You don't have to write units in a series.

AWKWARD CONSTRUCTIONS

Try to give your sentences the sound of talk, of natural speech. Don't break the continuity with intrusive passages.

I promised to, *if the expected raise came through,* take her to the Grand Hotel.
Her brother, *if we can believe local historians (and who can),* was a senator.

Any time your subject is eight words away from your verb, you're probably in trouble.

Avoid noun clusters. Business and technical writers sometimes seek a kind of forceful compression and talk of a "once-in-a-lifetime, million-dollar career-decision dilemma." In doing so, they produce sentences a person has to read twice to understand. It is better to write in a natural speaking voice.

Don't seek a poetic style by inverting word order. Don't write. "Quiet was the night" or "The reason for his suicide, we shall never know."

Keep it natural. Where it sounds all right, don't be afraid to begin a sentence with a conjunction or to end it with a preposition. ("And suddenly I realized where the money had come from.") And don't let some dated English textbook persuade you to say, "If Jim had been *I*, he would have paid the bill." You *know* how that sounds.

ABRUPT CHANGES IN TONE

Your tone is your personal voice, your way of saying things. This will vary with your audience and your subject. You talk one way to an intimate friend and another way to a visiting archbishop. You would use a formal style when writing a letter of application, and you might use colloquial—or even coarse—language in describing your brother.

It is important to keep your tone appropriate and consistent. Don't jar your reader by describing a United Nations charter provision as a "crapheaded experiment." And don't call a fraternity dining-room "a haven of calculated insouciance."

If your tone is light enough to permit contractions ("can't," "wouldn't"), use them right from the beginning of your essay. Don't begin to use them in the middle of a relatively formal paper.

Remember that any time your reader is more impressed by your writing than by your meaning, you have failed. No one can improve on the advice lexicographer Samuel Johnson gave in the eighteenth century. He said, "Read over your composition, and where ever you meet with a passage which you think is particularly fine, strike it out."

EXERCISES

Correct weaknesses in these sentences.

1. Saberhagen was pitching beautifully until the seventh inning, and then the fireworks fell in.
2. When reading late at night, the book should be held under a strong light.
3. Juan Perón's rise to power was a slow one. There were many pit stops.
4. We traveled for six days, and the car broke down. We hitchhiked to Laredo, and I took a job gardening. I had the car towed into town, but no one there could fix it.
5. I'm sorry about the story, Laurie. It's as bad as your messy essay. I warned you frequently to rewrite your work.
6. Mrs. L. Williamson earned her Ph.D. studying DNA at M.I.T.

7. Cancer hit my family with full force this year, sending two of my aunts to the Mayo Clinic.
8. Pamela was pretty, energetic, and carried a file of history notes.
9. The movie producers saw *Heaven's Gate* and immediately removed it from circulation. They could smell the handwriting on the wall.
10. Every engineer must get his work in on time.
11. Roman Catholics tend to be uptight about premarital sex. Baptists are more laid back.
12. When you go to the doctor, it costs you an arm and a leg.
13. Jim is tragically confined to a wheelchair. Fortunately, he is married to a woman doctor.
14. The treatment will take several months. You can't overcome over-confidence overnight.
15. The university published the names of faculty members broken down by sex.

RULE 8

Avoid Mechanical Errors

Due to a typing error, Gov. Dukakis was incorrectly identified in the third paragraph as Mike Tyson.

From a correction in the Fitchburg-Leominster (Mass.) Sentinel and Enterprise

To write effectively, you need to know a number of elementary rules of usage. But there are some you don't have to know. An important truth is expressed in this story.

> A man went to his doctor and described his ailment. Clinching his right fist tightly, he complained, "It hurts me when I go like that." The doctor prescribed the remedy. He said, "Don't go like that."

The story tells you many things about writing: how to punctuate long and involved sentences, where to put apostrophes in unusual constructions, the way to use quotation marks within quotation marks, and how to spell "bourgeoisie." The advice: "Don't go like that."

The following rules on punctuation, abbreviation, number, and spelling should take you through most writing situations.

PUNCTUATION

Use *Commas* to Make Your Sentences Easier to Read

Textbooks routinely tell you to put a comma before the conjunction in a compound sentence ("Pam is a good student, but she cannot learn economics"); after introductory clauses ("When I went home, I saw my brother's car"); and before the *and* in elements in a series ("I bought a suit, three ties, and a sweater"). The problem is that many professional writers don't punctuate like this. Hence you may be confused.

A good rule is this: Always use commas in these constructions *when the sentences are long.*

> Arthur had traveled 57 miles through the desert to meet the prince, and he knew that nothing in the world could make him turn back now.

299

When I saw that the young soldier was holding a gun on Martha and me, I became most obedient.

Suddenly Henry saw that the parable applied to him, that he must change his life, and that the time to start was now.

Similarly, you should always insert commas in these constructions when there is a danger of misreading. Consider these sentences:

The fox ate three chickens and the rooster ran away.

When they finished eating cigarettes were distributed to the soldiers.

They stopped looking for Irene became tired.

If you use normal word-order (a "talking" voice) and keep your sentences relatively short, you should have little difficulty with commas.

Use *a Semicolon* to Show That Two Independent Clauses Are Closely Related

Sometimes you want to indicate the particularly close relationship between two statements. Here you merge the statements into one sentence and connect them with a semicolon.

Her brother has been sick for years; now he is going to die.

To know her is to love her; to love her is a mistake.

This construction often occurs when the second statement contains "however," "therefore," "consequently," or "nevertheless."

The 747 was two hours late getting into O'Hare; consequently, he missed his connection to Reno.

Billy wanted to propose during final-exam week; he saw, however, that this would cause problems.

You can also use semicolons to separate the halves of a compound sentence, or the units in a series, when the separated passages have commas within them.

My boss, Patrick Henderson, was there; but before I could talk to him, he fell and broke his arm.

Among those present were Dr. Williams, an English professor; Mrs. Damico, head of the Presbyterian meeting; and Mrs. Milliken, president of the PTA.

If you have problems punctuating such long sentences, don't write them. You can write acceptable prose and never use a semicolon.

Use *a Colon* to Introduce a Unit

You use a colon to introduce something: an announcement, a clarification, or a formal series.

In May, the professor made his decision: he would leave the university.

The difference between fathers and sons used to be a simple one: fathers earned the money, and sons spent it.

Molly excelled in active sports: tennis, swimming, badminton, and gymnastics.

When a complicated sentence follows a colon, the first word may be capitalized—especially if the sentence is long. ("In May, the professor made his decision: He would leave the university, move to Cleveland, and take a position with the Pater Academy.")

In general, you shouldn't use a colon except after a complete statement. Don't write, "Her favorites were: Andy Williams, Tim Conway, and Brack Weaver." Write, "These were her favorites: Andy Williams, Tim Conway, and Brack Weaver." Or (even better) "Her favorites were Andy Williams, Tim Conway, and Brack Weaver."

It is permissible to use a colon after "the following." ("He did it for the following reasons: . . .") But when you can avoid it, don't write "the following" at all. It's not something you would *say*. (Write, "He did it for several reasons: . . ." or "He did it for these reasons: . . .")

Use *an Exclamation Mark* to Show Emphasis

Because adding an exclamation mark is an easy way to gain emphasis, you may be tempted to overuse it. Try to reserve it for "Wow!" or "Fire!" or a choice obscenity.

Never use two or more exclamation marks to seek additional emphasis. Never!

Use *a Question Mark* After a Direct Question

You will, of course, put a question mark after a question. But be sure it is a direct question.

What can they do in 12 minutes?

He asked, "Did you see Sylvia there?"

Don't use a question mark after an indirect question or after a question form that is really a polite command.

She asked if I knew the way to school.

Will you please hand in your blue-books now.

Use *Hyphens* to Form Compound Adjectives and to Divide Words at the End of a Line

Use a hyphen to join a compound adjective when it *precedes* a noun. You can write "the theory is out of date," or you can call it "an out-of-date theory." In such examples, the hyphens make your meaning clearer:

a Monday-morning quarterback
a dog-in-the-manger attitude
a long-term investment
germ-free research
a 40-pound weight

Remember there is a big difference between "an Oriental-art expert" and "an Oriental art-expert."

Hyphens are particularly necessary to make sense of the noun clusters that occur in technical writing. An engineer may refer to "polyethylene coated milk carton stock smoothness test results." What does that mean? It becomes clearer with hyphens: "Polyethylene-coated milk-carton-stock smoothness-test results." But it is always best to keep the hyphens and rewrite the phrase: "The results of smoothness-tests conducted on poly-ethylene-coated milk-carton stock."

When using combination words, you often don't know whether the form should be written as one word ("shutdown"), as two words ("check out"), or as a hyphenated unit ("loose-leaf"). If you can't find a rule to guide you, go ahead and hyphenate the words.

Use a hyphen to divide a word at the end of a line. But remember that you must divide the word between syllables ("when-ever," "in-tern," "pho-bia"). You should not divide a word so that only one letter appears on a line ("a-bout," "phobi-a"); and you should never separate a one-syllable word ("doubt," "called," "proved").

If you don't know where to divide a word, consult your dictionary. If you don't have a dictionary at hand, don't divide the word. Write it all on the next line. (That's how your word processor does it.)

Use *Parentheses* to Tuck in Extra Material

Parentheses are useful. They let you include additional information with-out breaking the continuity of your message. As these examples show, you can tuck in dates, examples, clarifications, and whatever else you want.

Nicholas wrote *Corners of Adequacy* (1981) to answer charges made against his father.

Dylan Thomas (1914–1953) was a Welsh poet and an alcoholic.

Some foreign words (*Gemütlichkeit,* for example) can't be easily trans-lated into English.

His wife (he married about a year ago) was barely five feet tall.

Don't misuse parentheses. Don't use them to set off material that is necessary in the sentence.

"Nice" (in the old sense of "discriminating") is seldom used any more.

And don't use parentheses so often that they call attention to themselves. If you use too many in your sentence (i.e., more than two or three), you can lose (or antagonize) your reader (especially if he or she is concerned about writing style).

Use *a Dash* Where You Need It

Like commas and parentheses, dashes can be used to set off an element. If you want to set off an idea that is closely related to your sentence, use commas. ("My father, who always loved fruit, died eating an orange.") To set off a unit that is less closely related, use dashes (or parentheses). ("My father—he would have been 39 next month—died eating an orange.")

Indeed, a dash—used in moderation—is acceptable punctuation in many circumstances.

Don't bet on Red Devil—he's a loser.

He thought about the situation for weeks—never able to get it all together.

It became clear that only one man could be the murderer—Dr. Dorrill.

The dash is a handy mark of punctuation. Just don't overuse it.

APOSTROPHES, QUOTATION MARKS, ITALICS, AND CAPITAL LETTERS

Use *Apostrophes* to Show Possession, to Indicate an Omission, and to Form Unusual Plurals

As a general rule, you show possession by adding *'s* to any singular or plural noun that doesn't end in *s*.

the dog's collar
the woman's hand
Michelle's trumpet
the men's boots

For nouns ending in *s*, you add either an *'s* or simply a final apostrophe. Punctuate it the way you say it; add the *'s* where you pronounce the extra syllable.

the girls' room
the Clardys' house
James's reign
the Harris's car

(In describing the Hiss-Chambers case, most commentators write of *Chambers'* accusations and *Hiss's* response.)

Sometimes you can avoid problems by not using apostrophes at all. The sentence "It is the company's policy to be ready for auditors' inspection," can also be written "It is company policy to be ready for auditor inspection."

In more complicated cases, it is best to avoid the issue. Don't speculate on how to punctuate "Charles and Bobs television," "Jesus parables," or "the last three months pay." Write "the television Charles and Bob bought last June," "the parables of Jesus," and "pay for the last three months."

You also use apostrophes to replace omitted letters or numbers in contractions ("I've," "couldn't," "the class of '45'") and to form unusual plurals.

A formal essay is not full of and's.
Today Ph.D.'s can't get jobs.
I got one A and four C's.

Usage is changing here. Many respectable authors no longer use apostrophes in these constructions. They write of "Ph.D.s" and "Cs" and "4s."

If you wonder whether you need an apostrophe with proper names (like "Veterans Administration") or brand names (like "French's mustard"), there is no rule to help you. The correct form is whatever the organizations use. In a difficult case, you may have to consult magazines, advertisements, or letterheads. You may have to phone for information or drive to your shopping center.

You need to include brand names in your writing because such details give color and interest to your prose. But the names do bring apostrophe problems, especially if you're trying to champion "Miller" beer over "Stroh's" and "Coors." This list gives some of the more common trade names and shows how complicated apostrophes can be.

Benson & Hedges cigarettes
Betty Crocker cake mix
Bride's magazine
Brooks Brothers clothes
Campbell's soup
Consumers' Research magazine
Diners Club
Dole pineapple
Elmer's glue
Folgers coffee
Häagen-Dazs ice cream
Hertz rent-a-car
Hunt's ketchup
Jergen's lotion
Johnson wax
Kellogg's cereal
Ladies' Home Journal
L'eggs pantyhose
Levi's jeans
L'Oréal hair products
McDonald's hamburgers
Myers's rum

Oscar Mayer meats
O'Shaughnessys' whiskey
Parents magazine
Parsons' ammonia
Phillips 66 gasoline
Phillips' milk of magnesia
Planters peanuts
Pond's cold cream
Popeyes chicken
Reader's Digest
Sears
Stroh Light beer
Wards
Wilson sporting goods
Woolworth's
Wrigley's gum

Nobody knows all these forms. The difference between a good and a bad writer is that a good writer takes the trouble to check out such things.

Use *Quotation Marks* to Enclose the Exact Words of a Source, Titles of Short Works, a Word Used as a Word, and (Sometimes) Words Used in an Odd or Ironic Sense
Use quotation marks to enclose material taken directly from a book or person.

> In 1955, Aaron Mitchell wrote that the failure of democracy would derive from the "continuing derision of the mob."

> Rankin said, "There is no reason to suspect murder."

But don't use quotation marks for a paraphrased statement.

> Rankin said that there was no reason to suspect murder.

Put quotation marks around titles of shorter works: magazine articles, short stories, poems, artworks, and songs.

> "A Rose for Emily"
> Frost's "Mending Wall"
> Picasso's "Three Musicians"
> "White Christmas"

Titles of longer works are put in italics.
Use quotation marks to indicate you are using a word as a word rather than as a meaning.

> I can never spell "surgeon."
> "Cellar door" has a pleasant sound.

The usage here varies. Many writers use italics in such instances.

Finally, use quotation marks to show the odd or ironic use of a word.

The Prime Minister lifted the first volume of the Encyclopaedia Britannica from his desk and "clobbered" his secretary.

These "teachers" are a disgrace.

Try not to use quotation marks this way. When you can, just write the words.

Where do you put end punctuation when you are quoting? The rules are uncomplicated. Put periods and commas inside quotation marks—*always*. (This doesn't seem reasonable, but do it anyway.) Put semicolons and colons outside. And put question marks and exclamation marks inside if they are part of the quotation; otherwise, put them outside. These examples show the pattern:

"When you come," Nick said, "bring your boat."

Molly had said, "I'll never forget you"; however, she forgot me in two weeks.

Rebecca asked, "How long has this been going on?"

Who wrote "the uncertain glory of an April day"?

All I can say is "Wow!"

I did too say "Monday"!

To show a quotation within a quotation, use single quotes.

Jack complained, "I can never remember who wrote 'to be or not to be.'"

A better suggestion: Reconstruct your sentence so you don't have to put quotes within quotes.

Jack said he could never remember who wrote "to be or not to be."

Use *Italics* for Titles of Longer Works, for Foreign Words, and (If You Have to) for Emphasis
You indicate *italic* type by underlining.

Use italics to mark titles of longer works: books, magazines, newspapers, TV shows, movies, plays, operas, and long poems, as well as the names of ships and airplanes. Consider these examples:

Walker Percy's *Love in the Ruins*
USA Today
Christian Century
Murphy Brown
Dances with Wolves
Carmen
Paradise Lost
the *Titanic*
the space shuttle *Columbia*

Do not use italics or quotation marks for the Bible—or books of the Bible—or for famous documents like the Declaration of Independence or the Magna Charta.

A good rule: Whenever you are in doubt whether to use quotation marks or italics to indicate a title, use italics.

Use italics for foreign words. But remember that many foreign words have now become part of the English language and do not need italics.

He was permitted to graduate *in absentia*.

Do not use clichés.

Kathy has a certain *élan*, but she acts like a prima donna.

What should you do about foreign words that have almost become English ("a priori," "coup d'état," "non sequitur")? When in doubt, don't italicize them.

Finally, you can use italics to give some word a special emphasis.

That's *precisely* the reason I am here.

Hilary didn't just act like a princess; she *was* a princess.

It is best not to use italics for emphasis, but sometimes you will want to.

Use *Capital Letters* with the Names of Specific Persons, Places, and Things

Knowing when to use a capital letter is not always easy, but the main rules are clear enough.

Capitalize the names of *people,* as well as their titles and words derived from their names; *places,* including countries (and national groups), states, counties, cities, and defined areas; *time units* like days of the week, months, and holidays; *religious entities; organizations,* their abbreviations and brand names; *historical events and documents; titles* of books, magazines, plays, poems, stories, movies, television shows, musical compositions, and art objects; and *structures* like buildings, monuments, airplanes, and ships. These examples show common usage:

Denise Shumock
Captain Kirk
Addison's disease
Shakespearean sonnet
Holland
General Motors
G.M.
Ovaltine
the Battle of Hastings
the Gettysburg Address
the Dutch
Europeans

the Riviera
California
Monroe County
Black River Falls
Tuesday
February
Memorial Day
God
Methodist
the Pope
the Archbishop of Canterbury
Genesis
the Magna Charta
Fear of Flying
Room 280
Epilogue
Newsweek
The Importance of Being Earnest
"The Killers"
"Mending Wall"
All My Children
"Margaritaville"
Beethoven's *Seventh*
the Empire State Building
the Washington Monument
the *Spirit of St. Louis*
the *Titanic*

You should have little problem with such examples.

Some words are capitalized in one context and not in another. They are capitalized when they name or relate to a specific entity. These instances show the distinction:

I knew Major Jones.
He rose to the rank of major.

I saw Mother there.
I will see my mother there.

I support the Democratic candidate.
I believe in the democratic system.

I attend Spring Hill Baptist Church.
We drove by a church.

I love the South.
We flew south.

This is the Sewanee River.
We swam in the river.

Turn to Chapter One.
Read the next chapter.

Any word is capitalized, of course, when it begins a sentence or when it begins a line of poetry.

Do not capitalize words like "spring" or "freshman."

Finally, there are the words that cause problems. In these cases, the usage varies with educated writers, and you may have to make your own decision. Here are some guidelines.

A.M. or *a.m.* Either form is correct. Just be consistent.

Coke or *coke.* When a product is vastly popular, its trade name may become the name of the product itself and thus lose its capital letter. This has happened to "ping pong," "thermos bottle," "kleenex," and "band-aid." It is now happening to "Xerox" and "Musak." Today it is probably best to write "Coke" when you specifically mean Coca-Cola, and "coke" when you mean any other soft drink.

Roman numerals or *roman numerals.* Sometimes a national reference becomes part of a common word and no longer conveys a sense of nationality; it may then lose its capital letter. You wouldn't capitalize "dutch treat," "french fries," or "turkish towel." Some words, however, are still changing. At present, you can write either "Roman numeral" or "roman numeral."

Psychology or *psychology.* You should always use capital letters with specific courses ("Psychology 201") and lowercase letters with the area in general ("I used psychology to convince my mother"). Capital letters, however, are sometimes used to discuss academic courses in a general way. You could write, "The University has strong programs in Psychology and Sociology, but it is weak in Languages."

Black or *black.* This can be a sensitive area, and there is no firm convention to guide you. A decade ago, the word was routinely capitalized. Currently, following the usage of noted black leaders, most writers no longer capitalize "black." But *Ebony* magazine still does. Judge the likely response of your reader before you choose to capitalize (or not capitalize) "black." No usage is correct if it offends someone you don't want to offend. (Today many people prefer the term "African-American.")

Despite the complexity of some of these examples, most uses of capital letters follow a simple rule. You capitalize proper names—the names of specific persons, places, things, and events.

ABBREVIATIONS

Because your writing should be an extension of the way you talk, you would do well not to write abbreviations at all. You say words, not abbreviations. Clearly, you'd sound funny talking like this:

We'll be there the second week in Feb.

In Madison, Wis., I worked for the Rogers Express Co.

This is the St., but I don't know the No.

However, many abbreviations *are* words. You would sound odd saying this:

I have to hurry to my Reserve Officers Training Corps class.

At two post meridiem, she drove her car into the Young Women's Christian Association parking lot.

The rule is to follow your voice. Write the word where you say the word and the abbreviation where you say the abbreviation. Thus you can write either "television" or "TV," either "CIA" or "Central Intelligence Agency." Probably you would never write "Blvd.," "MSS.," "e.g.," "anno Domini," or "University of California at Los Angeles."

There are a few exceptions to this rule. Standard usage dictates that "Mr.," "Dr.," "Mrs.," "Rev.," and comparable abbreviations be used before proper names. Similarly, it permits you to write "etc." instead of "et cetera." In general, however, you should not use abbreviations that are not also words. (And use "etc." sparingly.)

A common practice—especially in technical reports—is to write a complex term and then put the abbreviation after it is parentheses: "ethylenediaminetetraacetic acid (EDTA)." Once you do this, you can use the abbreviation throughout your document.

You use periods after most abbreviations ("B.C.," "p.m.," "M.D."). Some abbreviations, however, are so much a part of the language that they have become words themselves. You don't need to punctuate these acronyms:

UNESCO
YMCA
UCLA
FBI
NBC-TV

If you have doubt in such cases, you probably don't need to use the periods.

In writing addresses, use the U.S. Postal Service abbreviations for the states. Most of them are simply the first two letters of a one-word state name ("CA" for California) or the first letter of each word in a two-word name ("NY" for New York). Routinely, they are written without periods.

These are the only states for which the USPO abbreviation is not the first two letters or first letter of each word:

AK—Alaska
AZ—Arizona
CT—Connecticut
GA—Georgia

HI—Hawaii
IA—Iowa
KS—Kansas
KY—Kentucky
LA—Louisiana
ME—Maine
MD—Maryland
MN—Minnesota
MS—Mississippi
MO—Missouri
MT—Montana
NB—Nebraska
NV—Nevada
PA—Pennsylvania
TN—Tennessee
TX—Texas
VT—Vermont
VA—Virginia

You would do well to memorize this list. If you use these abbreviations (instead of "Wisc." or "Ala." for example), your writing will look more professional.

NUMBERS

The question is whether to write out a number in words ("three hundred and sixty") or to use numerals ("360"). The usage varies.

A good general rule is to write out numbers when they are small (say, ten or under) and when there are only a few of them in your essay.

There were seven people in the plane, but only two of them were injured.

On all other occasions, use numerals. When in doubt, write numerals.

You should always use numerals in dates, addresses, percentages, units of measure, page numbers, and hours followed by "a.m." or "p.m." Use these forms:

December 15, 1976
15 December 1976
639 Azalea Road
16 percent
4.2 minutes
page 37
8:20 a.m.
14,987 students

When writing large numbers, remember that numerals look bigger than words. If you want to justify America's national debt, put it down as "$1.7 trillion." If you want to protest it, write "$1,700,000,000,000.00."

When you want your readers to think a number is large, rub their nose in zeros.

If you have more than several numbers to express, use numerals throughout. But don't begin a sentence with a numeral.

Do not repeat numbers unnecessarily. Unless you're writing a contract, don't say "This happened seven (7) times."

SPELLING

The one best way to improve your spelling is to read extensively.

The best short-term way is to keep a dictionary at hand and to look up words you are in doubt about. You should have doubts when you face plainly difficult words, commonly misspelled words, and words you have had trouble with before.

You should never misspell "rhododendron," "ophthalmologist," "alumnae," or "hieroglyphic." You know these are difficult words; you should consult your dictionary and spell them right. (If you don't have a dictionary, consider using another word.)

Here are the most commonly misspelled words in English. Look over the list. If any one of the words looks unusual to you, circle it. Then try to memorize this correct spelling.

absence	apparent
accept	appreciate
accommodate	Arctic
achievement	athletic
acquainted	attendance
addressed	believe
advice	benefited
advise	Britain
AFFECT–EFFECT	bureau
aggravate	calendar
all right	capital
allusion	capitol
A LOT	category
amateur	cemetery
analyze	changeable
angle	choose
apology	colonel
committee	occurrence
comparative	omitted
compliment	pamphlet
conceive	parallel
conscience	perform
contemptible	permanence
cooperate	personnel
courteous	persuade
deceive	playwright

desert
dessert
dictionary
difference
dormitories
eighth
embarrass
environment
especially
exaggerate
excellence
existence
existential
fascinate
February
forehead
foreign
fourth
government
grammar
handkerchief
humorous
influence
initiate
intellectual
irrelevant
ITS–IT'S
let's
library
LOOSE–LOSE
mathematics
misspelled
ninth
occasion

politician
preferred
prejudice
PRINCIPAL–PRINCIPLE
pronunciation
prophecy–prophesy
psychology
questionnaire
RECEIVE
recommend
resemblance
reservoir
restaurant
rhythm
seize
sense
SEPARATE
sincerely
sophomore
stationery
subtle
syllable
temperament
tendency
than–then
THEIR–THERE
TO–TOO
truly
until
usually
Wednesday
were–where
whether
writing

Pay particular attention to the capitalized words on this list. They are the ones that cause the most trouble.

Start your own list. Keep track of words you have misspelled on your essays or on early drafts of your papers. Learn these words. There is no excuse for misspelling "separate" twice.

If you have a computer with a spell-check program, make use of it. But remember, it won't help you if you misspell a name, or write "short comings," or confuse "there" and "their."

EXERCISES

Punctuate these sentences. Insert commas, semicolons, colons, exclamation marks, question marks, periods, hyphens, and dashes where needed.

314   PART THREE   EIGHT RULES FOR GOOD WRITING

1. When the outfielder caught the second hand baseball he saw that the hide was torn
2. Charles Lackey the famous actor died on stage last week
3. He never complained he knew it would do no good
4. The nun asked me if I knew the way to Elm Street
5. During the summer I spent at least eleven thousand dollars on eighteenth century furniture
6. The price and I can't tell you how pleased I am to say it is only $4800.00
7. After six weeks of trying my brother finally learned to play hearts
8. The boy who won first prize a silver cup was our neighbor's son
9. I think *The Iceman Cometh* is the best American play written in this century and I absolutely refuse to teach it to this know nothing class
10. Would you kindly pay this bill by the first of the month
11. The wife got the stereo the television and the Thunderbird but the husband got to keep the dog
12. They insisted on waiting for Rex had never been there before
13. Then he wrote *Getting There from Here* 1955 a play about Nazi oppression
14. He studied seven year old children with personality problems
15. Our main concerns are the above ground hook ups and feed rates. During the shut down, we will install up to date equipment.

In these sentences, add apostrophes, quotation marks, italics, and capital letters when they are needed. Remove them where they are unnecessary.

16. My lawyer asked if I read georges mail. I said never in a million years.
17. My Mother loved to read the *Bible*, especially the story of Moses flight from Egypt.
18. It became an idée fix: he was sure he could find a word to rhyme with jeffersonian.
19. Kate said my favorite song is Bette Davis Eyes.
20. They worked hard on it, but the boys buick was still a wreck.
21. I prefer Yeats poem that celebrates Ulysses courage.
22. His first poem winter dreams was published in the Atlantic Monthly.
23. The Professor asked In what year did Coleridge write Christobel?
24. No wonder he gets straight Cs in mathematics. His 7s all look like 1s.
25. The details of the coup d'état were published in last sundays New York Times.
26. The best song in hello dolly is hello dolly.

Correct any errors in abbreviation, numbers, and spelling that you find in these sentences.

27. The suspect lived at 901 West Blvd. for 6 months. He burglerized a jewelry store, taking stones valued at ten thousand three hundred

and fifty dollars. He was indited and convicted, and his new adress is Rockway Prison, Temple City, Mich.

28. 15 percent of the students at the Massachusetts Institute of Technology do not plan to work in the U.S. Most want to get their doctor of philosophy degree, emigrate to Canada, and make fifty-five thousand a year working for the aircraft industry.

29. Your education already has cost me thirty-six hundred dollars. By the time you get you're M.A. in math, I'll be bankrup.

30. Citizens of Washington, District of columbia, loved Pres. Reagan. 10,000 of them attended his speech praising the C.I.A. and it's dedicated Personell.

31. We watched TV from eleven ante meridiem until after midnight. No more than ten % of the shows, however, were worth watching.

32. It's an odd occurence. Whenever we hire new personell, they expect to recieve top wages.

33. We bought a Nestles Crunch bar and carried it into Toys R Us.

34. So far this month, we have recieved only one (1) poster.

FINAL
REMINDERS

"Just say it."
—James Council

The eight rules for good writing should help to make you an effective writer. You may be further helped by these recommendations.

CREDIT YOUR SOURCES

In general writing, you do not need formal scholarly documentation. But often you will want to specify your sources. Don't use footnotes for this; few people read them. Put information about your sources in your text. Any of these forms is acceptable.

> According to Genie Hamner (*Bald Windows Revisited*, 1988), man has endured . . .

> In *Bald Windows Revisited* (1988), Genie Hamner argues . . .

> In her article "Decision Making in Washington Transportation Systems" (*Fortune*, June 1987), Kathleen Kelly describes . . .

> According to *Time* (February 15, 1991), President Bush has . . .

This kind of informal documentation need not be elaborate. But it is good to give your readers enough information so they can refer to the sources you used.

If you need formal documentation, see "The MLA System for Citing Sources" on page 354.

USE YOUR SPEAKING VOICE

Try to get your talking voice in your writing. You would never say, "This radio needed repair from the date of purchase"; you'd say, "This radio hasn't worked since I bought it." In talking, you tend to use short sentences, plain words, active voice, and specific details. You don't worry about beginning a sentence with "and" or "but." You don't use words like "shall" or "secondly" or "societal." You rarely say words in a series, and you'd never say, "My reasons were threefold" or "Quiet was the night."

Try to avoid long sentences full of paired or parallel constructions. Look at this example. (Italics and parentheses are added to show the pattern.)

> Children need generous amounts of *affection, guidance,* and *discipline* in order to develop into *intellectually* and *emotionally* mature adults. Children (who feel *rejected* or *unloved*) or (who are given *inconsistent* or *ineffective* discipline) tend to develop *serious* and *long-lasting* psychic disorders, such as *schizophrenia, alcoholism, drug addiction,* and *psychopathic personality.*

This is *written* language; nobody talks like that. Don't write this kind of social-science prose.

Trust your ear. What sounds like good spoken language—at a level suited to your subject and your audience—will be good writing.

Don't get hung up pursuing some hypothetically "correct" form. Don't trouble yourself about a choice like this:

> You will meet situations *where* all answers are wrong.
>
> You will meet situations *when* all answers are wrong.
>
> You will meet situations *in which* all answers are wrong.

All three usages are acceptable. Write the sentence the way *you* would say it.

Remember the "twelve garbagemen rule." The importance of simple language was stressed in a document addressed to practicing attorneys. It said, "When you begin your final summation to the jury, imagine that you're talking to 12 garbagemen who just stepped off the truck." That's good advice for anybody.

GET HELP FROM FRIENDS

In all likelihood, you will never be asked to write a document that someone else will read and judge immediately. Impromptu themes are sometimes assigned in college classes, but in the outer world you will always have time for reflection and revision. As part of your revision, have a friend, spouse, teacher, secretary, or colleague read through your essay for clarity and correctness.

Correctness in matters of punctuation, italics, number, idiom, and spelling is important. A misspelled "their" or "it's" can make a well-informed paper seem illiterate. An omitted comma can make an important sentence almost unreadable. A "not" that is typed "now" can cause big trouble.

Proofread your work carefully. Authors report embarrassing examples where "a bead" became "a bear"; "a political ideal" became "a political deal"; and "therapist" became "the rapist." A document from Senator Bill

Bradley's office in 1984 assured readers that, under his tax plan, a family with a $15,000-a-year income would pay only $16,000 in federal tax.

Of course, you should resort to a dictionary or an English handbook when you have difficulties. But serious errors may exist where you don't see a problem. If a piece of writing is important to you, ask a knowledgeable friend to look it over.

MAKE IT NEAT

Imagine you're applying for an executive position and are well qualified. Then you come to the interview chewing gum and wearing an old Batman sweatshirt. You're not going to get the job.

Similarly, if you write a first-rate letter of application and send it off in sloppy form (with bad handwriting, cross-outs, irregular margins, and on paper ripped from a spiral notebook), you won't get the job. If you send a messy manuscript to an editor, forget it. Major publishing houses and magazines now receive so many submissions that they immediately dismiss those that are cluttered or hard to read.

This is a reasonable response. The form in which you send out your material says something important about you and about your attitude toward your reader and your subject matter. Make it look good. There's a lot of truth in the ad: "If it's important, it belongs on Hammermill paper."

REMEMBER YOUR AUDIENCE

Keep in mind the kind of audience you are writing for. It makes a difference.

There is a danger in assuming that your reader knows what you know. This can lead you to commit what Edgar Dale calls the "COIK fallacy" and to write casually about Ken Maynard or Riverside Drive or real time because these terms are clear and meaningful to you. They are Clear Only If Known.

Addressing an educated audience, you can use words like "arcane" and "protean." Speaking to Southerners, you might venture "tump" or "cattywampus." Writing to a specialized group (scholars or athletes or priests), you can refer to Romantic poetry, a trap play, or John 3:16. But don't use such terms with a general audience; they won't understand you. Don't say, "They can look it up." They won't.

A problem arises when you are forced to use an obscure term. Here, along with the word, you should include an explanation of what it means. But you don't want to sound preachy or condescending. ("I suppose I have to explain to you that a 'shard' is a piece of pottery.") In such instances, you have to give the explanation in an indirect way. See how necessary clarification is included in these sentences:

> As spokesmen for the Jewish establishment, the *Scribes* and *Pharisees* were immediately hostile to the message of Jesus.

The *trap play* worked perfectly: The linebacker charged through the space we left open and was blocked out of the play.

No one ever understood what motivated Lizzie Borden. She remains an *enigma*.

The burden is always on you to make sure your reader understands your message.

Writing school assignments, you may have to violate many of the rules in this book. Your sociology teacher may assign a term paper and ask for 25 pages of text and dozens of footnotes. Your education professor may ask for a 200-page dissertation full of technical jargon. When teachers want that, give it to them. But remember, in the outside world, academic writing won't work for you. You're always better off keeping things clear, short, and talky.

Remember that some audiences are sensitive in particular areas. Writing to an African-American reader, be careful about using words like "negro" and "black." Don't tell Polish jokes in Milwaukee. Addressing women's groups, try not to say "chair*man*" or "spokes*man*" or to insist that "a surgeon really earns *his* money." Don't address a letter to *"Miss* Gloria Steinem" or to *"Ms.* Phyllis Schlafly."

Finally, recognize that some audiences cannot be reasoned with at all. When a zealot begins to talk about abortion or gun control, find a way to change the subject. Say, "Did you see the Dolphins play last Sunday?" Or, "What's your son doing these days?"

REMEMBER YOUR PURPOSE

The motto of one New York advertising agency is "It's not creative unless it sells." There is a lot of truth in that. Keep in mind the purpose of your writing. What is it you are trying to sell?

The eight rules of good writing just given are based on the assumption that you want to communicate information, to make an argument in a clear, forthright manner. But this isn't always the case.

Sometimes it's best to say nothing. Recent history provides examples of individuals who spoke out forthrightly when they shouldn't have. When the Democratic national headquarters at the Watergate was burglarized, Republican officials denied involvement before anyone had accused them of anything. When pro-life and pro-choice delegates conflicted at the 1980 Democratic convention, President Carter volunteered a middle-of-the-road statement on abortion. Addressing stockholders of Bendix, Inc., the board chairman announced that the young woman working as vice president for strategic services had won the job on her merits, not because of her personal involvement with him. In each case, silence would have been a more effective argument.

President Reagan learned this lesson well. After a few early (and conflicting) statements about the Iran/Contra affair, he resolutely kept quiet. He avoided reporters' questions and held few press conferences.

Only when the congressional committees had finished their investigations did he comment on the outcome.

Any time you are involved in an adversarial situation—that is, when you are responding to police officers, lawyers, newspaper and television reporters, relatives who enjoy lawsuits, an ex-spouse, or an insurance adjustor—don't be too quick to frame an argument, volunteer information, or write clever letters. They may return to haunt you. (Lawyers routinely advise accused clients to say nothing. They repeat the adage "There are no mutes on Death Row.")

In argument, it is always a mistake to lie. But there are times when truth won't do you much good. Always consider the virtues of silence.

There are also situations where you will want to express yourself indirectly. You might want to spare the sensibilities of your reader ("By the time he was twenty, Dudley had demonstrated a range of sexual abnormalities"). You might want to discredit an enemy ("The initial response to his book seems to be fairly favorable") or to veil a threat ("If you pay this bill promptly, your credit rating will remain excellent"). Such situations are not uncommon.

And sometimes you don't want clarity at all. Suppose, for example, you are obliged—in a school or business situation—to write on a subject you know little about. Now your purpose is to conceal your deficiency. You want to fill up a page, to sound fairly learned, and to avoid any specific assertion that will demonstrate your ignorance.

So you reverse many of the rules in this book. You will add "which" clauses and sprinkle modifiers (like "truly," "more or less," and "on the other hand") to ensure that no sentence has fewer than 30 words. You will write of *quintessential* issues and suggest that *procrustean* tactics are the *ne plus ultra* of folly. (This will obfuscate your message.) You will avoid proper names by using the passive voice ("a decision has been made that" or "word was received that"). You will write of vague entities like "business leaders," "the former," and "fair play." These can be described as "adequate" or "unfortunate"; but if you want to avoid even this minimal level of judgment, you can call them "notable," "meaningful," or "significant." (These words don't mean good or bad or much of anything.)

Write all this in small print (either in cramped handwriting or in 9-point type) and put it in long block paragraphs. The final work will be meaningless and unreadable, but in particular situations—where you can't or don't want to communicate directly—this may be the kind of writing you want.

Most of the time, however, you write to say something specific. You want to persuade your audience that marijuana should not be legalized, that gas rationing is essential, or that Sacco and Vanzetti were guilty. You want to describe your new boat. You want someone to give you a job, to buy mutual funds, or to settle that insurance claim in your favor. In such cases, the eight rules for good writing will help you get the effect you want.

Anything that thwarts the purpose of your writing (misspelling, wordiness, errors of fact, or even direct and meaningful statements) should be avoided. And anything that furthers your cause with a particular audience (even such features as expensive paper, folksy language, neat typing, and footnotes) should probably be used.

Good writing may not always win you the final effect you want—that job, that insurance adjustment, that sale. But it will do all that language can do to achieve that end.

BE SMART

Here is an important question: How many of these topics do you need to know about to be a persuasive writer?

alcohol and baldness
Antarctica
Apollo 13
biorhythms
the causes of homosexuality
competition in China
creationism in court
Senator Bob Dole
Freudian psychology
friendly fire
a googolplex
Halley's comet
Sherlock Holmes
modern cryptography
monkeys and sign language
Rubik's Cube
Duke Snider
St. Croix
The Tales of Hoffmann
tax-free bonds
true believers
ufologists
zen tennis

The answer, of course, is all of them. Nothing is irrelevant in persuasion.

Remember that every book you read, every movie you attend, every town you visit, every TV show you see, and every relative and bartender you talk to is giving you material you can use in writing.

The lessons in this book will be useful. But you also have to read a lot of books, talk to all kinds of people, and stay alert if you want to be a first-rate persuader. It's a worthy goal.

Go for it.

APPENDIXES

APPENDIXES

EXERCISES FOR REVIEW

How valid are these arguments? Identify examples of induction, deduction, expert testimony, semantic argument, analogy, argument in a circle, post hoc, begging the question, ad hominem argument, extension, the either–or fallacy, and statistical manipulation.

1. "Crisco'll do you proud every time."—Loretta Lynn

2. Of course you favor federal aid to education. You're a teacher. You stand to profit on the deal.

3. "Our cheese is like a good love affair."—Rondele

4. A Tampax poll found that 22 percent of the respondents thought menstrual pain is psychological.

5. "Each ring is Solid 14 Karat Gold; the Stone is guaranteed to be a Genuine 17-faceted, .25 pt. Diamond, anchored in a Solid Sterling Silver setting."—Ad for a ring costing $9.95

6. Asking Britain to desert Northern Ireland is like asking the United States to give up Texas.

7. "Seven out of ten Americans cheat on their income tax."—Professor R. Van Dyke Ellington III

8. I never knew an Auburn football player who could read or write beyond the eighth-grade level.

9. In March 1987, Peter Holm filed an alimony suit against actress Joan Collins, giving a breakdown of his estimated $960,000-a-year expenses.

10. *Poll Question:* Should the United States continue providing support to people in Central America who are fighting for their independence from Soviet-backed Marxists? Yes _____ No _____

11. One Pass: "The fastest way to touch down almost anywhere in the world free."—John Elway, Denver Broncos

12. It takes 400,000,000 years to make a bourbon as good as Old Granddad.

13. We should not ban laetrile just because it didn't prove effective in laboratory tests. Pretty soon, they'll want to ban holy water.

14. In 1985, Ann Landers polled her female readers. She asked, "Would you be content to be held close and treated tenderly, and forget about 'the act'?" Over 90,000 women wrote in, and nearly three-quarters of them said "Yes." I guess that proves something.

15. "There is no proof that sugar confectionary gives rise to dental cavities."—*Association Internationale des Fabricants de Confiserie*

16. I don't believe drugs, alcohol, and gambling are addicting habits. Pretty soon they'll claim that Billy Cannon had a counterfeiting sickness and Jesse James had a train-robbing sickness.

17. Why not a 45-mph speed limit? Wouldn't that save more lives?

18. Over 60,000 doctors recommend Preparation H, according to a survey of doctors who recommend OTC products.

19. Snickers—"The official snack food of the 23rd Olympiad."

20. *The Husband* (a novel by Sol Stein): "The dilemma of countervailing demands on the sensual man of good will . . . rich and true . . . modulated with a respectful reserve . . . handled with hardly a false note."—*New York Times*

21. "For every rape that is reported, from 9 to 23 are not."—Southwest Radio Church

22. "When the fish-pond that was a meadow shall be mowed.
Sagittarius being in the ascendant,
Plagues, famines, death by the military hand,
The century approaches renewal." (Prophecy of Nostradamus)

23. What did you do to deserve Beefeater?

24. If your name is Makay, Malloy, or Murray, beware of drink. According to John Gary, director of the Council for Alcoholism in Glasgow, Scotland, people whose last names begin with the letter "M" may be eight times more prone to alcoholism than others.

25. *Miss MacIntosh, My Darling* by Marguerite Young: "What we behold is a mammoth epic, a massive fable, a picaresque journey, a Faustian quest, and a work of stunning magnitude and beauty . . . some of the richest, most expressive, most original and exhaustively revealing passages of prose that this writer has experienced in a long time."—William Goyen, *New York Times*

26. We scientists working on astrological data expect to be criticized. We know that Newton and Einstein were ridiculed in the past.

27. All this effort to register and confiscate handguns will not help us fight crime. Violence rises from the souls of men.

28. It's not safe to walk on the streets of New York City. I'm glad I live in Cleveland.

29. "Ever wonder why kids instinctively go for soft drinks in bottles?"—Glass Container Manufacturers Institute

30. *Miss MacIntosh, My Darling* by Marguerite Young: "In fact, this is an outrageously bad book, written by an author with very little of interest to say and very little skill in saying it . . . wholly unreadable."—*Time*

31. The accident can't be my fault. I have no-fault insurance.

32. If you smoke, please try Carlton.

33. "Smaller-chested women can't make it."—Donna Rice

34. A clever magician can always perform tricks, but a genuine psychic can sometimes produce paranormal effects and sometimes not. Uri Geller produced no effects at all when he appeared on the *Tonight Show*. He is a true psychic.

35. On a typical television poll, an early-evening newscaster poses a yes or no question, asking viewers to phone one number to vote "yes" and another to vote "no." Then a late-evening newscaster reports the results—for example, that 72 percent oppose socialized medicine.

36. If secular humanism is a religion, what isn't?

37. What I want to know is who masterminded the plot to impeach Richard Nixon.

38. How about a law to compel anybody publically lobbying against abortion to have a baby, or two or three, or else go to jail. Same thing.

39. "One Out of Two Marriages Has Serious Sex Problems"—*National Enquirer* headline.

40. Dial. The most effective deodorant soap you can buy.

41. Do you approve of pornographic and obscene classroom textbooks being used under the guise of sex education? Yes _____ No _____

42. I disagree with Abby Van Buren when she says no woman should be forced to have a baby she doesn't want. A lot of people have parents they don't like, but we don't let them go around murdering their fathers and mothers.

43. "Will $1 million be enough to solve your problems for the moment?"—Poll question from an ad offering "Your Golden Astral Number"

44. Athletics teach our young people how to play the game of life.

45. Naval ROTC should be abolished. I'm learning nothing from it.

46. Read *One in Twenty* by Bryan Magee—an adult, plainly written study of male and female homosexuality.

47. "I lowered my vibrations to be able to come to Earth and pay off a debt I owed to a girl in a previous lifetime—a karmic debt."—Omnec Onec, a visitor from Venus, speaking at the World UFO Congress held in Tucson in May 1991.

48. Everyone knows that America's greatest threat is not from foreign powers, but from within.

49. We can't get family counseling from a priest. What does he know of marriage?

50. Homosexuality is no illness. It is a widespread practice, like vegetarianism. The homosexual has a sexual preference for members of the same sex; a vegetarian has an alimentary preference for noncarnivorous foods. In neither case is there any impairment of function or any disease.

51. All I say is that a baby shouldn't have to suffer for a mother's convenience.

52. "You wouldn't sweep dust under the rug—so don't put clean food in a dirty oven!"—Easy-Off Oven Cleaner

53. Gordon's—"Largest selling gin in England, America, the world."

54. To All Citizens and Taxpayers. QUESTION: "Do you favor our city and county governments devoting more of our present tax money to police protection?" Yes _____ No _____

55. "A good club soda is like a good woman: it won't quit on you."—Canada Dry advertisement

56. How can you deny the power of the moon's influence? The oceans have tides; women have periods; and emergency rooms are full on moonlit nights.

57. "The execution of a person possibly in the state of mortal sin and spiritual unreadiness potentially sends that person to eternal damnation and thus constitutes the most egregious violation of the Eighth Amendment's proscription of cruel and unusual punishment and the First Amendment's guarantee of religious liberty."—A legal claim made by the Alabama Representative Resource Center

58. I can't decide which Supreme Cutlery setting to buy. I'm choosing between Ron de Vu, Bamboo, Arctic, Marchese, Colonnade, Ionic, and Snowflake.

59. *Playboy* estimated that, among news reporters and editors working on the Bakker and Hart sex scandals, the number who were faithful to their wives was .0000001 percent.

60. "Cougar is like nobody else's car."

61. Ford LTD—"700% Quieter."

62. A new study interviewed more than 500 men and women who had recently suffered cardiac crises and compared them to over 500 healthy men and women. Out of the sick group, over half said they were nonreligious. But in the healthy group, only one in five were nonreligious. This proves religious men and women suffer signifi-

cantly fewer heart attacks than people who don't believe in God or go to church regularly.

63. Lawyer Peter Wold said that his client, a Northwest Airline pilot, wasn't drunk while flying a Boeing 727 from Fargo to Minneapolis. The pilot did drink 17½ rum-and-diet-cokes the night before, but he was an alcoholic and had a tolerance for alcohol.

64. If Lisa Olson doesn't like locker-room humor, let her stay out of the locker room.

65. "The West wasn't won on salad."—a North Dakota billboard promoting beef.

66. I have found an interesting pattern in U.S. history that tells me we're due for a war. The WWI soldier fathered a son in 1918; that boy was 23 in 1941, just the right age to fight a war. The WWII soldier had a son in 1945; the child was 20 years old in 1965, just right to fight at the start of the Vietnam War. The Korean War soldier had a child in 1951; the boy was 18 in 1969 when the Vietnam War was at its height. You see the pattern? Now consider a child fathered in the middle of the Vietnam War; he's 19 today. And he's ready.

67. Dialogue overheard at a school board meeting:
    WIFE: I see that David Millar, who used to be the Marlboro man on television, just died of emphysema.
    HUSBAND: How old was he?
    WIFE: Eighty-one. Some people never learn.

68. My cousin Kathy is asking the insurance company to pay for her breast enlargement. She calls it correcting a birth defect.

69. "Eighty percent of people who think their mates are cheating are right."—Irwin Blye, New York City private detective

70. If you think the jails in this state are bad, you should see the jails in Iran and Turkey.

71. "I am not asking you to subscribe to a magazine."—The first line of a sales letter from *Sojourners.*

72. "I want to be the type of football player the Lord would be if He played football."—Herschel Walker

73. "The average man makes up his mind in six short seconds whether or not he wants to know a woman better."—Dr. Joyce Brothers

74. *Lost in Yonkers* by Neil Simon. 1991 Pulitzer Prize winner. Winner of the 1991 Tony Award for "Best Play."

75. Feminists are rejoicing at the recent Supreme Court ruling that women cannot be denied access to jobs working with lead batteries,

simply because this involves serious risk to their reproductive organs. Hooray for civil rights!

76. *Lost in Yonkers* by Neil Simon. "There's not one glimmer of honesty or authenticity in this family melodrama by Neil Simon."—*New Yorker*

77. Asked why U.S. intelligence reports were poor prior to the Grenada invasion, Admiral Wesley McDonald explained, "We were not micro-managing Grenada intelligencewise during that time frame."

78. "The risen Jesus Christ, when He came back to earth, the first food He ate was bee pollen. God had Him use bee pollen symbolically, to show that bee pollen should be an integral part of everyone's diet."—TV ad for High Desert Bee Pollen

79. So Pee-wee Herman was caught at an adult theater. I can understand that. What I can't understand is why they sent a dozen cops to raid a showing of *Nancy Nurse*. Don't Sarasota police have anything better to do?

80. Figures given by the Institute for Sex Research, at Indiana University, suggest that sooner or later 35 to 40 percent of American wives are unfaithful.

81. We can't keep Dan Quayle as Vice President. My God, what if the President died?

82. "We don't go for fakes. And neither should you."—Ad recommending "genuine G.M. parts"

83. "Some things you can just count on. Like a good friend and the great taste of Maxwell House Coffee."

84. "Thank You for Not Speaking in Tongues"—Placard distributed by the Tobacco Institute

85. A man wrote "Ask Marilyn" with the question: "Can you give me just one good reason why I shouldn't look for an attractive woman to marry, rather than an ordinary one?" The answer: "A good-looking set of china doesn't make the meal taste better."

86. "Earth is being spied upon by several extra-terrestrial civilizations."—From an 8-inch-thick, supersecret NATO report compiled by top-level military experts, scientists, astronomers, historians, theologians, sociologists, and psychologists. The existence of the report was revealed by former U.S. Army master sergeant Robert Dean in an article in the *National Enquirer*.

87. *There is a Cure for Arthritis*—A book by Paavo O. Airola, N.D.

SUBJECTS FOR ARGUMENTATIVE ESSAYS

abortion rights
academic writing
Academy Award winners
acid rain
ACT test scores
acupuncture
adoption by unmarried couples
adoption by gay couples
adult children who don't leave
 home
affirmative action
Agent Orange
aging American population
AIDS as God's punishment
AIDS testing
airbags
airline accidents
alcoholism as a disease
Mohammed Ali
Alice in Wonderland
alimony payments
All My Children
Alzheimer's Disease
American vs. Japanese cars
animal experiments in research
anorexia
Antichrist
antitrust laws
aphrodisiacs
Arizona and Martin Luther King
 Day
arthritis cures
aspirin to prevent heart attacks
astrological signs
astrology in the White House
—athletes' salaries

bad teachers
Jim and Tammy Bakker
baldness cures
banning cigarette ads
banning textbooks

Barbie dolls
Mayor Marion Barry
baseball cards
battered wives
beef as a health threat
bending spoons with mind
 power
betting on *Monday Night Football*
the Bible as literature
the big-bang theory
Bigfoot
bikini bathing suits
bilingual education
biorhythms
Bird vs. Magic vs. Michael
birth control devices
birth order
black vs. *African-American*
"Bo Knows"
Ivan Boesky
bombing abortion clinics
bottle water vs. tap water
professional boxing
brainwashing
Tawana Brawley
breast enlargement
breast-feeding
William Buckley's prose
bulimia
Delta Burke's weight
busing to achieve racial balance

cable TV
California earthquakes
cancer cures
carbon dating
Johnny Carson
the success of Catholic schools
cats vs. dogs
Edgar Cayce's powers
celibacy

censorship of books and
    magazines
census figures
chain letters
the *Challenger* explosion
channeling
chemotherapy choices
the Chernobyl accident
child abuse
childhood obesity
children whose parents divorce
chiropractors
Christian Science
Christmas with the family
the CIA
cigarette ads
cigarette smoke and the
    nonsmoker
circumcision
circumstantial evidence
civil rights for men
civil rights for minorities
Governor Bill Clinton
cloning
coaches' salaries
cocaine as a recreational drug
cohabitation
Coke vs. Pepsi
cold fusion
colorizing black-and-white films
Christopher Columbus, hero or
    villain
communism
competency tests for teachers
computer dating
the Condon Report on UFOs
conscientious objectors
consenting adults
conspiracy theories
the core curriculum
correct English
cosmetic surgery
crack
crack babies
creationism in public schools
credit card problems
crop circles

Nancy Cruzan
Cuba
cultural illiteracy
cybernetics

Dalcon shield
date rape
day-care centers
daylight saving time
Dear Abby
death penalty
death penalty for minors
declining educational standards
deconstructionist criticism
the defense budget
deficit spending
Desert Storm
designated drivers
the designated hitter
designer-label clothes
Designing Women
dialects
diet pills
dioxin
dirty lyrics
disarmament treaties
discrimination against overweight
    people
divorce laws
Jeane Dixon
docudramas
dog racing
dousing
Dungeons and Dragons
Senator David Durenberger

E prime
Earth Day
Easter Island
Eastern Airlines
ecology
ecumenical Christianity
effects of a full moon
Electoral College
El Salvador
Elvis today
empty-nest syndrome

endangered species
English teachers
entrapment by police agents
entropy
Equal Rights Amendment
escort services
extra-sensory perception
euthanasia
evolution
exorcism

faith healing
fashion trends
father–daughter relationships
father–son relationships
fear of flying
fear of public speaking
the fetus as a human being
high-fiber diets
fire walking
the First Amendment
flag-burning laws
fluoridation fears
Larry Flynt
Jane Fonda
food stamps
foreign language requirements
four-letter words
free speech on campus
Freud
Friday the 13th
Friday the 13th
frozen embryos
fundamentalism
funding public schools
fur coats

Zsa Zsa Gabor
gambling
gangs
gay rights
Gaza Strip
Uri Geller
gene therapy
genetic engineering
German reunification
ghosts

Glasnost
glossolalia
Bernhard Goetz
good manners
good taste
Mikhail Gorbachev
Graceland
grammar vs. usage
Grenada invasion
gun-control laws

Halcion
Halley's comet
handwriting analysis
health-care costs
health-food stores
health nazis
Patty Hearst
Heaven and Hell
heredity vs. environment
Pee-wee Herman
modern heroes
high school pregnancies
Anita Hill
the Hillside Strangler
John Hinckley
Jimmy Hoffa's disappearance
holistic medicine
the homeless
homosexual teachers
homosexual clergy
horror movies
Howard Hughes
Saddam Hussein
hyperactive children

Lee Iacocca
illegal aliens
inflation rate
insanity plea
insecticide manufacturing
insider trading on Wall Street
instant replay
instinct
interracial romance
intuition
IQ test results

Iran/Contra investigation
Iraqi casualties in Desert Storm
Ireland vs. Northern Ireland
Israel
the IUD

J, the Old Testament author
Jack the Ripper
Jesse Jackson
Michael Jackson
Japanese trade competition
Jesus
jogging
junk bonds
junk foods
junk mail
"Just a housewife"
"Just say no"

KAL Flight 007
Erica Kane
the Keating Five
Kitty Kelley biographies
Senator Edward Kennedy
the Kennedy assassination
Kennedy family scandals
Dr. Jack Kevorkian
Ayatollah Khomeini
killer bees
Martin Luther King
Rodney King
Korea
Ku Klux Klan
Kurdish refugees

L.A. police brutality
labor unions
laetrile
latchkey children
Latin classes
the Latin Mass
lawyers
lead poisoning
leash laws
legal insanity
John Lennon

lesbians
libel laws
lie-detector tests
life in space
life-support systems
Rush Limbaugh
literature classes
living alone
lobbyists
the Loch Ness monster
state lotteries
Lourdes miracles
love relationships
lucky numbers

Madonna
the Mafia
man as animal
Nelson Mandela
mandatory jail sentences
Manhattan Project
Marla Maples
marijuana laws
marriage adjustments
math scores of U.S. students
medical school quotas
Medjugorje
Meese Report on pornography
menopause
the Mexican debt
MIAs and POWs
Michael Milken
Milli Vanilli
miniskirts
minoxidil
Miss America pageants
the missing link
Miss Manners
modern painting
modernism in the church
Marilyn Monroe's death
Moonies
personal morality of candidates
Jim Morrison and the Doors
mother–daughter relationships
movie critics
movie ratings

multiculturalism
Muslims

the effect of names
names of automobiles
national debt
National Endowment for the Arts
National Enquirer
NATO
natural law
Nazi party
NCAA Proposition #48
NCAA rules on recruiting
negative ions
the New Age movement
the new Coke
new morality
Nicaragua
1984
Nintendo
Noah's Ark
No-Doz
no-fault insurance
noise pollution
non-English-speaking Americans
no pass–no play
Norplant
Colonel Oliver North
Nostradamus
National Rifle Association
nuclear power plants
nuclear waste
nudist colonies
numerology

oat bran
off-track betting
oil prices
oil spills
Lisa Olson
one-night stands
one-parent families
"Onward, Christian Soldiers"
opera
organ transplants
overachievers

overweight people
ozone depletion

PACs
palimony
palm reading
papal infallibility
paranoia
paroles and pardons
patriotism today
People for the American Way
Peristroika
Ross Perot
perpetual motion
PG-13 movies
phobias
teaching phonics
memorizing pi to 100 places
pit bulls
the placebo effect
plagiarism
Playboy
Pledge of Allegiance
PLO
PMS
Polish jokes
political correctness on campus
polling systems
pollution levels
poltergeists
polyunsaturates
population growth
pornography
POSSLQ
postal rates
prayer in public schools
prenuptial financial agreements
preservation of historic buildings
Princess Di
prisoners' rights
privacy-invading reporters
private clubs
private schools
Procter & Gamble and devil
    worship
modern prophets
prostitution as a crime

Prozac
psychoanalysis
psychokinesis
psychometry
public smoking laws
the public's right to know
public television
Purgatory
pyramid power

quack doctors
quasars
Dan Quayle
Joan Quigley
Karen Quinlan
job quotas

race and capital punishment
racial superiority
racism on campus
ransoming hostages
rap music
readers vs. nonreaders
Nancy Reagan
Reagan the communicator
recruiting top athletes
rednecks
redshirting freshmen
reincarnation
replacement workers
required courses
retarded citizens
retirement age
Book of Revelation
right to bear arms
right to die
right-to-work laws
rights of the accused
rights of the victim
Rolex watches—real and
    imitation
Roman Catholicism
Pete Rose
Julius and Ethel Rosenberg
royal jelly
RU-486, the abortion pill
Rubik's cube

running as a religious experience
rural vs. urban living
Salman Rushdie
Nolan Ryan

saccharin
Sacco–Vanzetti
safe sex
salt as a health threat
Santa Claus
Sarah, the woman with 21
    personalities
Satan worship
savings-and-loan scandals
General Schwartzkopf
Scientology
mandatory seat-belt laws
secular humanism
selling college degrees
sex-change operations
sex education
sexist language
sexist language in the Bible
sexual harassment
sexually explicit textbooks
Shakespeare's plays
shock treatments
shoplifting
the Shroud of Turin
Sikhs
Bart Simpson
666
skyjacking
slander and libel
sleeping pills and tranquilizers
smoking and health
smoking on airlines
soap operas
social-science classes
Social Security funding
solar power
Son-of-Sam laws
boycotting South Africa
space creatures
space programs
speed limits
speed reading

spelling reform
Star Wars weaponry
statute of limitations
statutory rape
Stealth bombers
steroid use by athletes
Stonehenge
student illiteracy
students' rights
sugar vs. NutraSweet
teenage suicides
sun tanning
Super Bowl games
Supreme Court decisions
Supreme Court nominees
surrogate mothers
Jimmie Swaggart

tabloid advertisements
tabloid stories
a talisman
talking animals
Jerry Tarkanian
tarot cards
tax reform
tax relief for private schools
Elizabeth Taylor
Zachary Taylor's "poisoning"
teacher strikes
teenage parents
telephone company competition
televangelism
television commercials
television ratings
term-papers for sale
forms of territoriality
test-tube babies
thalidomide
Third World loans
Three Mile Island
salvaging the Titanic
tithing
the tobacco industry
the top 40
toxic wastes
transactional analysis
translating the Bible

Trilateral Commission
Trivial Pursuit
true believers
Donald Trump
Ted Turner
Robyn Twitchell
2 Live Crew
Mike Tyson

UFOs
unemployment compensation
United Nations effectiveness
Universal Product Code
unlisted phone numbers
U.S. saving bonds
USSR turbulence
utopias

vampires
the Vardogr effect
Vatican II
VCRs
vegetarianism
Velikovsky
veterans' rights
the vice presidency
victimless crimes
Vietnam War
Virgin Mary apparitions
virginity
vitamin C
vitamin E
Klaus von Bülow
Erich von Däniken
vote fraud

want-ad dating
Watergate
wedding extravaganzas
weight-lifting for women
welfare for unwed mothers
Wellesley College and Mrs. Bush
Western Civilization courses
Dr. Ruth Westheimer
wheatfield circles
whiskey ads
Vanna White

white-collar crime
woman's role
women candidates
"womyn" in "herstory"
worker-protection laws
professional wrestling

X-rated movies
X-ray treatments

yoga
the Yugo
Yugoslavian turbulence
yuppies

Zionism
zoning laws

GOOD WORDS, BAD WORDS, AND PERSUASIVE WORDS

GOOD WORDS

In these lists, the word on the left may be correct on a particular occasion. Most of the time, however, the word on the right is clearer, more direct, and less clichéd. Write with everyday words.

achieve	do, make
advise	tell
and/or	and, or
approximately	about
attempt	try
benefit	help
commence	start, begin
conclude	end, stop
contribute	give
deem	think
demonstrate	prove, show
depart	leave
desire	want
dialogue with	talk to
disclose	tell, show
discontinue	stop
due to the fact that	because
e.g.	for example
enumerate	count
exhibit	show
expertise	skill, ability
the fact that	(omit)
failed to	didn't
finalize	complete, finish
for a period of	for
the following	these
Gentlemen:	Dear Mr. Clark:
has the ability to	can
herein	here
i.e.	that is
in addition	besides, too
in order to	to
in regard to	about
in the event that	if
in the near future	soon, Wednesday
invaluable	valuable
it is noted that	(omit)

last but not least	last, finally
the latter	(repeat the noun)
locate	find
the majority	most
the month of	(omit)
my intention is	I will
notify	let me know
not later than	by
not only . . . but also	and
numerous	many, two dozen
observe	see
obtain	get
parameters	limits
perform	do
personnel	people, Molly and Ed
possess	own, have
prepared	ready
prioritize	rank
prior to	before
probability	chance
provided that	if
purchase	buy
regarding	about
relative to	about
remainder	rest
remuneration	pay, payment, $50
request	ask
secondly	second
share with	tell, talk to
similar to	like
state	say
state-of-the-art	latest
submit	give, send
sufficient	enough
terminate	end, stop
therefore	so
this point in time	today, now
touch base with	talk to
transmit	send
truly	(omit)
until such time as	until
utilize	use
very	(omit)
viable	practical, workable
whenever	when
whether or not	whether
with reference to	about

with the exception of	except
the writer	I, me

BAD WORDS

These words will weaken any argument you try to write. They make you seem vague, illiterate, clichéd, angry, insensitive, and pretentious. Avoid them.

the above	let's face it
am of the opinion that	logistical
and . . . was no exception	mesdames
asinine	mode
bastard	Mr./Ms.
bimonthly	N.B.
cognizant	Negro
crap	nitty-gritty
datum	per
Dear Sir:	*per se*
down through the ages	peruse
enclosed please find	Polack
falsa lectio	quintessential
first and foremost	Sear's
goddam	seperate
his or her	shall
his hope was that	societal
history teaches us	some people
idiotic	stated
ignorant	syndrome
in lieu of	thirdly
in life	To Whom It May Concern
in view of the fact that	truly
keratectomy	viz.

PERSUASIVE WORDS

After you have made your best case, you can enhance it by using some of the favorite words of professional persuaders. These ten may be particularly useful.

Claim—This is a word to apply to your adversary. You *say* (*insist, prove*) vitamin C cures a cold; he *claims* it does not.

Clearly—You can use this to begin any sentence: "Clearly, John Hinckley was framed."

Colonel—People with titles love to hear them. Use them often. Work *Colonel* (or *Mayor* or *Doctor*) into every fourth sentence.

Fair—This, of course, describes your position. Because it cannot be specifically defined, *fair* (like *positive, realistic, just,* and *reasonable*) is a key word in politics and commerce.

Integrity—Write of "personal integrity," "family integrity," "professional integrity," "instructional integrity," etc. The terms mean pretty much what you want them to mean.

Mature—This sounds like a compliment, but you can use the word to suggest your opponent is old and his ideas are obsolete. Other double-edged words are *young, sensitive, free-spirited, witty, experienced,* and *intellectual*.

Notable—This is an important word when you have to evaluate something and don't want to call it either good or bad. *Notable* (like *meaningful* and *significant*) means almost nothing.

Pro—On every issue, you want to be *pro* rather than *anti*. Call yourself pro-life or pro-choice. Describe your opponent as anti-baby or anti-woman.

Relatively—This is a useful qualifying word. You can talk of "a relatively short time" or a "relatively inexpensive product." This can mean anything.

Superficial—Because your opponent's argument cannot treat every conceivable detail involved in the issue, you can always dismiss it as *superficial*. Another useful adjective is *unrealistic*.

Unfortunate—This is the perfect word when you have to say something negative and don't want to assign blame. You can speak of "an unfortunate decision," "an unfortunate incident," or "an unfortunate choice of words."

These persuasive words won't win an argument for you unless you have your facts, authorities, and statistics in order. But they can help.

WRITING A BUSINESS LETTER

Probably the main form in which you will write persuasive prose is the business letter. You'll want to convince someone you deserve a job or a raise. You'll want to make a sale or get a larger insurance adjustment. You'll want to pacify someone who has written an angry letter to you.

Business letters take a fairly standard form.

Read the two letters on the following pages. Both are effective examples of business writing.

Now consider the seven parts of a business letter as illustrated in these examples.

THE RETURN ADDRESS

Notice that this is omitted if you write on letterhead stationery. Always use the two-letter U.S. Postal Service abbreviations to indicate the state. (See page 310.) And always include the ZIP Code, in its five- or nine-digit form.

THE DATE

Either of the two forms shown is acceptable. Just be consistent.

INSIDE ADDRESS

If your letter is at all important, send it to someone by name.

On pedestrian matters, you can address "Subscription Office" or "Catalog Department," but never address anyone simply as "Personnel Manager," "Chairman," "Publisher," or "President." If you use your library and your telephone, you can get the name of the person you want to write to.

If you raise the question, you will probably find that friends of yours (either through their jobs or their relatives) have access to a WATS line. This can be immensely useful when you have to write to the personnel manager at Philip Morris, or to Mr./Ms. Leslie Rogers.

THE SALUTATION

Write "Dear Mr. [or *Mrs.* or *Miss* or *Ms.*] Name." This is always followed by a colon. Writing to a friend, you can use "Dear Bill" but this too must be followed by a colon.

Try never to write "Dear Sir," "Dear Madam," "Dear Sir or Madam," or "Gentlemen." These forms, which prevailed some years ago, now seem offensively vague and sexist. If you don't have a name to write to, address a title. You can get by with "Dear Editor" or "Dear Manager." You might try "Dear Red Cross Representative."

But it's always best to take the extra time and find a name.

862 Callaway Drive
Medford, WI 54101
15 December 1986

Mr. George Blazdon, President
Silver Shadow Pen Company
1515 Vermont Street
New York, NY 10009

Dear Mr. Blazdon:

Last year I was given one of your Silver Shadow pens (Model 364A) for an anniversary present. I love its looks, but I'm having trouble with it. I wonder if you can help me.

After a few months, the point no longer came out when I twisted the pen. I had kept all the original papers and followed the warranty instructions. I sent the pen to your Atlanta office, and they fixed it and returned it.

At the same time, because I can't seem to find refills locally, I sent for half a dozen red-ink refills. You sent them, along with a bill for $18. This seemed pretty steep to me, but I had no choice if I wanted to use the pen, so I paid it.

Now the pen is broken again. When I twist it, the point doesn't come up. I phoned your Atlanta office to see if the pen was under warranty. They said it wasn't, but that they'd be able to fix it for $10.75.

I'm not sure I should have to pay this amount. Either the pen was defective in the first place or repaired poorly in the second place. Should I have to pay for your mistakes?

I'm not a consumer crank, Mr. Blazdon, but I don't think this situation is fair. What do you advise me to do?

Sincerely,

Thomas Ridgeway
Thomas Ridgeway

SILVER SHADOW PEN COMPANY
1515 Vermont Street
New York, NY 10009

December 21, 1986

Mr. Thomas Ridgeway
862 Callaway Drive
Medford, WI 54101

Dear Mr. Ridgeway:

Thank you for your letter of December 15. I'm pleased you like our Silver Shadow pen, and I'm sorry it's giving you trouble. I hope this information helps you.

Your pen is indeed out of warranty. You have used it for over a year. I'm sure you understand that we cannot offer a lifetime guarantee with our products.

You can purchase refills for your pen at Redman's Office Supplies in Medford or at Quality Stationery Company (3201 West Lane) when you drive into Milwaukee. The refills do cost $3 each, but these are jumbo-cartridges containing 2½ times as much ink as usual ballpoint refills.

May I offer a compromise, Mr. Ridgeway? You don't want to be without your Silver Shadow pen, and we can't afford dissatisfied customers. I suggest you have the pen repaired in Atlanta and pay the $10.75. Thereafter, if the same problem recurs, send it to me and it will be repaired free of charge.

I hope you have a pleasant holiday.

Sincerely,

George Blazdon

George Blazdon
President

GB:itm

THE BODY OF THE LETTER

Usually a letter has at least three paragraphs, with the first acting as introduction and the last as conclusion.

The first paragraph should be short and should define the issue. Your reader should never have to move on into the second paragraph to know what your letter is about. If you are answering someone, it is a good idea to begin, "Thank you for your letter of July 17." Giving the date lets the reader check the appropriate file and refer to the original message. Saying "thank you" sets a positive tone.

Through the body of your letter, use the forms that mark good writing anywhere. Use short sentences, plain words, active voice, and specific detail. Sound like yourself talking. At all costs, avoid "letterese," the clichés of business writing:

am cognizant of

are in receipt of

as per your request

at your earliest convenience

do not hesitate to

enclosed herewith

thanking you in advance

under separate cover

with reference to

Work particularly hard to avoid the words "advise," "acknowledge," "per," and "transmit." They are deadly.

Keep your language plain. Remember, you're not answering a letter. You're answering a person.

It is often effective to repeat the name of the person you're writing to. ("I am genuinely sorry, Mr. Metcalf, but there is no possibility we can give you a loan at this time.") Save this for an important sentence.

Never express anger in a business letter. You can feel it, but don't write it.

The concluding paragraph should be short, general, affirmative, and personal. Even if your letter expressed criticism and unhappy truths, finish on as positive a note as you can. ("I'm sorry I have to give you this bad news, Bill. But I know you can handle it.") And even if you've been speaking for your company and using "we" throughout your letter, use an "I" in the final paragraph.

THE COMPLIMENTARY CLOSE

A simple "Sincerely" or "Sincerely yours" is best. If you're writing a governor or an archbishop, use "Respectfully."

THE SIGNATURE

Always type your name beneath your signature. And put your title (if you have one) on the line below that.

If someone else types your letter, the typist indicates the fact by putting the author's initials, then his or her own, on the left margin below the signature.

A final word about the overall appearance of your letter. Keep it on one page if at all possible. Center the writing so that the white space around it seems to frame it. Double-space between paragraphs, and begin a new paragraph often. All this will make your letter more inviting to read.

In general, your business letter will be most effective and persuasive if it is short, informed, natural-sounding, and marked by unrelenting goodwill.

You can learn a good deal from the following example. It was published in the *ABCA Bulletin* under the title "The World's Worst Business Letter: A Candidate."

PROCANE INSURANCE
5111 Lincoln Avenue
Mobile, Al.

Feb. 22nd. '84

Anarda Bonding Co.
1601 Mirrabel St.
Locksley, Ala.

Attn: Mrs. Sally Hall

RE: Truckstop Ranch
Mobile, Alab.
QAP #958-254-8927A

Dear Madam,

Per our telephone conversation this date, please be advised of the fact that we are no longer insurance carrier for the above referenced company. We regret we cannot, pursuant to your request, transmit information in regard to the record of said account in the area of fire-protection viability. Enclosed please find documentation in reference to the referenced account. Be advised that during the month of January and subsequently, the above company and/ or its personnel did not honor our requests to forward data describing interface between manpower and fire-protection hardware capability. Again, permit me to remind you that insurance was carried on the subject company only for the period from June 1973 to December 1982. Transition data relative to specific transactions prior to termination date are indeed available. In the event that you can utilize aforementioned documentation (in lieu of requested information), do not hesitate to contact me at your earliest convenience or at any point in time thereafter. Feel free to direct your request to the writer (at the above address), and we shall transmit required data by return mail.

Thanking you in advance, I remain

Very cordially yours,

J.D.R. McMann, Jr.

Thomas D. R. McMann, Jr.
B.S.C.

TDRMc/MH/jp

MAKING A SPEECH

Another form in which you may have to make an argument is the platform speech. You may have to make a case to a civic club, a church organization, a union group, or a town meeting. You may want to sell some product or service or idea. You're going to have to stand before an audience and talk.

It is not difficult to make an effective speech if you're willing to give necessary time to the job.

PREPARING THE SPEECH

Most of the suggestions about good writing apply equally to effective speaking.

In preparing your speech, you need to choose a subject that lends itself to detail, get specific facts, narrow the topic, organize the material, and express it in an everyday talking voice. But a speech is different from a written essay in several ways.

Here are rules to remember:

1. *Make Your Organization Clear.* Because your audience has no paragraphs to look at, you have to be more specific in announcing the outline of your talk. You might say, "I have three reasons for opposing the construction of a nuclear power station in Arneson," then follow this with markers "first," "second," "third," and "in conclusion." (This would be mechanically offensive in an essay, but it helps a speech.) You can get the same effect with a time reference ("Every day last week, I thought of a new reason to vote for the school tax") or with an extended metaphor ("If the Patman Bill was a used car, you wouldn't buy it"). Your audience should always have a general idea of how far along your speech is and where it's going.

2. *Make Your Introduction Short and Provocative.* Don't dawdle around. Greet the audience. ("Good morning, ladies and gentlemen.") Add a note or two of personal goodwill. ("I'm pleased to be here with you today.") Announce your subject. ("I want to talk to you about our new turbines.") And make it interesting. ('They're giving us strange problems, and they're costing us money.") Then get on with your talk.

    In platform speaking, you have about 30 seconds in which to "catch" your audience. If you don't win them then, you probably won't do it at all. If you begin saying "In 1895, the Senate of the United States . . ." or "Young people today . . .", you've said all anybody is going to listen to.

    Don't begin your speech with a joke unless it is particularly related to your topic. The isolated opening joke is now a cliché. It suggests the speaker has a frivolous attitude toward the audience and the subject. You can, of course, offer any amount of relevant humor as your speech moves on. But don't begin, "Being here today reminds me of the story of the monkey and the artichoke." Spare your audence that.

3. *Refer to the Audience and the Local Scene.* Don't talk *to* an audience, talk *with* an audience.

   Address them as "ladies and gentlemen" or "gentlemen" or "friends" or "you" or "we" (meaning you and them together). Speak to them courteously and directly. ("Please follow this now; this is important.") Refer to people in attendance. ("Tom here can tell you what happened.") Never let your talk become so abstract and objective that it loses this "you and me" note.

   Refer to what is going on around you. Mention other features of the occasion: the preceding speaker, the orchestra, the meal, the awards ceremony, a special guest, whatever. Use immediate objects as illustrative props. ("It's like this saltshaker; if you don't shake it, nothing comes out.") Mention things everyone is concerned with at the moment (Christmas shopping, unusual weather, inflation, an upcoming election, the Super Bowl, etc.). These things tie you and your audience together.

4. *Don't Let Your Speech Get Boring.* You know how quickly you lose interest in a sermon on "faith" or a graduation speech on "responsibility." When a book becomes dull, you can skim a few paragraphs and get on to the more compelling material. When a speech gets dull, it just drones on, and you begin counting the bricks in the wall.

   In preparing your talk, therefore, it is important to narrow your subject to a richly specific topic. Then talk about real things and use proper names. Say "for instance" and "for example" a lot.

   Don't give long lists of names, facts, or statistics. These might be acceptable in an essay, but they're deadly in a speech. Put such material on a chart or a handout sheet; then refer to it.

   Always edit your speech to make sure you're not saying the same thing over and over.

   Unless you are singularly eloquent, don't let your speech go beyond 20 minutes. And shorter is better.

5. *Keep Your Concluding Remarks Brief.* When you've said what you have to say, quit. Never pad out a speech to fill up some artificial time frame.

   Have an upbeat final line. Don't trail away with a dull sentence. ("That's pretty much what I have to say about those turbines.") Make it more dramatic: "We *can* make these turbines work, but it won't be easy. We must begin tomorrow morning."

GETTING READY FOR THE EVENT

Besides preparing an effective speech, you can do other things ahead of time to ensure the success of your talk.

1. *Rehearse*. Practice your speech. Give it over and over. Talk to anyone who will listen to you: your spouse, your brother, your golden retriever, anybody. If you plan to use an opaque projector or flip charts or a pointer, practice with these props.

    You might even have a dress rehearsal. Invite over a few friends, ply them with food and drink, and make them listen to your speech. Pay attention to their response.

2. *Make Yourself Look Good*. In a speech, everything counts. The audience is looking at you and making judgments. While a writer is happily invisible, a speaker has to be concerned about appearance. A man might want to buy a new suit; certainly he should have a haircut and shoeshine. A woman should never wear clothes or accessories that draw attention away from her message. For an important occasion, you might want to lose 5 or 10 pounds.

    These things may sound trivial. But they're all part of the total impression you make. They are part of the persuasive process.

3. *Arrange the Setting*. Get to the speaking site half an hour early and look over the scene.

    Make necessary arrangements. Check the lighting. Make sure there is a speaker's stand, and adjust it to the right height. See that the microphone works. Get props and audio-visuals ready. Make sure that you have a blackboard (or a flip chart) if you need one and that there is something to write with. Sometimes you can even arrange the chairs so the audience will sit where you want them.

    None of these things happens by itself. Many speaking problems can be avoided if you check things out ahead of time.

DELIVERING THE SPEECH

Finally, the moment arrives. It's time to stand up and give that talk. This counsel should help you.

1. *Stand Facing the Audience*. If you can avoid it, never give a speech or deliver a report sitting down. And when you stand, don't slouch in an effort to look supercasual.

    Face the front. Don't make extended references to a blackboard or flip chart and talk with your back to the audience. When pointing to things on a chart, stand directly beside it so you're still facing your listeners. Don't make them listen to your profile.

2. *Control Any Nervousness*. The best way to avoid nervousness is to prepare a first-rate speech and rehearse it a lot. If you're confident you can do a good job, you'll have less reason to be nervous.

    Even if you are uncomfortable, don't mention your nervousness to your audience. Unless you are shaking or falling down, they won't know you're nervous. It doesn't show.

3. *Sound Natural.* Don't be intimidated by a formal term like "platform speaking." You've been talking to people all your life. Speaking in public isn't that much different.

    Always sound like one human being talking to another human being. (Don't use "speech" words like "auspicious," "incumbent," and "threefold.") In a formal speech, you'll want to talk somewhat slower than you usually do and, if you don't have a microphone, you'll have to speak somewhat louder. Nevertheless, keep your tone as conversational as the audience, subject, and occasion will allow.

    Don't use any models. Don't try to sound like Dan Rather or Ronald Reagan or Barbara Walters. Sound like yourself.

    Never sound (or look) like you're reading a document to the audience.

4. *Speak from Notes or from a Full Text.* Once you have written your speech and rehearsed it and rehearsed it, you can decide whether you want to bring the full text to the speaking event or whether you want to rely on outlined notes. Either way has advantages.

    Never memorize your speech; you could black out in the middle of it. Because you want to look like you're "just talking" with the audience, however, you shouldn't keep looking down to card notes or sheets of paper you're holding in your hand.

    If you are comfortable speaking extemporaneously, simply put an outline of your speech on the speaker's stand and resort to that when necessary. This allows you to sound conversational and to talk more directly at your audience. (You can also put an outline of your talk on a chart and have it up front for the audience to look at. The lines on the chart are, in fact, *your* notes.) Not being tied down to the exact words of a written-out text, you're freer to modify your talk so it meets the responses of the audience.

    If you need the security of the full text, you must take care that it's written to sound like natural speech and that it doesn't freeze you so you can't change your lines when necessary.

    In general, it is better to speak from notes than from a full text.

5. *Use Whatever Gestures Come Naturally.* As you address your audience, don't simply stand motionless, and don't move in any way that feels artificial to you.

    Remember you have many props to occupy your hands. You have the speaker's stand, your pockets, a pointer, chalk, your glasses, and so on. Feel free to use these.

    And move your feet if you want to. You can step away from the podium, go over to your flip chart, walk toward your audience, whatever. Move any way that seems natural to you.

    Be careful of mannerisms that draw attention away from your message. Don't fiddle with a paper clip or with your hair or tie. Don't click your ballpoint pen. Watch out for those collapsible point-ers. Almost invariably speakers begin opening and closing them and look like they're playing an accordian.

If you can relax and get involved with what you're saying, whatever gestures come naturally will be fine.

6.   *Use Common Sense.* Sometimes all your preparations aren't enough. Before or during your speech, unexpected things happen. Here you have to make common sense adjustments.

If you are one of a series of speakers and those preceding you have all run overtime, what do you do? If you rise at 5:10 P.M. and have a 15-minute speech to deliver, forget it. Say one or two ingratiating things, then sit down.

If you discover your audience is more conservative or more hostile than you expected, skip over material they are likely to find offensive.

If you are in the middle of your speech and find you are taking longer than you should, paraphrase a long section into a sentence or two. If you find you're going to end sooner than you expected, don't pad. Let the talk end.

If you misspeak, correct yourself. ("Excuse me, I should have said *Henry* Kissinger.") Then go on.

Watch your audience. You can tell when they are with you and following your argument. You can also tell when they start to shift around in their chairs and the glaze comes over their eyes. If you feel you're losing them, you may want to insert a quick, stimulating line ("Now get this; this is important" or "Anyone who doesn't understand this next point is going to lose money"). You may also need to end your speech as soon as possible. An audience always wakes up when it hears, "In conclusion."

If during your speech a water glass tips over or your manuscript falls on the floor, mention the accident ("I'm sorry about that"), then get back to your talk. Don't panic or giggle or make jokes about the event; that just draws attention away from your subject.

These are just a few of the unexpected things that can happen during a speech. When they happen to you, make the necessary adjustments. Use your common sense.

The best way to give a good speech is to have a good speech. When you stand before your audience, all that time you took researching and writing and rehearsing your talk will pay off handsomely.

THE MLA SYSTEM
FOR CITING SOURCES

When you're writing longer arguments or working from a number of books and articles, you need a formal system to identify your sources. The method recommended in the *MLA Handbook for Writers of Research Papers* (1988) will serve you well. This is an efficient system. With it, you don't have to repeat information or write footnotes.

It is a two-step process. First, you list alphabetically all the works you used. This goes at the end of your paper in a section called "Works Cited." Then, in the text, when you express an author's idea or quote an author's words, you use a brief parenthetical insert citing the source and the page. That's all there is to it.

CITATIONS

The citations refer the reader to the "Works Cited" list at the end of the paper. This gives bibliographic information about the books and articles you used. (It is written in a prescribed form that will be detailed later.) Part of the list could look like this:

Jackson, Thomas P. "Prisoners Alone." *S.A.G. Newsletter* Aug. 1988: 5–8.

"Knowing it All." Editorial. *Nationality* 28 Mar. 1987: 4–5.

Linder, Chuck. *Ghost of the Past.* New York: Regency, 1979.

—. *Haunted City.* New York: Regency, 1981.

Muster, Thomas, and Albert Meyer. *Where Are They Going?* San Antonio: Richland, 1989.

This list allows readers to check your sources.

In the text, you will refer to the authors you listed. Based on the entries given, the citations might look like this:

Few prisoners are ever reformed by incarceration (Jackson 6).

As Thomas Jackson reminds us, few prisoners are reformed by incarceration (6).

Many school systems in the city are approaching bankruptcy ("Knowing" 4).

Ghosts have been described as "inner-outer counterprojections" (Linder, "Haunted" 51).

[This takes a longer citation because the author has more than one title on the "Works Cited" list.]

The cultural literacy of young Californians has been called "bad and/
or absent" (Muster and Meyer 141).

Muster and Meyer have called the cultural literacy of young Californians "bad and/or absent" (141).

These are the main citations you will use. Be sure to follow the forms
exactly as they are shown here.

WORKS CITED

This is the MLA form for entries in "Works Cited." Put the list at the end
of your paper, and always begin it on a new page. Follow the spacing,
punctuation, and abbreviations exactly as they are shown here. Notice
that the list is typed double-spaced and that publishers' names are routinely abbreviated.

BOOKS

The general format for books is this: Author. *Title,* Edition. City of Publication: Publisher, year. Below are the main forms you will use.

A Book By a Single Author

Tuchman, Barbara. *The Zimmerman Telegram.* New York: Macmillan,
1958.

[With a book published before 1900, you can omit the name of the publisher and put a comma rather than a colon after the city.]

Dewey, John. *The Study of Ethics: A Syllabus.* Ann Arbor, 1894.

A Book By Multiple Authors

Hanna, Michael S., and James W. Gibson. *Public Speaking for Personal
Success.* Dubuque: Wm. C. Brown, 1987.

[If there are more than three authors (or editors), you have a choice. You
can name them all, or you can name just the first and add "et al."]

A Book By a Corporate Author

American Medical Association. *The American Medical Association Family Medical Guide.* Rev. ed. New York: Random, 1987.

An Anthology

Lawn, Beverly, ed. *Literature: 150 Masterpieces of Fiction, Poetry, and
Drama.* New York: St. Martin's, 1991.

A Work in an Anthology

Chekhov, Anton. "The Kiss." *Themes in World Literature.* Ed. George
P. Elliott, et al. Boston: Houghton, 1975. 334–348.

Mixon, Janet. "The Admission of Women to the Catholic Priest-hood." *Read and Write: A Guide to Effective Composition.* Ed. James F. Dorrill and Charles W. Harwell. San Diego: Harcourt, 1987. 319–21.

An Introduction, Preface, Forward, or Afterward

Le Carré, John. Introduction. *The Philby Conspiracy.* By Bruce Page, David Leitch, and Phillip Knightley. Garden City: Doubleday, 1968. 1–16.

Material Reprinted from Another Source

McCown, J. H. "The Truth About Nicaragua." *Catholic Week* 26 Oct. 1984:2. Rpt. in *The Language of Argument.* Ed. Daniel McDonald. 5th ed. New York: Harper, 1986. 170–71.

A Multivolume Work

Churchill, Winston S. *A History of the English-Speaking People.* 4 vols. New York: Dodd, 1956–58.

[or]

Churchill, Winston S. *The Age of Revolution.* New York: Dodd, 1957. Vol. 3 of *History of the English-Speaking People.* 4 vols. 1956–58.

An Edition Other Than the First

Alison, Alexander, et al., eds. *Norton Anthology of Poetry,* 3rd ed. New York: Norton, 1983.

Chaucer, Geoffrey. *The Works of Geoffrey Chaucer.* Ed. F. N. Robinson. 2nd ed. Boston: Houghton, 1957.

A Translation

Borges, Jorge Luis, and Adolfo Bioy Casares. *Chronicles of Bustos Domecq.* Trans. Norman Thomas Giovanni. New York: Dutton, 1976.

A Republished Book

Montagu, Ewen. *The Man Who Never Was.* 1953. New York: Bantam, 1964.

[The book was first published in 1953.]

A Pamphlet

Weigle, Charles F. *A Deck of Cards.* Grand Rapids: Zondervan, 1976.

[Treat a pamphlet as if it were a book.]

ARTICLES

This is the general pattern for articles: Author. "Article Title." *Journal Title* Volume Number (Date): pages. The main forms are shown below.

An Article From a Newspaper

Grandy, Fred. "NEA's Job is to Battle Mediocrity." *USA Today* 22 June 1990: 10A.

[Notice that between the journal title and the date, there is no punctuation and only one space.]

O'Neil, Cindy. "The Curse of Satan's Corner." *Weekly World News* 21 Jan. 1992:5.

[Except for May, June, and July, all months are written as three-letter abbreviations.]

An Article From a Periodical

Clemente, Vince. "Meeting Mozart." *Negative Capability* 11.1 (1991): 119–24.

[This refers to volume 11 and issue 1 of the magazine.]

Marion, Robert. "The Mystery of Cassandra." *The Saturday Evening Post* Jan.–Feb. 1991: 26+.

[The "26+" means the article began on page 26 and was continued later in the journal.]

Wilson, Gerald L. "An Analysis of Instructional Strategies for Responding to Illegal Selection Interview Questions." *Bulletin of the Association for Business Communication* Sep. 1991: 31–34.

An Article in a Journal with Continuous Pagination Throughout Volume

Davis, Fred E. "Hi-Fi Audio Pseudoscience." *Skeptical Inquirer* 15.3 (1991): 250–54.

[The article apppeared in volume 15, issue 3 of the journal.]

Sheridan, Daniel. "Changing Business as Usual: Reader Response in the Classroom." *College English* 53.7 (1991): 804–14.

A Government Publication

Cong. Rec. 7 Feb. 1973: 3831–51.

An Editorial

"Mayor Halfway." Editorial. *New York Times* 5 Jan. 1992: 12E.

An Anonymous Article

"Compromising on Clean Air." *Time* 12 Mar. 1990: 25.

A Letter to an Editor

Bailey, Susan F. Letter. *Chronicle of Higher Education* 27 Nov. 1991: B4.

Sinclair, Robert. "Schools Have Enough Money." Letter. *Mobile Press* 6 Jan. 1991: 7A.

A Review

Braestrup, Peter. Rev. of *Live from Baghdad: Gathering News at Ground Zero*, by Robert Wiener. *New York Times Book Review* 5 Jan. 1992: 9.

An Interview

Lansbury, Angela. Interview. *Off-Camera: Conversations with the Makers of Prime-Time Television.* By Richard Levinson and William Link. New York: Plume-NAL, 1986. 72–86.

Mitchell, Hilary. Telephone Interview. 12 Mar. 1991.

MATERIAL FROM REFERENCE WORKS

"Apus." *American Heritage Dictionary of the English Language.* 1969 ed.

"Kansas." *World Almanac and Book of Facts.* 1990 ed.

Pochmann, Henry A. "Washington Irving." *Encyclopaedia Britannica.* 1970 ed.

[With less familiar reference works, give full publishing information.]

Crystal, David. "Language vs. Dialect." *Cambridge Encyclopedia of Language.* Cambridge: Cambridge UP, 1987.

"Matthew B Brady." *Webster's American Biographies.* Ed. Charles Van Doren and Robert McHenry. Springfield: Merriam, 1975.

These examples will get you through most writing situations. If you need a bibliographic entry that is not shown here, refer to *The MLA Handbook for Writers of Research Papers* (1988). It is probably in your library or at your local bookstore.